ALLIED INTERVENTION IN RUSSIA

ALLIED INTERVENTION IN RUSSIA

John Bradley

UNIVERSITY
PRESS OF
AMERICA

LANHAM • NEW YORK • LONDON

CONTENTS

MAPS

MAPS BY ARTHUR BANKS OF SURREY ART DESIGNS

PREFACE

The intervention by the western Allies in Russia after the bolshevik *coup d'état* in 1917 is still a controversial subject. But this is mainly so because neither side has yet ventured to publish relevant archives *in toto*. Since there are so many important gaps in the story of the intervention, ideologues, apologists and politicians on both sides, have often drawn on it and sometimes made it a political issue of great topicality, instead of a historical study. Thus even now, almost fifty years later, the intervention is capable of stirring up passions on both sides and for that reason is shunned by historians.

But the story of the intervention is also a complicated subject. It involved in the Russian revolution and the subsequent civil war many countries and nations. Thus sources in many languages must be studied and formidable distances coped with to consult the limited available material. Obviously the greatest pity is that the most fundamental source, the Soviet archives, has remained closed, inaccessible to Soviet and western historians alike.

Fortunately in Western Europe large holdings of documents are now open for consultation. The principal source in Great Britain is the Milner Papers which were left by the former War Secretary to New College, Oxford. These papers cover both military and diplomatic aspects of the intervention and throw a new light on British attitudes towards and actions in Russia. A complementary collection of documents on the intervention, especially in the north, was consulted in the National Maritime Museum, London; it made many of the Milner documents more meaningful apart from clarifying other obscurities. The Foreign Office library has proved another important source.

In France the harvest of documents has proved even more plentiful than in Britain. The archives of the French army yielded some outstanding new documents explaining many aspects of the French involvement in the intervention. Perhaps a little paradoxically they also yielded many documents shedding light on British military plans and actions, documents inaccessible in Britain. The diplomatic

side of the intervention from the French point of view can be naturally studied in the archives of the French Ministry of Foreign Affairs
in Paris. However, these diplomatic documents had several times been
displaced and their consultation is therefore very difficult. The
archives were twice set on fire during the last war and after the war
they have been slowly re-constituted from the French embassies in
capitals unoccupied by the Germans. The Germans had also seized
large quantities of documents from the ministry archives; these in
turn were captured by the Russians. All the same it is possible to
reconstruct the French side of the intervention from the existing
documents.

Many important documents on the intervention from the German
point of view are scattered throughout the archives of the *Auswärtiges
Amt*. These are mainly captured German sources open for consultation in Washington (National Archives), London (Cabinet Office),
Paris (Quai d'Orsay) and Bonn itself. German military documents
can also be consulted in Washington, or more conveniently at the
Bundesforschungsinstitut at Koblenz where they are now concentrated. Still other German documents are in the custody of the
University of California and St Antony's College, Oxford. Manchester University has also a small collection of these documents.
These German sources are often invaluable for 'cross-checking',
though sometimes, when Germany is directly involved in the intervention (German internationalists in the Red Army) they are of
primary importance.

Similarly the Austrian *Staats-* and *Kriegsarchiv* in Vienna. They
both contain documents which are useful for 'cross-checking' of
Allied intentions and actions in Russia, but also yield new information on the formation of the International Units and the Czech Legion
which were the two important factors in 1918 in 'forcing' the western
Allies and the Japanese to intervene. It is unfortunate that the
military archives for 1919 and 1920 are still inaccessible.

The last chapter of this book deals with the Russo–Polish conflict
in 1920. Though it is impossible to consult the Polish archives in
Warsaw an important part of them had been evacuated to the West
in 1939. These sources can now be studied at the Pilsudski Institute
in New York. Among these documents are, for example, the handwritten letters of General Weygand to General Rozwadowski, telegrams from the Poles in Siberia, as well as important reports from the
Denikin HQ in South Russia.

The White Russian movement and its involvement with the Allies can only be meaningfully studied in the United States. It is true that there are still some military sources in Brussels and France, but the greater part of political material has found its way to America. The chief holdings of White Russian documents in the American East are at Columbia University in New York; in the West, the Hoover Institution in California has another outstanding collection, especially on Siberia. It should also be mentioned that the Trotsky Papers at Harvard University can now be consulted at Amsterdam, while the microfilm copies of the Smolensk Archives, also originally at Harvard, are at Manchester University.

Last but not least I must express my thanks to many individuals and acknowledge my indebtedness to many institutions. In the first place I must thank my own University for generous financial and other encouragements, and particularly to Professor W. J. M. Mackenzie, who had helped me with critical suggestions and leaves of absence. The former librarian, Dr M. Tyson, was very helpful in buying up the masses of documents I brought back from my research peregrinations.

In France I owe most to the President of the French Archives Commission, Monsieur le Doyen Pierre Renouvin, who had helped me both with advice and countless interventions which enabled me to consult French archives. I must also thank the Director of Archives at the Quai d'Orsay for his kind permission to consult documents there, as well as General de Cossé Brissac, Director of the French Army archives.

In Austria Dr Kirchschläger of the *Aussenministerium* was very kind and helpful, as well as Dr Blaas and Dr Wagner of the *Staats-* and *Kriegsarchivs* respectively. In Germany Dr Arenz of the *Militärgeschichtlicher Forschungsinstitut* in Freiburg was most obliging.

In America Professor P. Moseley and Dr Magerovsky of Columbia University deserve my special thanks. The latter went to endless trouble to show me many rare documents which were of great value to me. I must also thank Colonel Koc and Professor Jędrzejewicz for permission to consult the Polish sources at the Pilsudski Institute. My thanks go also to Dr Sworakowski of the Hoover Institution and Dr Allen of the Library of Congress, Washington. Dr Koutník and Dr Wandycz of Harvard University both helped greatly with advice for locating sources.

A*

In Great Britain I am indebted to the Librarian and the Deputy Librarian, Mr C. J. Child, O.B.E., of the Foreign Office for their kindness and assistance. My thanks go also to Mr A. W. H. Pearsall of the National Maritime Museum (Manuscript Department) as well as to Mr D. J. Footman and the fellows of St Antony's College, Oxford. I owe special thanks and gratitude to Sir William Hayter, Warden of New College, Oxford, for many kindnesses, encouragements and 'diplomatic interventions' on my behalf. He and the Librarian also kindly permitted me to consult the Milner Papers in the college library. Dr L. Kochan of East Anglia University, Professor R. Auty of Oxford and Dr Andreyev of Cambridge, deserve many thanks for their aid, advice and encouragement.

Of the institutions I must specially single out the Astor Foundation whose two research grants enabled me to travel and consult archives in the United States. Various financial help was received from the following: the Centre National de la Recherche Scientifique, Paris; Deutsche Akademische Austauschdienst, London; the Humboldt Foundation, Bonn; the Austrian Ministry of Education, Vienna; the Hayter Committee Fund and the Austrian Institute, London.

Manchester University

                                                        J. F. N. B.

BIBLIOGRAPHICAL INTRODUCTION

The historian who will want to undertake to write the complete story of the Allied intervention will have to face many hazards and sometime quite absurd situations. On the western side the chief obstacle to free access to documents will be the various legal regulations governing the availability of archives. But on the eastern side he will have to cope with political considerations as well as utterly irrational phenomena.

It is well known that in 1919–20 in Siberia whole railway coaches of White and Allied documents fell into bolshevik hands. But for some unfathomable reasons only very few of these have since been published. We would undoubtedly know much more about the intervention had the Soviets opened for consultation various captured holdings. It is true that they published about a hundred French documents which they had seized from the Germans.[1] But the important Denikin Papers transferred to Moscow after their capture in Prague after the Second World War have not seen the light of day, neither have the White documents collected in Jugoslavia or Bulgaria.

The official Soviet publications on the intervention, and in a wider context, on the period of the civil war, suffer from a strange paucity of relevant material. Thus Lenin's works offer a historian a more interesting selection than the whole series of Soviet foreign policy documents.[2] In 1941 I. Mints and E. Gorodetsky brought out a collection of documents which only touches on the beginning of the Allied intervention.[3] It might have been better had the subject been completely ignored. A more recent collection of documents again skips over the intervention as if it were a simple and tedious affair: the imperialist Allies were bent on the destruction of the young

[1] They are scattered throughout the three volumes of *Iz istorii grazhdanskoy voyny*, Moscow, 1960–61.

[2] V. I. Lenin, *Sochineniya*, vols. 30, 31, 32, 33, 35, 28, Moscow, 1948 et seq.; *Dokumenty vneshney politiki SSSR*, vol 1 and 2, Moscow 1957–58. Also V. I. Lenin, *Ob innostrannoy interventsii i grazhdanskoy voyne v SSSR*, Moscow, 1956.

[3] *Dokumenty po istorii grazhdanskoy voyny v SSSR*, vol. 1, Moscow, 1941.

communist state. This thesis can be 'easily' proved by 'skilfully' selecting documents from the American and British official publications and the memoirs of Lloyd George, General Ironside and the writings of W. S. Churchill.[1]

Simplifications and inaccuracies inevitably arise from the few captured documents that were actually published in the Soviet Union. Thus in 1918 Commandant Pichon's reports to his government had been intercepted by the Soviet intelligence. They were then published under a characteristic title: *The Allied Intervention in the Far East and Siberia*.[2] Not only was Commandant Pichon a minor figure in the huge complex of the Allied intervention, but he certainly was not in the position of making French, or for that Allied, decisions on the Siberian intervention; at best he drafted recommendations. Subsequently I. Mints brought out a much better collection of Japanese documents, perhaps in contradiction to the simplifications of Pichon.[3]

There is a curious gap in Soviet documentation on Siberia in 1919. Thus apart from a few articles in the *Krasny arkhiv* based solidly on official papers,[4] there are only M. M. Konstantinov's surveys of the end of Admiral Kolchak (late 1919–20) and the partisan warfare which deal partially with the Allies in Siberia in a documentary manner.[5]

The few Soviet collections, published after the intervention had failed, emphasize the unsavoury aspects of this Allied action. A whole series of these documents deal with atrocities committed by Allied troops, or with their demoralization in the Ukraine, southern Russia and the Crimea.[6] The other group of documentary publications originating mainly from the Cold War period deal with the Allied conspiracy led by the United States whose aim it was to destroy the USSR.[7]

[1] *Iz istorii . . .* , cf. 1.

[2] *Soyuznaya interventsiya na Dalnem Vostoke i v Sibiri*, Moscow–Leningrad, 1925.

[3] *Yaponskaya interventsiya 1918–1922 gg. v dokumentakh*, Moscow, 1934.

[4] K istorii interventsii v Sibiri, *Krasny arkhiv*, 1929, 3 (34): 126–65.

[5] *Posledniye dni kolchakovshchiny*, Moscow–Leningrad, 1926.

[6] *Osvobozhdeniye Kryma ot anglo-frantsuzskikh interventov*, Simferopol, 1940; V. Konovalov, *Innostrannaya koleggiya*, Odessa, 1958; *Antanta i Vrangel*, Moscow–Petrograd, 1923; M. Kamen, *Zamysly frantsuzskikh imperialistov protiv SSSR*, Moscow–Leningrad, 1928.

[7] A. Berezkin, *SShA–Aktivny organizator i uchastnik voyennoy interventsii protiv Sovetskoy Rossii*, Moscow, 1952; A. I. Melchin, *Amerikanskaya inter-*

If the documents are selected to fit a political thesis, Soviet interpretations are produced only to re-emphasize it.[1] Sometimes, though
slanted they at least have the form of historical works;[2] the majority,
however, are simply propaganda exercises often with sensational
titles.[3]

While apart from propaganda exploitation the Soviets simply neg-
lect the intervention, the White Russians are curiously silent about it.
From the early documentary publications we learn very little of what
went on between the Whites and the Allies.[4] It is true that the greater
part of the White documents was captured or re-captured by the
Soviets after the war, but sometimes the silence strikes as a conspiracy, especially, in the various histories of the White movement.[5]
Even White memoirs maintain the 'conspiratorial' silence, so perhaps
we shall find more about White-Allied relations, if and when the
Soviets finally decide to publish the captured White sources.[6]

It may be that the United States was made the arch-villain of the
intervention only because so many documents about it and interpretations of it were published there. Of the documents the series
Papers relating . . . is of greatest importance.[7] It is, in fact, the key to
any western attitude to, and decision on, the intervention. But the
Americans were also fortunate to have published the personal papers
of the statesmen who had made the decisions in 1917–20.[8] In addition

ventsiya v 1918–1920 gg., Moscow, 1951; A. E. Yunina, *Proval amerikanskikh
planov zavoyevaniya mirogovo gospodstva v 1917–1920*, Moscow, 1954; K. G.
Seleznyev, *Krakh zagovora*, Moscow, 1963, etc.

[1] I. K. Koblyakov, *Ot Bresta do Rapallo*, Moscow, 1954.

[2] V. P. Potemkin, *Istoriya diplomatii*, vol. 2, Moscow, 1945.

[3] F. D. Volkov, *Krakh angliyskoy politiki interventsii i diplomaticheskoy izolat-
sii sovetskogo gosudarstva*, Moscow, 1954.

[4] P. N. Milyukov, *Rossiya na perelome*, Paris, 1927; A. Zaytsov, *1918 god*,
Paris, 1934; etc.

[5] *Le livre jaune*, issued by the Denikin HQ, 1919; Ocherk vzaimootnosheniy
vooruzi *zhennykh sil Yuga Rossii i predstaviteley frantsuzskogo komandovaniya*,
May 1919.

[6] K. N. Khagondokov, *Vozpominaniya*; B. M. Brofeld, *Vozpominaniya i
vpechatleniya*; C. Mandraty, *Vozpominaniya*.

[7] *Papers Relating to the Foreign Relations of the United States: Russia 1918*,
3 vols., Washington, 1931–32; *Papers Relating . . .: The Lansing Papers, 1914–
1920*, 2 vols., Washington, 1940.

[8] R. S. Baker, *Woodrow Wilson, Life and Letters*, 8 vols., New York, 1939;
C. Seymour, *The Intimate Papers of Colonel House*, 4 vols., New York, 1928.

the political and private papers of these and other men concerned with the intervention as well as official documents not previously printed are available for consultation in the United States.[1]

The Americans have also published the most valuable collections of documents dealing with Russia in the context of the revolution and the civil war.[2] Their soldiers disputed publicly intervention policies with their politicians who had sent them to Russia in 1918.[3] Their journalists defended or debunked the intervention; many more or less competent interpretations appeared.[4] Of the latter perhaps the best is G. F. Kennan's.[5]

There is an excellent official publication of documents in Britain. But this series unfortunately only covers the years 1919–20. Somehow the vital years 1917–18 were completely left out.[6] W. P. and Z. K. Coates published a curious collection of official and unofficial statements on the intervention, but on the whole the published British documents are hopelessly incomplete.[7]

W. S. Churchill's apologia of the intervention is probably the most important and interesting of the works devoted to the intervention.[8] It is also in a sense his memoirs. Lloyd George's memoirs are, of course, of capital importance.[9] Some useful information about the decisions in London may be gleaned from Lord Riddell's and Sir Henry Wilson's diaries.[10] Interesting details come out of Wickham

[1] The Francis Papers at St Louis; the House Papers, Yale University; the Lansing Papers, Library of Congress; the Morris Papers, Library of Congress, etc.

[2] J. Bunyan, H. H. Fisher, *The Bolshevik Revolution 1917–1918* Stanford, 1934; R. Varneck, H. H. Fisher, *The Testimony of Kolchak and other Siberian Materials*, Stanford, 1935; P. C. March, *The Nation at War*, New York, 1932.

[3] W. S. Graves, *America's Siberian Adventure, 1918–1920*, New York, 1931; G. Stewart, *The White Armies of Russia*, New York, 1933.

[4] J. R. Moore, *The History of the American Expedition Fighting the Bolsheviki*, Detroit, 1920; E. M. Halliday, *The Ignorant Armies*, New York, 1960.

[5] G. F. Kennan, *Soviet–American Relations*, 2 vols., Princeton, 1956–58.

[6] *Documents on British Foreign Policy 1919–1939*, series 1, vol. 3, London, 1949.

[7] *Armed Intervention in Russia 1919–1922*, London, 1935.

[8] *The World Crisis. The Aftermath*, London, 1929.

[9] David Lloyd George, *War Memoirs*, 6 vols., London, 1933–36.

[10] *Lord Riddell's War Diary*, London, 1933; Major-General Sir C. E. Callwell, *Field-Marshal Sir Henry Wilson, Bart., His Life and Diaries*, 2 vols., London, 1927.

Steed's and Sir Basil Thomson's autobiographies.[1] Many participants
and observers at Versailles wrote about the British point of view on
the Russian problem at the peace conference.[2] British diplomats and
soldiers on active service in Russia also produced their records, some
highly interesting, but mostly cautious or incomplete.[3]

However, British historical literature lacks interpretations of the
intervention. E. H. Carr only touches on it; R. H. Ullman treats it
more fully but his sources are limited.[4]

In France no official documents have as yet been published. A
volume on the early Franco–Soviet relations is in preparation,[5] but
apart from this only the monumental series of the army documents
ending rather inconveniently for the intervention, contains some
relevant documents.[6] E. Moulis's and E. Bergonier's unofficial
selection of documents is highly biased as much as Xydias' version
of the French intervention in the south, but in the opposite sense:[7]

Clemenceau left behind no suitable explanation of his decisions on
Russia, though his biographer records some interesting details.[8]
J. Noulens, French Ambassador, left behind his memoirs; other
soldiers and diplomats on active service in Russia left theirs under
different guises.[9] Sadoul, the 'deserter', left a sort of diary and

[1] W. H. Wickham Steed, *Through Thirty Years*, London, 1924; Sir Basil
Thomson, *The Scene Changes*, London, 1939.

[2] Lord Riddel, *Intimate Diary of the Peace Conference*, London, 1933; H.
Nicolson, *Peacemaking, 1919*, London, 1933; R. H. Beadon, *Some Memories
of the Peace Conference*, London, 1933; H. W. V. Temperley, *History of the
Peace Conference of Paris*, London, 1924.

[3] Sir George Buchanan, *My Mission to Russia and other diplomatic memoirs*,
2 vols.; R. H. Bruce Lockhart, *Memoirs of a British Agent*, London, 1932;
Major-General Sir Alfred Knox, *With the Russian Army*, 2 vols., London, 1921;
Sir P. Dukes, *Red Dusk and the Morrow*, London, 1922; ——, *The Story of ST 25*,
London, 1938; F. McCullagh, *A Prisoner of the Reds*, London, 1921, etc.

[4] E. H. Carr, *A History of Soviet Russia*, 3 vols., London, 1950–53; R. H.
Ullman, *Intervention and the War*, Princeton, 1961.

[5] Cf. *Survey*, January 1964, pp. 97–106.

[6] *Les armées françaises dans la Grande Guerre*, Paris, 1930–38, 28 vols.

[7] *Documents réunis: la guerre entre les Alliés et la Russie*, Paris, 1937; J.
Xydias, *L'intervention française en Russie, 1918–1919*, Paris, 1927.

[8] *Grandeur et misère d'une victoire*, Paris, 1930; J. J. H. Mordacq, *Le ministère
Clemenceau, journal d'un témoin*, Paris, 1931.

[9] J. Noulens, *Mon ambassade en Russie soviétique, 1917–1919*, Paris, 1932;
P. Janin, *Ma mission en Sibérie*, Paris, 1933; J. Rouquerol, *L'aventure de l'amiral
Koltchak*, Paris, 1929; etc.

A. Marty his story of the mutinies of the French fleet in the Black Sea.[1] From the biography of Marshal D'Esperey come plentiful details of Odessa, and French embarrassment there.[2]

Not only is there a great paucity of published material on the intervention in Russia proper but also on its last episode, the Russo–Polish conflict in 1920 and France's rôle in it. It is true that several versions of the Piłsudski offensive have been recorded, unanimous in the praise of the Marshal, but we completely lack any French documentary evidence or even memoir treatment of these events.[3]

As for interpretations in French there are none; P. Renouvin treats the whole intervention within a wider context and his is the only overall scholarly version of it.[4]

Of the minor Allies involved in the intervention the Czechs were the most important. Their Corps' revolt against the bolsheviks provoked the actual military action. They have not published many official documents either; but Dr. Beneš's *Memoirs* contain a representative selection of both French and Czech documents on the Czech involvement.[5] Additional French documents were published in Czechoslovakia recently; these were the copies of papers passed on to the Czechoslovak National Council in Paris by the Quai d'Orsay and the Slavonic Committee of the French Army.[6]

But while documents are rare there exist several highly useful official histories, first written by the participants themselves, later by the communist critics.[7] All the main personalities which took part in

---

[1] J. Sadoul, *Notes sur la Révolution bolchevique*, Paris, 1919; ——, *Quarante lettres de Jaques Sadoul*, Paris, 1922; André Marty, *La révolte de la Mer*, Paris, 1932.

[2] P. J. L. Azan, *Franchet d'Esperey*, Paris, 1949; also F. J. Deygas, *L'Armée d'Orient dans la guerre mondiale*, Paris, 1932.

[3] General Camon, *La manoeuvre libératrice du Maréchal Pilsudski contre les bolcheviques*, Paris, 1929; Capitaine C. Kuntz, *L'offensive militaire de l'étoile rouge contre le Pologne*, Paris, 1922; etc.

[4] Pierre Renouvin, *Les crises du XXe siècle*, vol. 1, Paris, 1957.

[5] E. Beneš, *Světová válká a naše revoluce*, Prague, 1927–1928, 3 vols.

[6] V. Vávra, Francouzské dokumenty k přípravě protisovětského vystoupení čs legií, *Historie a vojenství*, Prague, 1963, pp. 476–98.

[7] F. Šteidler, *Naše vystoupení v Rusku*, Prague, 1923; J. Papoušek, *Proč došlo k bojům legii se Sověty*, Prague, 1928; J. Kratochvíl, *Cesta revoluce*, Prague, 1928; J. Muška, J. Hořec, *K úloze čs. legii v Rusku*, Prague, 1953; J. Veselý, *Češi a Slováci v revolučním Rusku*, Prague, 1954; V. Vávra, *Klamná cesta*, Prague, 1958; J. Kvasnička, *Československé legie v Rusku*, Bratislava, 1963.

the revolt and the Siberian intervention wrote their reminiscences.[1] Interpretations, however, are few: the participants were preoccupied with establishing facts while the communist critics with demolishing them. The latter furthermore suffered from ideological unbalance. Thus they sometimes claimed that the revolt was deliberately provoked by Trotsky who was then an Allied agent.[2] My monograph on this subject is based mainly on French documents.[3]

The Poles have not yet published a systematic collection of their relevant documents. But they did issue occasionally, similarly to the Soviets, selected documents supporting their point of view.[4] Sometimes valuable documents were concealed in the reports of various commissions set up after the first world war;[5] on other occasions in memoirs of men who took part in the events.[6] However, in all the cases the problem basically dealt with was Polish–Soviet relations, or the lack of them; the Allies come in only incidentally.

There is no scholarly treatment of the complex of the Allied–Polish–Soviet–White relations, though several works are on the borderline.[7] Memoir literature is extensive, but unfortunately largely apologetic.[8]

Until recently the International Units of the Red Army were a forbidden subject. Only after the establishment of the communist

[1] T. G. Masaryk, *Světová revoluce*, Prague, 1925; R. Gajda, *Moje Paměti*, Prague, 1921; F. Polák, *Sibiřská anabase čs. legií*, New York, 1961; etc.

[2] Vávra, *op. cit.*, p. 173, 202–3, 212–13, 223–4.

[3] *La Légion tchécoslovaque en Russie 1914–1920*, Paris, 1965.

[4] *Livre rouge. Recueil relatif des documents relatif aux relations entre la Russie et la Pologne*, Moscow, 1920; *Akty i dokumenty dotyczace sprawy granic Polski na konferencji pokojowej w Paryzu 1918–1919*, Paris, 1920; *Polish–Soviet Relations 1918–1923*, Polish Embassy, Washington, n.d.

[5] *Delegacje polskie w komisjach reewakuacyjnej i specjalnej w Moskwie*, Warsaw, 1922–23; *KPP w obronie neipodległości Polski*, Warsaw, 1954.

[6] J. Pilsudski, *L'année 1920*, Paris, 1929; L. Sikorski, *Le campagne polono-russe de 1920*, Paris, 1928.

[7] A. Przybylski, *La Pologne en lutte pour ses frontières*, Paris, 1929; T. Komarnicki, *Rebirth of the Polish Republic*, London, 1957; A. Zoltowski, *Border of Europe*, London, 1950.

[8] T. Kutrseba, *Wyprawa kijowska 1920 roku*, Warsaw, 1937; S. Stronski, *Pierwsze lat dziesiec*, Lwów, 1928; W. Jedrzejewicz, *Rokowania borysowskie w 1920 roku*, *Nereipodleglosc*, London, 1951; General Dowbor-Muśnicki, *Moje wspomnienia*, Warsaw, 1935; E. de Henning–Michaelis, *Burza dziejowa*, 2 vols, Warsaw, 1928.

régimes in Eastern Europe, and above all after Stalin's death, have the Soviets published selected documents about these units.[1] The subject was in fact so neglected that some western historians even doubted its existence. But after the Soviet example a whole spate of Czech,[2] Slovak[3], Hungarian[4] and Rumanian[5] publications followed. Now even the East Germans have come out with reminiscences and memoirs if not documents.[6]

In the Federal Republic, apart from the limited pre-1933 sources (mostly reports on the PoWs) nothing significant has come out.[7] The Austrians have also ignored the subject while the Jugoslav participants were glorified in the USSR.[8] It is obvious that the research on the International Units is still in an initial stage and that many findings will for some time remain provisional.

The Japanese, with the exception of the Official Gazette, containing mainly declarations and government decisions, have not published their documents. However, several scholarly studies based on relevant documents released by the Japanese after the last war have appeared since.[9] We shall still have to wait for an extensive edition of documents or a comprehensive Japanese interpretation.

Of the other documentary collections throwing some limited light on Allied intervention in Russia the most important are the *Documenti diplomatici italiani* and J. Degras's two collections of Soviet documents.[10]

[1] *Boyevoye sodruzhestvo trudyashchikhsya zarubezh nykh stran s narodami Sovetskoy Rossii*, Moscow, 1957; L. N. Zharov, V. M. Ustinov, *Internatsionalnyie chasti v boyakh za vlast sovetov*, Moscow, 1960.

[2] J. Křížek, *Penza, slavná bojová tradice čs. rudoarmějců*, Prague, 1956.

[3] *Bojová pieseň zněla*, Bratislava, 1958.

[4] *Vengerskiye internatsionalisty v Velikoy Oktyabrskoy socialisticheskoy revolyutsii*, Moscow, 1959; *Velikaya Okt. Revolutsia i Vengriya*, Moscow, 1959. These are translations from Hungarian.

[5] V. Liveanu, in *Studii*, issue 1, January–February 1956.

[6] *Weltenwende-wir waren dabei*, Berlin, 1962.

[7] E. Brandstrom, *Among the Prisoners of War in Russia, and Siberia*, London, 1930; K. von Bothmer, *Mit Graf Mirbach in Moskau*, Tübingen, 1922.

[8] Aleksander Dunayevsky, *Oleko Dundich*, Moscow, 1960.

[9] J. W. Morley, *The Japanese Thrust into Siberia, 1918*, Columbia, New York, 1957; Chitoshi Yanaga, *Japan since Perry*, New York, 1949; *Japanese Intervention in the Far East*, Washington, 1922.

[10] *I documenti diplomatici italiani*, sesta serie, vol. 1, Rome, 1955; Jane Degras, *The Communist International, 1919–1943*, 2 vols., London, 1956–60; ——, *Soviet Documents on Foreign Policy*, 3 vols., London, 1951–53.

This survey is obviously not exhaustive but rather a comprehensive selection suited for the purposes of this study. However, not even a correlation of all the printed sources would significantly elucidate the strange story of Allied intervention. For a more complete and definitive version of it we shall undoubtedly have to wait another century, when the passions still surrounding it will have perhaps died out and all the archives will have been published or thrown open to the fortunate historian.

CHAPTER ONE

ALLIED DOUBTS AND HESITATIONS

I

November 1917–March 1918

On 15 September 1914 France, Russia and Great Britain solemnly signed the Pact of London. Subsequently all the other belligerent countries, Serbia, Luxemburg, Belgium, Japan (October 1914), Italy (30 November 1915) and Rumania (1915) adhered to the Pact. One vital stipulation of this treaty was that none of the Allied governments would conclude a separate peace with the Central Powers.

In addition to the Pact Russia had also signed the Constantinople (12 March 1915 with Great Britain and 12 April 1915 with France) and the Sykes–Picot agreements (16 May 1916). Both these agreements concerned the Turkish Empire and its future. Both were to the advantage of Russia: the former promised her control over the Straits and the latter large chunks of the Turkish territory.[1] For all this Russia had to fight faithfully with the other Allies to the very end.

Thus there was obvious legal and moral justification for the Allies to intervene against a new Russian government which repudiated the vital undertaking of the government it replaced. But this was a new problem and its solution far from simple. The Pact of London contained only the impossibility of a separate peace, but did not envisage a course of action to follow if such a move was contemplated. It is true that there were several precedents of 'intervention': eleven Anglo-French divisions were rushed to Italy after the disaster of Caporetto in 1917. There was even a Russian brigade in France which (rather reluctantly) fought on the western front alongside its allies. But all these interventions were undertaken by invitation.

An intervention without invitation was obviously a more complicated matter. But this seems to have been the only possibility the Allies had in Russia, when on 21 November 1917 the new bolshevik

[1] Documents cited in this chapter were consulted in the Ministère de la Guerre and Ministère des Affaires étrangères in Paris. The Milner Papers in Oxford as well as the Admiralty and Foreign Office archives were consulted.

government officially requested the Allies to initiate peace negotiations with the Central Powers. The Allies were unwilling even to consider such negotiations and simply refused to release the new government from the obligations of the Pact of London. But because of the war the logical solution of this impasse, namely a direct military intervention against the bolshevik government proved impracticable. Hence the Allies had to content themselves with solemn warnings[1] and with the preservation of the *status quo* in Russia, i.e. maintaining the Eastern front in existence and keeping as many German troops there as long as possible.

II

For very few among the Allies in Russia or students of Russian affairs outside Russia was the bolshevik *coup d'état* a surprise. Barely a month earlier on 9 October 1917, Allied Ambassadors in Russia protested collectively to the Prime Minister Kerensky against the disintegration of the Russian Army and chaos in the rear.[2] Kerensky knew of this situation full well, but he somehow expected help rather than protests. But the Allies never did offer him real aid. It is true that plans were in the air. Many special missions and agents appraised the situation in Russia and reported to their governments. Thus for example it was decided that the Americans were going to reorganize Russian railways, the British to streamline Russian shipping and water transport, while the French would help with the re-forming of the Russian Army. However, all these projects were for the future, and even some of the soundest and most realistic ideas had come too late. It was only on 6 November 1917 that Ambassador Francis suggested that his government should send two US divisions to Russia to raise public morale.[3]

While the Provisional Government was left unaided many Allied representatives in Russia knew that a bolshevik attempt to seize power would be made on 7 November. Kerensky, who also knew, tried in vain and too late to hinder it. Allied diplomats, military representatives, agents and journalists remained passive: they became

---

[1] Lloyd George in the House of Commons, 20 December 1917 (*Parliamentary Proceedings*, vol. 100, col. 2222).

[2] The *démarche* of the British, French and Italian Ambassadors, 26 September 1917.

[3] Francis to Lansing, 6 November 1917.

puzzled and sometimes malicious spectators of the events of the *coup d'état*. This passivity was in marked contrast to their busyness during the Kornilov crisis. But by 7 November everyone seemed terrifyingly apathetic and more concerned with their own predicaments.[1]

The reasons for this apathy were manifold. Practically all the Allied personnel in Russia, after witnessing the chaos that followed on and gradually increased after the March revolution, became convinced that Russia 'was lost' and had become useless as an ally. The passivity was, of course, also induced by ignorance of and lack of contact with the bolsheviks. But while the latter were instinctively hated for their pro-German reputation, anti-war 'demagogy' and 'wild' social ideas, the idea of a bolshevik coup was quite liked, especially by those Allies who for various reasons disliked the Provisional Government and did not engage themselves fully on its behalf. For all of them agreed with the many non-bolshevik Russians that the bolsheviks were too weak to last long. It seemed obvious that once in power the bolsheviks would suffer from the same disunity and lack of purpose as the previous régime and consequently would also collapse. The secret and cheering thought was that the *coup d'état* would act as an awakening, that it would drive together the best and naturally pro-Allied forces in Russia, who would stage a comeback and resuscitate Russia for the Allied cause.

Thus during the day of 7 November 1917 Allied representatives went about their routine business as usual, with the exception of two American diplomats who had to walk to their office because their car had been requisitioned by Kerensky who needed it 'to get loyal troops to the capital'. In the evening Ambassador Noulens heard the cruiser *Aurora*'s shots and laughed at their inaccuracy. Sir George Buchanan also took the events of the coup in his stride; he took his regular walk as if nothing had happened. Only the Allied military, propaganda and Red Cross missions, though also passive, seemed put out. All the personnel slept armed fearing assassination at the hands of the bolsheviks, possibly with good reason. The young socialist Captain Sadoul, of the French Mission, set out to reconnoitre the centre of the insurrection, the Smolny Institute.

In Allied capitals the news of the *coup d'état* in Petrograd was taken

[1] M. P. A. Hankey to War Cabinet, Summary of Policy of the War Cabinet Relative To Revolutionary Governments of Petrograd (hereafter referred to as *Hankey Memorandum*), 23 February 1918; also Buchanan to Balfour, 7 September 1917; Buchanan to Balfour, 22 October 1917.

stoically. The American President did not concern himself with the events in Russia until 18 November, though he did utter a few inaccurate remarks on the happenings in his speeches during the preceding days. The press on the whole hoped that the bolsheviks would continue in the war, which seemed the main concern of the Americans as well as of the European Allies. In London Lord Milner noted in his diary that the news from Russia was bad and threw a new complexion on the war. The British press commented on the coup by apportioning the blame for it; animosity towards the bolsheviks came out later when they published their peace proposals. The members of the British War Cabinet had no summary of the events in Petrograd until 9 November. Even then, no attempt was made to interpret them.[1] In France the government had been in power for less than two months and the Foreign Minister Barthou in office only since 28 October. There was another governmental crisis during the events in Petrograd. The French press reported the events in Russia, but no aggressive answer came until 15 November when Clemenceau emerged as Prime Minister. France had had its mutinies and traitors. The press echoed the hope that Clemenceau and Pichon would deal with the Bolsheviks in international politics as they would deal with mutineers and traitors at home. However all this was to happen later; for the moment all the Allied governments waited for further information on subsequent developments, for the final denouncement and the actual attitude of the new rulers of Russia, if indeed they survived, towards the Allies and the war.

III

In a sense the bolsheviks revealed themselves, as far as peace negotiations were concerned, on 8 November when they passed the decree on peace. This undoubtedly was not a surprise to the Allies, for the bolsheviks had consistently advocated the ending of the war and peace negotiations. However, it was reasoned that to conclude a peace took two sides, and that so far only the bolsheviks had declared such intentions publicly; it was a long way from the proclamation of intentions to the actual conclusion of peace negotiations, as the bolsheviks themselves were going to find out. In any case the peace decree was overshadowed by the events of the day: the imminent comeback of Kerensky and the final showdown in the capital.

[1] Summary of Intelligence, 11th series 1917, no. 8, 9 November 1917.

The Allies in Petrograd had more immediate problems to face than to take notice of the declaration by the 'usurpers'. On 8 November they knew that the bolsheviks were masters of the capital; while the fighting still went on and the attitude of the new rulers was uncertain, the problem of the safety of the embassies and foreign nationals loomed large. At a meeting in the British Embassy it was decided that each embassy or legation should take measures individually to ensure safety. Immediately the thorny problem of making contact with the bolsheviks arose. But the problem was not insuperable. Captain Sadoul had already gained access to Smolny and, on the same day as the joint meeting took place, Major-General Knox called there to request the release of the women's battalion captured during the siege of the Winter Palace.[1] The women were released, so in a sense contacts were established. The following day, 15 November 1917, another Allied meeting was held in the British Embassy and the upshot of this was that the Military Attachés of Britain, France, and the United States called on the Petrograd Military HQ and demanded protection for the Embassies. Once again the request was granted, and the bolsheviks sent military cadets to guard the buildings. On the same day 'Colonel' Robins, of the American Red Cross Mission, called on Trotsky, without informing his Ambassador, and discussed Red Cross activity. Thus unofficial or semi-official contacts were established, and the embassies and their governments had a steady, supply of information on the new masters of Russia.

Still these initial contacts meant little while Kerensky was at large preparing his counter-coup. On 9 November Sir George was again assured by Avksentev, one of the SR leaders, that the bolsheviks would not last long.[2] Trotsky later alleged that Sir George gave money to the Committee for the Salvation of Russia. Avksentev was its leading member – but this is doubtful. At this stage all the Allies, partly through fear for the safety of themselves and their nationals, partly for lack of instructions from their Governments, remained strictly neutral and aloof from both the political struggle and actual fighting. The anxiety to appear neutral did not go as far as to make the Allies sever all contacts with the Russian opposition to the bolsheviks, but it went far enough. Thus when rumour had it that the French were actually fighting the bolsheviks in Moscow, the

[1] Buchanan to Balfour, 9 November 1917.
[2] Buchanan to Balfour, 20 November 1917.

5

Ambassador and the Military Mission were most emphatic in denials. Noulens even instructed Sadoul of whose contacts with Trotsky he knew, to explain in Smolny that the French officer captured in an armoured car in Petrograd was a Foreign Legion Lithuanian and not a Frenchman at all.

The period of passive waiting and half-hearted attempts to find out more about the bolsheviks lasted until 12 November 1917. On 10 November the embassies exceedingly enjoyed the rumours of Kerensky's imminent arrival in the capital and the mounting tensions in Smolny. Again the warning signs were ignored: Gots and Zenzinov were arrested trying to reach Kerensky. The bolsheviks were still very much the masters. On 11 November the embassies had yet another proof of bolshevik strength. The officer-cadets, provoked by false rumours of bolshevik collapse, left their academies and, in some cases, took over public buildings. Their merciless suppression prompted some of the Allied diplomats to reflect. Noulens came to the conclusion that whoever ultimately achieved power in Russia – Trotsky, Kerensky or Chernov – would do the same: sue for peace and carry out agrarian reforms.[1]

On 12 November the struggle was over. While Noulens thought that the civil war was about to start, it had in fact ended, at least for the time being. After an inconclusive engagement at Pulkovo Heights, the Cossacks of General Krasnov retired and thus sealed the fate of the Russian opposition. On the same day, the Stavka, the supreme HQ of the Russian Army, issued paper protests against the bolshevik seizure of power, since all its other efforts had failed. At the same time in London, a Foreign Office memorandum speculating on the future of Russia expected the Generals to save Russia for the Allied cause. Thus events proved the memorandum wrong, even at the moment of its appearance. However, once the issue was decided, it was time to devise new plans, to initiate action.

The following day Sir George recognized that Kerensky had failed and informed his government of this. Noulens, who much disliked Kerensky, did likewise. Francis offered no political advice to his government, though the day before he had urged the State Department to stop all credits to the Russian government. M. Destrée, the Belgian Minister in Petrograd and also a leading Belgian socialist, went to Smolny the same day to have a chat with Trotsky. He found himself in total disagreement with him, perhaps not surprisingly.

[1] Buchanan to Balfour, 21 November 1917.

Despite all the evidence, some Allied officials still thought that the energetic bolsheviks could be won over and persuaded to give up their 'peaceful' idea.

Both the French and the British cabinets knew on 14 November that 'heavy fighting' had taken place near Tsarskoye Selo and that Kerensky had been defeated.[1] Some action was urgently needed, but it was only on the following day that the French governmental crisis was resolved and Clemenceau emerged as the new Prime Minister. Decisions, everyone hoped, would soon be forthcoming. The embassies in Russia lacked guidance and were in a difficult position as it was becoming increasingly evident that the bolsheviks could not be ignored much longer. On 16 November 1917 Sir George asked the Foreign Secretary what relations he should establish with the bolsheviks. For a negative answer from the Secretary he had to wait until 20 November.[2] But Sir George's reaction was perhaps typical of the British attitude to a *fait accompli*: why not recognize it and come to terms with it? Noulens (perhaps equally typically for a Frenchman) reacted by switching his attention almost exclusively to establishing contacts with the opposition. He heard of the Don and sent the journalist Marchand there as his personal agent, but he never reached General Kaledin or Alekseyev. Instead, after setting out, he fell ill in Moscow and shortly afterwards 'joined' the bolsheviks. Ambassador Francis would not hear of establishing contacts with the bolsheviks, but his subordinates were much less scrupulous and he wasted his time fighting them over this issue. But the centre of gravity shifted from the capital to the Stavka at Mogilyov for the moment.

Sadoul's supply of information kept the French at least *au courant*. It was becoming obvious that the bolsheviks were serious about implementing their peace decree. So far the bolshevik coup had been an internal Russian affair, but any peace move was of vital concern to the Allies. However indifferent the Allies might be to the fate of the non-bolshevik Russians, bolshevik peace moves were forging a new alliance, or better renewing it. Both the Russian opposition and the Allies had reached the conclusion that the Stavka would become the focal point of further development, and Clemenceau chose it as the first challenge to the bolsheviks by the combined forces of the opposition and the Allies. On 19 November 1917 the War Office made it clear to

[1] Summary of Intelligence, 11th series 1917, no. 12, 14 November 1917.
[2] Buchanan to Balfour, 22 November 1917.

the British Cabinet that a separate peace by Russia would prolong the war considerably despite the imminent American participation in it.[1] Next day both the French and the British Cabinets were informed of the orders to General Dukhonin, the acting Supreme Commander, to initiate armistice negotiations with the Germans. Throughout 21 November the Stavka prevaricated. Meanwhile the Russian opposition leaders were gathering at Mogilyov to form a new government and launch a crusade against the bolsheviks under the protection of the generals. On 22 November Lenin and Stalin spoke to the reluctant Dukhonin again, and when he refused to obey their orders they dismissed him and appointed Ensign Krylenko as his successor. The implications of the dismissal excited the Allied missions at the Stavka. On 23 November they received their instructions from their governments which accepted the impasse at the Stavka as a suitable challenge and threw their lot in with the Russian opposition gathered there. But this move misfired, possibly because of bad coordination. The Italians delivered two notes contradicting each other. The Americans delivered an unauthorized one. Of the two 'coordinated' notes the French was violent in its tone and inflammatory in its contents.[2] But it did not inflame the Russian High Command nor inspire the gathered Russian politicians. The challenge failed, the first failure in a series of joint enterprises. Both sides had now shown their hands and both were preparing for the next venture. The Allies, however, had first to sort out the confusion in order to determine what form the venture should take.

IV

After so much indecision the situation in Russia had become dangerous. Apart from the obvious interest in keeping Russia in the war the Allies had important financial, economic and personal interests in the country. Pre-war and war credits had cost France, Britain and lately the United States considerable sums, and these would be lost if an open rupture occurred between the Allies and bolshevik Russia. Allied nationals and their economic interests in the country were another factor which made rupture impossible. At the same time, as long as a peace treaty had not been signed there was still hope that the bolsheviks could be either deflected from signing it

[1] Milner Memorandum, 19 November 1917.
[2] Clemenceau to Colonel Fagalde, 22 November 1917.

or forced by unfavourable conditions to refuse to sign it. It was imperative to maintain tenuous contact with the bolsheviks and to avoid an open rupture. It was equally imperative to try and overthrow them.

On 10 November 1917 the London *Morning Post* called for direct intervention in Russia aimed at the suppression of the bolsheviks and their replacement by friendly Russians. But this was an impracticable proposition and it remained what it was, a piece of irresponsible propaganda. It is true that some French diplomats also held this view, but both Noulens and Clemenceau were resolutely against it. On the other hand there were a few Allied representatives who advocated a *rapprochement* with the bolsheviks. But their views did not prevail either, at least for the time being. The most plausible way of thwarting the bolsheviks seemed to be to challenge them indirectly by means of the opposition forces on the spot. Thus a dual policy *vis à vis* the bolsheviks was adopted by all the Allies, namely keeping in touch with both the bolsheviks and the opposition and aiding the latter.

The adoption of the dual course was not surprising. From the beginning the Allies had been persistently baited by the bolsheviks. Even their peace proposals were broadcast first to the people of Allied countries and not to the governments. Bolshevik appeals to the peoples of Egypt and India to rise and overthrow their oppressors also disturbed the British government. When on 19 November Trotsky found the 'secret' treaties and on 23 November published them in *Izvestiya* the bolsheviks had very few friends left among the rulers of Western countries. The arrogance and offhandedness with which Allied diplomats were treated did not endear the bolsheviks to them either.[1]

The avoidance of a rupture did not by now mean passivity. The Allies were determined to give the bolsheviks as hard a time as they were getting. This struggle was conducted mainly at the diplomatic level. This 'diplomatic war' consisted of mutual harassing which sometimes did not lack a humorous side. Official recognition of the bolsheviks was not contemplated, but this did not unduly worry Trotsky who announced himself as the new Foreign Minister on 21 November. All his notes, *démarches* and threats were officially ignored. The Ambassadors took to answering them indirectly through the newspapers or press conferences.[2] But they also had more concrete

[1] *Hankey Memorandum*; also Buchanan to Balfour, 23 November 1917.
[2] Buchanan to Balfour, 24 November 1917.

problems which had to be resolved directly: the recognition of passports, visas and bolshevik representatives. The British fought a battle with Trotsky over Chicherin and Petrov, who were under arrest in Britain, and duly lost it. Trotsky stopped exit visas for British subjects in Russia and on 14 December Britain capitulated and released the detained bolsheviks. But there were also 'victories'. When early in January 1918 clashes occurred in Rumania between Russian and Rumanian troops the bolsheviks arrested the Rumanian minister in Petrograd. A collective *démarche* by Allied diplomats finally brought about his release, though the Rumanian gold reserve which was in Russia for safekeeping was not retrieved. However, between December 1917 and February 1918 Allied embassies were kept out of the real action which was undertaken by Allied military missions in centres of resistance to the bolsheviks.

V

All four Allied powers had military missions in Russia throughout the war. However, the missions differed considerably in importance. While Italy had only a few officers attached to the Russian army and its HQ, the Americans and the British, in addition to their Military Attachés, had quite important Red Cross and propaganda missions in Russia, as well as individual military representatives attached to various fronts and bases where they had particular interests. Compared with the French all the other Allied missions seemed insignificant.

General Niessel was the head of the French Military Mission in Russia and had a large contingent of officers and men under him in Petrograd. Until their departure from the Stavka the French had another large group of officers there under the command of General P. Janin. A smaller mission was at Kiev under General Tabouis. It maintained liaison with the Ukrainian authorities, ran two French hospitals at Kiev and Odessa, and also looked after an aviation base at Kiev. Another large contingent of French soldiers, mainly artillery experts and instructors were attached to various armies and fronts. Thus there was also a small mission at Tiflis and repatriation and shipping offices at Murmansk. Another large mission, soon to come under General Niessel, was in Rumania headed by General Berthelot. All missions and 'sub-missions' were headed by experienced officers of general rank with technocratic background (most of them were Polytechnic graduates).

The bolshevik *coupd' état* deprived General Niessel of effective control over many of the sub-missions. The Stavka ceased to be important when the Allied missions withdrew *en masse* shortly before Krylenko seized it.[1] Thus the two most important centres of French influence became Iassy and Kiev, both outside Great Russian territories. Since the French, as well as the British, had become disillusioned with the ethnic Russian element they 'abandoned the Russians' for the peripheral nationalities. Since in the north the bolshevik Russians were already negotiating a separate peace, definite support for the south or some kind of intervention was envisaged.

But from the outset there was no unity in Allied thinking on, and planning for the 'intervention'. The British on the whole favoured direct intervention as soon as this became feasible, if ever. However, in the Caucasus, much too near to their sphere of interest, they were ready to support separatists and local nationalists whom they opposed in other areas. The Americans favoured centralized power in Russia, consequently some sort of non-bolshevik Russians. The French supported the nationalities but even they were willing to make exceptions, if suitable Russian leaders or followers could be found. However, throughout their intervention in Russia the French did not really get on well with the Russians, consequently they preferred to deal with the local nationalists.

It is not quite certain when the French cabinet decided to support the anti-bolshevik opposition actively, but since the French seem to have been one step ahead of the British it was probably some time in late November. On 3 December 1917 the British Cabinet decided in principle to support General Kaledin and his South Eastern (Cossack) Union, and any other centre of opposition to the bolsheviks.[2] However, this support in principle did not amount to anything. First, batches of telegrams were sent out seeking information about Kaledin. Captain Noel from Tiflis was sent to the Don and his report finally contradicted all the optimistic reports about the Don which had reached the Embassy in Petrograd, the Consulate in Moscow and the British Mission at Iassy.[3] Thus on 14 December the

[1] Buchanan to Balfour, 28 November 1917.

[2] *Hankey Memorandum*; Buchanan to Balfour, 25 November 1917.

[3] Balfour to Barclay, 22 November 1917; Buchanan to Balfour, 23 November 1917; Knox to Radcliffe, 29 November 1917; Buchanan to Balfour, 30 November 1917; Wardrop to Balfour, 4 December 1917; Knox to Radcliffe, 5 December 1917; Buchanan to Balfour, 5 December 1917; Barclay to Balfour, 9 December 1917; Captain Noel via Knox to Radcliffe, 6 December 1917.

Cabinet, conscious of urgency, approved the first real help to the Russian opposition: large sums of money were to be disbursed to them.[1] However, the problem of getting the money to the opposition remained unsolved, and it can be assumed that no British money ever reached Kaledin or the Volunteer Army in the Don.

Though the French appeared more flexible and thorough than the British in helping the non-bolsheviks, their efforts likewise came to nothing. The decision to support the opposition found its expression in a special commission for Russia which was created on 7 December 1917. General Janin was its chairman and among others Dr. Beneš and Major Štefánik, the Czechoslovak exiles, were members. The commission was to study political problems in Russia, launch a propaganda campaign and prepare ways for action.[2] The composition of the commission showed a marked bias towards the nationalities, but perhaps also recognised their importance in Russia at that moment. The Czechs were obviously the cornerstone for any future action, though by now the French were already disappointed by their refusal to leave the Ukraine and take up positions against the Germans on the Rumanian front.

Both Britain and France hoped that the inter-Allied conference to be convoked in Paris at the end of November 1917 would bring some order into Allied actions in Russia. Instead the conference dealt only with the armistice and bolshevik peace proposals. Since the bolshevik proposals touched on Allied war aims there was sharp disagreement among the Allies on the problem. The French and Italians advocated the resolute pursuit of agreed war aims; the British vacillated under the pretext that such a resolute pursuit would completely alienate the bolsheviks from the Allied cause and drive them into an alliance with the Central Powers. The Americans were for a revision of war aims more in line with the bolshevik demands. Thus disagreeing on this fundamental question, the Allies also disagreed as to the form their support of the Russian opposition should assume. Though the Americans agreed that support for the opposition was necessary they refused to do anything practical. The only coordinated decision reached at this conference was to send an unofficial Anglo-French military mission to the Don.[3]

But even this modest coordinated move failed. For some reason

---

[1] *Hankey Memorandum.*
[2] Ministère des Affaires étrangères arrêté, 7 December 1917.
[3] War Office to General Ballard, Iassy, 3 December 1917.

General de Candolle, the British representative, did not leave Iassy for the Don till early in 1918. The French representative Colonel Hucher arrived at Novocherkassk on 22 December 1917. Curiously, the American Vice-Consul Poole also arrived there at the same time, but this was the result of private initiative by the Ambassador. After conferring with General Alekseyev and Professor Milyukov, and calling on Kaledin, both Poole and Hucher sent out messages urging their governments to support financially and otherwise the Cossacks of Kaledin and the Volunteers of Alekseyev.

In the meantime the French and British Cabinets made an effort to coordinate their policies in Russia. So far lack of liaison and contradictory advice had fanned confusion. There was no real agreement on the Caucasus, the South Eastern Union and the bolshevik north. On 21 December 1917 the British Cabinet discussed the situation in Russia in some detail. The Prime Minister, Lloyd George, received R. Bruce Lockhart, the recently returned Consul from Moscow, and told him that he would be the unofficial British agent with the bolsheviks. On the same day the Cabinet decided to continue to follow the dual policy, namely maintain unofficial contacts both with the bolsheviks and with the opposition forces in the south, the Caucasus, Siberia and the Cossack Voyska, especially the South Eastern Union.[1] After their decision the British made an effort to rationalize their approach to Russia and to coordinate actions with the French. Lord Milner, Lord Cecil and General Macdonogh left for Paris and discussed their respective positions throughout 22 December. An agreement was reached and on 23 December a convention was signed by the two parties. This convention has, ever since it was divulged in the thirties, become a target of abuse for the bolsheviks, the Whites and even for the Americans. For the two former it was an imperialist plan for the dismemberment of Russia, for the latter a rather cynical division of spheres of interest with which they disagreed. More recently some historians have argued that the convention was in fact a purely military one in which purely military tasks were dealt with. Others have claimed that it was the expression of the economic interests of the two Allies. There is probably some truth in all these arguments, except perhaps in the bolshevik and White one, for the British and French had never considered dismembering Russia, however desirable it might have seemed at the time. In the light of subsequent events, the convention appears a

[1] *Hankey Memorandum*; Balfour to Buchanan, 3 December 1917.

purely theoretical attempt by the far-away Allies to sort out policy problems and to allot each other tasks for future eventualities. There are many factors which support this view. First of all the convention did not embody the *status quo* in Russia. The 'allocation' of territories was done on a hypothetical basis. Thus the Don was allocated to the British, but it was the French who had a small mission there while there was no Briton anywhere near the territory, or at best the Briton was still *en route*. As for the Caucasus, the forces and interests of the Allies there were about equal, though the French mission at Tiflis probably exercised more influence than the British. The allocation of the Ukraine to the French did not mean that the British were excluded from it. In fact the British agent Bagge arrived there at about this time and helped the French, especially in financing pro-Allied forces. Neither was the convention meant as a long-term policy; most probably it was the result of Allied anxiety to organize some kind of resistance in the east against the Germans and the Turks and to support the suddenly deserted Rumanians as soon as practicable.

Thus despite the convention the French continued to look after the Don area. Early in 1918 General Berthelot at Iassy sent Captain Bordes with two French soldiers to deliver to Colonel Hucher at Novocherkassk 7 million francs for the Whites. After an adventurous journey Bordes and his soldiers reached Novocherkassk with their money intact. They were very disappointed when they found the whole mission, Colonel Hucher, Captains de Courson and Bernier in the local jail. The South Eastern Union had ceased to exist a few days previously after the suicide of Kaledin and the retreat of the loyal forces into the steppes south of the Don. Bordes procured the mission's release, gave Hucher 3 million francs and sent him with the others on to Moscow. Bordes then continued his peregrinations of southern Russia in search of the Whites, leaving behind him significant sums with various honorary French Consuls in the area for 'future use'.[1] Thus ended another attempt by the Allies at supporting the non-bolshevik Russians.

VI

In the Ukraine the situation was more complex but also more promising for the Allies. General Tabouis, who was in command of

[1] *Dossier Bordes.*

the French Mission in Kiev, had made contacts with the Ukrainians even before the *coup d'état* in Petrograd. But the friendly attitude of the Ukrainians to the Allies was influenced much more by two other factors: the presence of organized units of pro-Allied nationalities, especially the Czechoslovak and Polish Army Corps, and the position of Rumania in the war. It was obvious that Rumania could not continue in the war without food supplies from the Ukraine (the Don was too far). It was also obvious that the Rada, the Ukrainian government, very much depended on the military support of the Czechs and Poles, two close Allies of the French. Thus on the spot the Franco-Ukrainian alliance seemed a mutually profitable partnership.[1]

The Rada began to derive benefits from this 'partnership' as soon as the bolsheviks seized power in Petrograd. The 2nd Czech regiment which went into action against it on behalf of the Russian Military HQ in Kiev was withdrawn by the Czechoslovak Council two days after the fight for power started. The Czechs were followed by the Cossacks, and the HQ was forced to conclude an armistice leaving the Rada as the undisputed ruler of Kiev. Though the Rada at first ruled with the bolsheviks, the latter were expelled very shortly after the armistice in Kiev. Bolshevik organizations were suppressed by the Rada after the meeting of the 'suppressed nations' on 16 December 1917. The Rada made use of Polish troops in this operation. But even after this internal stabilization the Rada continued to depend on Czech and Polish troops for internal security, guard duties and the maintenance of order in the provinces. At the same time the Rada's position was made precarious by the existence of two external foes, the northern bolsheviks and the Germans.

Probably the Ukrainians could have held the Russian bolsheviks at bay with their own troops (which amounted to some three regiments and many irregular units) and the Czech and Polish troops, provided the western Allies lent all three their full support. As for the Germans, no one in the Ukraine had any illusions; it was obvious that at the first sign of activity on their part the Ukrainians would conclude a peace and the Czechs and the Poles would have to fly. However, how long the Rada could balance between the two external foes depended much on the diplomatic skill of the Allied representatives on the spot, on their determined leadership and on their unity of action, as well

---

[1] Buchanan to Balfour, 11 December 1917; Balfour to Buchanan, 15 December 1917; General Berthelot to Clemenceau, 7 December 1917.

as on the backing they could get from the cabinets in London and Paris.

On 24 December 1917 the Supreme Allied Council announced that everybody in Russia bent on continuing the war would get Allied support. At the same time the supply problems, which made the declaration void of any meaning, were raised.[1] On 1 January 1918 in a secret memorandum the situation in Russia was dealt with in more concrete terms. The French were already organizing the Ukrainian Army, and American engineers were about to be sent to Southern Russia to improve transportation. In case of renewed hostilities the Ukraine and Rumania were to be supplied via Persia and Siberia and for that purpose the Trans-Siberian Railway was to be put under Allied control. Allied landings, even if only temporary, would have to be contemplated. The memorandum concluded with a call for an inter-Allied bureau of intelligence.[2]

From the memorandum it can be concluded that the Allies had by now thrown all their weight behind the south Russian opposition forces, especially behind the Ukraine. It is also clear that not much progress had actually been achieved in organizing the opposition: even the intelligence services had not been coordinated. It is also obvious that all these steps had so far been taken for Rumania's sake. French reports confirm this view. On 3 January 1918 General Berthelot reported from Rumania that the Rumanian Army was still a good fighting force, but that the nationalities of Southern Russia would take long to train.[3] On 4 January 1918, however, the Foreign Office again discussed the situation in Russia and from the minutes of the meeting it is obvious that depression had by now crept in. Lord Cecil spoke of a desperate situation . . . 'so are our risks'. Five hundred million rubles were required to make Allied support really effective in Southern Russia and everyone was appalled by the risk involved. Even at this stage little was known of Novocherkassk, and the report of General de Candolle was awaited before taking a decision to offer any real help to Kaledin and Alekseyev.[4]

The Allies vacillated at home and feared the risks, Allied representatives on the spot acted likewise. It is clear that in January 1918 the

<hr />

[1] Memorandum on Suggested Policy in Russia signed by Lords Milner and Cecil, Clemenceau and Pichon, 23 December 1917.

[2] *Foreign Office Memorandum*, 1 January 1918.

[3] Berthelot to Clemenceau, 3 January 1918.

[4] *Sir George R. Clerk Memorandum*, 4 January 1918; Also General de Candolle to General Radcliffe, 6 January, 22 January, 28 January, 9 February 1918.

crisis in Russia reached its height, and resolution and firmness were needed, above all in the Ukraine. The bolsheviks had started their operations against the Don and were getting ready to launch an invasion of the Ukraine. The Rumanians could be counted on and the Allies still had under their control the two Polish and the Czechoslovak Army Corps. According to Colonel Nielsen, the Polish Corps under General Dówbor-Muśnicki was an excellent fighting force which, however, lacked artillery and other equipment. In Nielsen's opinion the Corps would be completed early in 1918 despite the Bielgorod Poles' opposition.[1] Apart from this corps, resolute action could create another Polish Corps, which was being formed by General Michaelis in Kiev. The Allies could also hope to form a second Czechoslovak Army Corps and reassemble the various Serbian detachments scattered throughout Russia. Together with the Rada forces it seemed that quite a large army could be put together and used in the field against the bolsheviks and even against the Germans.

But somehow Allied leadership failed completely. Not that the various schemes were not tried out. On 2 January 1918 Major Vanier informed the Czechoslovak Council in Kiev that henceforth a common recruiting commission would deal with Polish, Rumanian and Czech recruits. A new supply commission was formed for the Ukrainians, Poles, Czechs and Rumanians. All these nationalities and the newly formed units would come under a special military HQ in Kiev. No one objected to this rationalization, but vigour and purposefulness were lacking and hardly anything of this project was implemented. Time was running out.

The 1st Polish Corps was out of the way but there were attempts to make it fall in with the French plan to resist both the Germans and the bolsheviks in the Ukraine. The plan was divulged on 20 January 1918. General Tabouis who in the meantime became the French High Commissioner to the Rada, ordered the Czech Corps to move to the Vinnitsa-Mogilyov line under General Lafont's command. Thus it would have on its right wing the Polish Corps and on its left the Ukrainians, 2nd Polish Corps and the Rumanian Army.[2] Though this front-line was intended against the Germans it could be defended against the bolsheviks, if the situation so required. The order, however, was more of a test case. If the Czechs obeyed and moved, the Southern Bloc could become reality, and the limited re-establishment

---

[1] General Panouse to Clemenceau, 13 December 1917.
[2] Panouse to Clemenceau, 2 April 1918.

17

of the Eastern Front effected. Divided, the Ukraine and the nationalities did not stand a chance against either the bolsheviks or the
Germans. United under the Allied command they could mean much.
But the Allies could not enforce unity; neither could they have simple
military orders obeyed. The Czechs refused to move, and everything
collapsed. By 23 January 1918 Tabouis and Bagge knew that the
Rada was ready to conclude a peace with the Germans.[1] On 22
January 1918 the declaration of Ukrainian independence was issued
and the Ukrainians went to Brest-Litovsk to sue for peace. Events
then followed swiftly. The 1st Polish Corps tried to fight but was
defeated by the bolsheviks and forced to join the Germans, who
disarmed it. The bolsheviks, after proclaiming their own Rada at
Kharkhov, invaded the Ukraine.[2] Without Czech and Polish support
the Rada was easily defeated. Kiev fell on 7 February and the Rada
had to fly and only returned with the invading Germans three weeks
later. But when this happened, in March 1918, there were no more
Polish Corps, the Czechs were retreating disorganized, the Don and
the Volunteers were in the steppes and Rumania had just concluded
a separate peace. Now only the bolsheviks were left opposing the
Germans, and the Allies, disappointed with the non-bolsheviks were
now tentatively ready to turn to them.

VII

The success and energy of the bolsheviks prompted some Allied
representatives in Russia and outside to advocate *rapprochement*
with them. Ambassador Noulens commented on their energy shortly
after the *coup d'état*; however, this very energy made him ultimately
a determined supporter of a direct Allied intervention. General
Niessel's attitude was more complicated; he could not fail to recognize bolshevik enthusiasm and energy, and at times favoured
rapprochement. With him much depended on immediate circumstances.[3] It is, however, clear that the British agent in Russia, Bruce
Lockhart, advocated an alliance with the bolsheviks almost without
reservation. Despite his efforts, both Paris and London remained
indifferent. Thus on 6 February 1918 Lockhart cited in support of his
arguments for the *rapprochement* bolshevik successes in Finland, the

---

[1] Panouse to Clemenceau, 23 January 1918.
[2] Panouse to Clemenceau, 18 February 1918 (General Barter to Radcliffe).
[3] General Niessel to Clemenceau, 2 March 1918

Ukraine and the Don. But as General Panouse commented on this telegram, forwarding it to Paris: 'these successes against our friends were precisely the reasons why the bolsheviks should not be supported'.[1]

By February 1918 Lockhart, Sadoul and Robins were not the only ones to advocate a *détente* with the bolsheviks. On 16 February General Poole also thought that if the Allies recognized the bolsheviks they would turn anti-German and join the Allies.[2] Indeed when the peace negotiations at Brest were broken off on 11 February Allied speculations about the bolsheviks became wild. Many of the representatives on the spot performed a daring *volte face* and began to see an advantage in the peace negotiations which they had found so catastrophic when they had opened. Now it appeared that 'Colonel' Robins, benefiting from the negotiations, was able to send a subversive mission of Russian bolsheviks to Germany to start a revolution there.[3] The bolsheviks, especially Trotsky, were coming round to the Allied point of view, namely that it would be impossible to satisfy German imperialism. All the same the bolsheviks made it clear that they were turning anti-German because they thought that German militarism was the more dangerous of the two imperialisms and that it had to be defeated first.[4]

The direct courting of the bolsheviks started in January 1918. By 12 February it was so advanced that even such a staunch opponent of theirs as Noulens lent himself to a collective *démarche* offering the bolsheviks Allied aid in case of German attack. On 13 February 1918 *Pravda* used this offer tactically in public to impress the Germans. But the Germans refused to heed 'paper tactics'; they knew of Allied weakness in Russia, which in the minds of the Germans made the Allies responsible for bolshevik successes and the gradual elimination of pro-Allied Russians. On 18 February 1918 they denounced the armistice and launched an attack against the bolsheviks.

On the same day Noulens and Lindley, the British chargé d'affaires, let it be known to the bolshevik foreign Ministry that Allied aid would be forthcoming if requested.[5] Still it was with evident relish that the Allied military commentators wrote of the German army

[1] Panouse to Clemenceau, 6 February 1918.
[2] General Poole to Radcliffe, 16 February 1918.
[3] Panouse to Clemenceau, 9 February 1918.
[4] Lockhart to Balfour, 16 February 1918.
[5] Balfour to Lockhart, 4 March 1918.

dispersing 'bolshevik bands'.[1] Indeed the collapse of the bolshevik bands was so complete that even Trotsky began to entertain the idea of Allied aid seriously. On 21 February 1918 Captain Sadoul asked the Ambassador what France would do for Russia. Noulens went out of his way to telephone the answer to Trotsky. While he asked General Niessel to get a defence plan ready he radioed Paris and through Paris all the other Allies urging them to support the bolsheviks at this juncture. Trotsky in the meantime told Lockhart that the bolsheviks were ready to retreat to the Urals but would not stop fighting.[2] This was obviously an exaggeration, for by then the bolsheviks were waiting for German consent to sign the peace treaty, but in the circumstances the exaggeration worked. All the Allies, with the exception of the United States, approved aid to the bolsheviks. Immediately all over Russia Allied (i.e. mainly French) officers joined the retreating bolshevik detachments as demolition experts and began to blow up rail communications to delay the German advance.[3]

On 22 February 1918 General Niessel had his defence plan ready and approved by the Allied governments. But it took him two more days to see the 'belligerent' Trotsky. When he finally saw him and explained it, Trotsky, who by then knew that the Germans had just accepted the bolshevik request to sign the peace and consequently halted their advance, told the General that the plan was good but of no use. He did not enlarge on his reasons. Though on 25 February Lockhart again reported that the bolsheviks were going to raise an army and make use of Allied help in organizing it, it was obvious that for the moment at least the game of cooperating with the Allies was up. Allied embassies were leaving the capital, and the Germans were expected to take it at any moment. Bolshevik forces offered resistance to the Germans only in few places. On the whole they preferred to fly.[4] Bolshevik power seemed to crumble; there were disagreements in the leadership on the crisis. The end seemed at hand. But then suddenly the Germans, who had occupied all the territory they wanted, stopped their advance. In any case the bolsheviks signed an even worse treaty on 3 March 1918 than that originally proposed. When on 15 March 1918 Lenin finally brought off the ratification of the treaty against vigorous opposition during the 4th Congress of the

[1] Summary of Intelligence, 13th series, no. 10, 12 March 1918.
[2] Lockhart to Balfour, 22 February 1918.
[3] *Dossier Bordes*.
[4] Lockhart to Balfour, 25 February 1918.

Soviets, a new era opened for both the bolsheviks and the Germans.

Another Allied move had failed and the situation in Russia had become even more confused than previously. The Allies were now scattered all over Russia, largely isolated from each other. The centres of influence disappeared from the south and moved out to the extreme north. Siberia became overnight the most important centre of attention. With the Japanese landing shortly after the Brest crisis the question of direct intervention arose again. Still the problem was: would the bolsheviks be defeated internally as a result of their collapse against the Germans, or would intervention be necessary to bring about their downfall. If the latter was inevitable under what pretext could it be carried out?

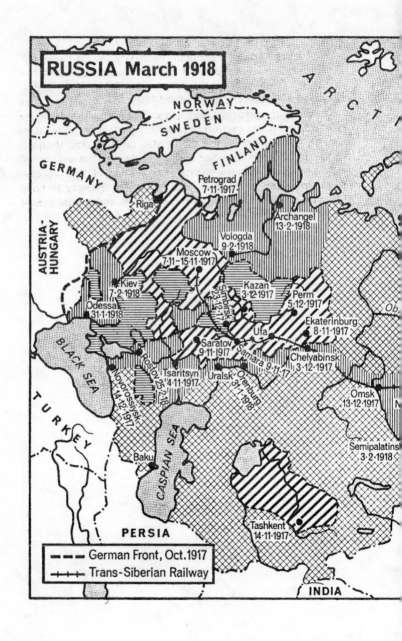

RUSSIA March 1918

NORWAY
SWEDEN
FINLAND
GERMANY
AUSTRIA-HUNGARY
ARCTIC

Petrograd
7·11·1917

Archangel
13·2·1918

Riga

Vologda
9·2·1918

Moscow
7·11-15·11·1917

Kiev
7·2·1918

Odessa
31·1·1918

Simbirsk
23·12·17

Kazan
3·12·1917

Perm
5·12·1917

Ekaterinburg
8·11·1917

Ufa

Ob

BLACK SEA

Rostov 25·2·18

Novorossisk
14·12·1917

Saratov
9·11·1917

Samara 9·11·17

Chelyabinsk
3·12·1917

Tsaritsyn
4·11·1917

Uralsk

Orenburg
31·1·1918

Omsk
13·12·1917

TURKEY

Baku

CASPIAN SEA

Semipalatins
3·2·1918

PERSIA

Tashkent
14·11·1917

German Front, Oct.1917

Trans-Siberian Railway

INDIA

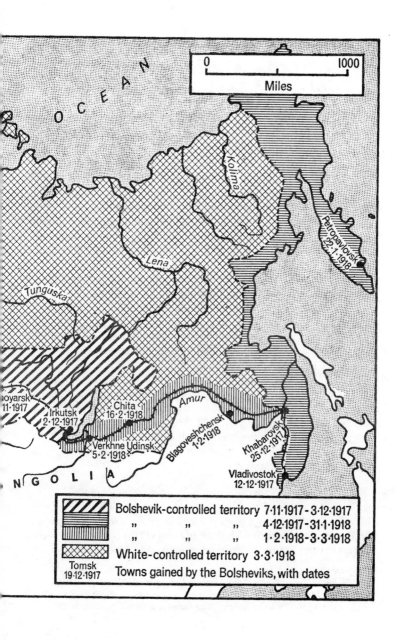

Bolshevik-controlled territory 7·11·1917 – 3·12·1917

" " " 4·12·1917 – 31·1·1918

" " " 1·2·1918 – 3·3·1918

White-controlled territory 3·3·1918

Tomsk
19·12·1917 Towns gained by the Bolsheviks, with dates

CHAPTER TWO

JAPAN AS ALLIED MANDATORY

I

The first Japanese landing at Vladivostok took place on 5 April and was of short duration. Captain Payne of HMS Suffolk also landed a few of his sailors to help in guarding the British Consulate. This 'joint action' by the local commanders, Admiral Kato and Captain Payne, while reflecting the spirit which animated Allied intervention in the Far East, proved abortive. This time another ally, the United States, joining paradoxically the bolsheviks, was able to thwart British and Japanese intentions. Within a month the Japanese marines and the British sailors were back on board their ships in the Vladivostok harbour.[1]

However, when on 3 August 1918 the Japanese 12th Infantry Division began to disembark at Vladivostok it was there to stay for a long time. By 21 August additional 12,000 soldiers had passed through the city on their way to Manchuria. On 26 August still 10,000 more arrived and by November 1918 the Japanese had more than 70,000 troops in Siberia. This then was a massive indication of Allied intervention in the Far East.

But in fact the Japanese were in Siberia not as an intervening force of the Western Allies against the Central Powers but as self-declared helpers of the Czech Corps which was in difficulty after its revolt against the bolsheviks in May 1918. Above all this was not the beginning of a massive intervention, but its climax. Nonetheless, the Japanese were in Siberia by the grace of British diplomatic and French political initiative.[2]

II

After the early warnings from the special British and French envoys in Russia, Henderson and Thomas, in July 1917 the two Allied governments began to think seriously of military aid to Russia in terms of

[1] Vide Chapter I.

[2] Documents cited in this chapter were consulted in the Ministère de la Guerre and Ministère des Affaires étrangères in Paris. The Milner Papers in Oxford as well as the Admiralty and Foreign Office archives were also used.

combat units. It was vital to keep the Russian Army in the field and without the help of Allied divisions this seemed unlikely. It was therefore necessary to find and transport such fighting units to Russia.[1]

The search for the units to prop up Russian morale was difficult and after 7 November 1917 further complicated by the fact that the new government would probably not welcome them. Thus even if the troops could be found they would have to be an intervening rather than Allied force. By then it was also obvious that the Allied countries which could raise the necessary troops were the Americans or the Japanese. But the Americans proved quite unreceptive to the idea of sending their troops to fight in Russia. Thus the Japanese were the last hope, and if persuaded to intervene, were tactically well placed to reinforce the newly reconstituted eastern front.

It seemed logical that the Japanese intervention in Russia should be actively considered by the interested Allies. The two Allies who had most to gain from the Japanese aid to Russia were, of course, France and Britain. Thus both governments made their first decisions concerning Japan and her intervention in Russia as early as November 1917.

Though in 1918 all the Allies were interested in Japan's entry in the war against Germany and its allies, there was no agreement among them where and in what form this should be achieved. Britain which thought that the Japanese contribution to the active war would be most beneficial to her was the first to take up the issue and remained throughout the moving force behind the pressures to secure Japan's active participation until its successful solution in August 1918.

Britain could always count on full French support. But while French reasons remain obscure Britain certainly had specifically her own. With the collapse of Russia, Siberia and the Russian south, Turkestan, Kazakhstan and the Caucasus found themselves in a power vacuum and there was a danger that if the bolsheviks and Germans arrived at an agreement, or even without it, by an unilateral action of Germany, India could be threatened from the north. This was the primary reason for the British to urge a full-scale intervention in Eastern Russia (a loose term for Siberia and south). Naturally the British even when in special need of the Japanese were cautious enough not to give them a free hand. This is possibly the reason why the negotiations between the Allied partners were so tortuous and ultimately futile. All the same Japanese intervention in Siberia was the result of British initiative.

[1] Vide Chapter IV.

III

While the bolsheviks were victorious in European Russia Siberia remained passive and uneasy. Bolshevik progress there was slow; of the Siberian cities only Krasnoyarsk turned bolshevik in November 1917 – Vladivostok had its Soviet on 12 December 1917. It was perhaps this inexplicably slow progress which caused chaos and confusion to increase. The increasing chaos prompted a British observer in the Far East, Commander Locker-Lampson, to send a memorandum to London in which he asked for the Allied occupation of Vladivostok and for the protection of the war stores in the city. The French government had similar reports and recommendations from the French Consul, André.[1]

Another reminder of the chaos in the Russian Far East was Sir John Jordan's telegram from Pekin in which the Ambassador conveyed the Chinese government's request for Allied troops to protect foreign nationals at Kharbin in Manchuria.[2] After these and other warnings the British government took up the problem of the Far East.

On 7 December 1917 the situation in the Far East was discussed by the War Cabinet. It was thought that the simplest solution would be if Japan intervened in the area. But since American opposition to the Japanese intervention was well known it would have to be overcome first. In any case at that moment a direct Japanese involvement seemed premature: it would have forced the bolsheviks into German hands. It was quite possible that if the Japanese were let loose on them the bolsheviks might even join the Germans and fight their former allies. No active measure was therefore decided upon. But pressure was to be put on the United States to change its non-intervention policy and permit, or even join Japan in intervening in the Far East, if the situation there deteriorated still further.

As a result Britain embarked on a series of diplomatic and political *démarches* in Washington. But the Americans persevered in opposing Japanese intervention very resolutely.[3] Japan on the other hand was most reluctant to move without American support. The Japanese, however, made a clear distinction between an intervention and the defence of national interests. While they were reluctant to start the former they did not hesitate to send several troop ships to Vladi-

[1] André to Paléologue, 2 May 1917; André to Ribot, 19 July 1917.
[2] Sir John Jordan to Balfour, 19 November 1917.
[3] Sir Cecil Spring-Rice to Balfour, 11 December 1917.

vostok, where a Soviet had at long last been established and Japanese interests in the city threatened. These ships arrived on 12 December, but after American protests no troops were landed. Shortly afterwards an American ship also arrived at Vladivostok and Admiral Knight's presence in the city 'had a salutary effect on the Russians who were becoming restive'. Thus the American ship moored alongside the Japanese troopships exemplifying the check in which the two nations held each other.[1]

While the American involvement in Vladivostok was welcome by the Russians the Japanese took it rather badly. Viscount Motono, Japanese Foreign Minister, told Sir Cunnyngham Greene, British Ambassador in Tokyo, that American interference was very unpopular in Japan. However, for the present he could but ignore it; but he was very interested in subsequent American intentions. After this message Balfour saw quickly to it to find out Washington's plans using the Japanese enquiry as a pretext. By then Balfour had also the military opinion on the subject of the Far Eastern intervention: the Imperial General Staff thought a joint Japanese-American action there would be very useful. It would be to everybody's advantage if the two countries agreed to guard the stores in Vladivostok and to assume the control of the Trans-Siberian Railway.[2]

But the Americans had not changed their views *vis-à-vis* Japan. Lansing, Secretary of State, told the British Ambassador that the United States were aware of Japan's readiness to protect the Japanese colony in the Russian Far East. But a Japanese or a joint Japanese-American intervention in that area was quite a different matter. Both were out of the question at present.[3] All the Americans concerned with the Far East were completely unanimous at this stage. Thus Colonel Stevens, who was in the Far East with his Railway Mission, also opposed Japanese or joint intervention. He thought that such an effort would drive the bolsheviks into the hands of Germany and would unite them in their opposition and hostility against the Allies. He was therefore even against the landing of his own mission (some 400 experts) in Vladivostok.[4]

It is true that the British (and the French for that) were anxious to

[1] Buchanan to Balfour, 14 December 1917.

[2] Sir Cunnyngham Greene to Balfour, 15 December 1917; Chief of the Imperial General Staff to Balfour, 20 December 1917; Balfour to Spring-Rice, 21 December 1917.

[3] Lansing to Spring-Rice, 22 December 1917.

[4] Morris to Lansing, 26 December 1917.

use the Japanese in the Far East. However, British national interests would have been best served if the Americans joined the Japanese in order to keep an eye on this Asian ally. Britain therefore never pressed the United States to give Japan a *carte blanche*. Viscount Chinda, Japanese Ambassador in London, showed his surprise and puzzlement, when, during an interview with Lord Cecil at the Foreign Office he was told that Japan should aim at a joint action with the United States. Chinda was after all only responding to British pressure when he had previously assured Lord Cecil that Japan would sooner or later act unilaterally and land forces in the Russian Far East.[1]

This perhaps rather indiscreet revelation was immediately exploited by the British in Washington. The Americans were asked how they would react to such unilateral action. They reacted very strongly and in the wrong quarter. The Japanese Ambassador in Washington had to deny the story: Japan had never entertained such an intention.[2]

While this cautious sounding out and diplomatic preparation for intervention by Japan was going on the Western Allies completely disregarded both the Russian bolshevik and White opinion. The Japanese still thinking of the possibility of being invited to intervene cultivated the Whites. The Russian Ambassador in Tokio, Krupensky, was consulted from time to time by Motono and agreed to Japanese intentions. The Russians were also asked by the Japanese to make their views known in the West.[3]

The new Russian initiative pleased the British, for it strengthened their case for a Japanese intervention. But obviously the Russians were only used by the Japanese. At the first interview the timid Russian Ambassador was simply told of Japanese plans. Motono also complained that the Japanese could not move against the bolsheviks because of Allied pressure. But despite this he was prepared to consider landing Japanese forces in Vladivostok, if local conditions required it and local authorities asked for it. On 23 January 1918 the Ambassador was suddenly told Japan was ready to take an independent action in Siberia as soon as it became necessary and ignore Allied public opinion. The Ambassador did not even have time to protest. He was personally opposed to an unilateral Japanese action but did not say so. Instead he pleaded for Japanese aid to Ataman Semenov hinting thus as to the form Japanese intervention should assume.

[1] Chinda to Cecil, 27 December 1917.
[2] Ishii to Lansing, 28 December 1917.
[3] D. I. Abrikosov, *Memoirs mss.*, pp. 10–11 (Columbia University archive).

But Motono refused to discuss the matter any further. He knew that the Ambassador would pass on this information to the Western Allies and this seems to have been the sole purpose of the 'consultation'.[1]

This message from Tokio did not fail to alarm London. It was delivered with suitable oral commentary by Nabokov, the Russian chargé d'affaires in London, who made it clear that even the White Russians were seriously opposed to a direct intervention by Japan. The British Consul in Vladivostok and Lindley, the British chargé d'affaires in Russia, soon confirmed that the Soviet Russians were equally opposed to Japan. But the Western Allies also thought it highly undesirable that the Japanese should suddenly threaten to take a direct action without consultation.[2] The British desire to see Japan actively intervening was being foiled by the Japanese themselves who by insisting on acting independently were asking for trouble from the other allies, especially, from the Americans.

Balfour therefore tried again to slow down the Japanese. When his Ambassador in Tokio reported early in January 1918 that the Japanese were disappointed with the previous British suggestion that they should act jointly with the United States in Siberia the Ambassador was instructed to explain more fully British views.[3] But the Japanese had probably understood the implication of this suggestion and refused to listen to the Ambassador. Instead they sent two notes to London, in which they argued for a direct and unilateral action in the Far East.[4] A new formula to cover this Japanese contingency had to be found and the Foreign Secretary, after he had ascertained the urgency of Japanese intervention, promptly produced one.

Late in January 1918 the War Office produced a memorandum on the situation in the Far East in which the necessity of Japan's direct involvement in the war was stressed. Grave risks were involved if Japan failed to join in. Lord Milner then urged Balfour to find a political solution to the Japanese military involvement.[5]

On 26 January 1918 Balfour sent out notes to all the Allied governments in which he elaborated the new formula. He asked the Allied powers to recognise Japan as their mandatory in the Far East whose task would be to secure the war stores in Vladivostok and the Trans-

[1] Motono to Krupensky, 23 January 1918.
[2] Greene to Balfour, 1 January 1918.
[3] Balfour to Greene, 10 January 1918.
[4] Chinda to Cecil, 11 January 1918; Greene to Balfour, 14 January 1918.
[5] Milner to Balfour, 20 January 1918.

Siberian Railway line. The mandate excluded any territorial expansion of Japan in the Far East, but the Japanese action was thought of as vital for the success of Allied war effort. The French government immediately approved this new formula and agreed with the British government on all points. On 31 January 1918 the two governments agreed to ask the Japanese jointly to study the problems connected with the protection of the Trans-Siberian Railway.[1]

Surprisingly enough the Italians objected to this new way of getting the Japanese to fight in the war. They saw in an unilateral intervention by Japan a danger to western prestige: the yellow race fighting successfully the white race: but they tempered their objection with an addendum: the Italians had only very slight interests in the Far East.[2] The new proposal, however, hinged on the American reaction to it.

In the United States Lord Reading and Sir William Wiseman put concerted pressure on the Americans to react favourably to this new formula. But despite their efforts the Americans rejected it. They were unwilling to intervene at this stage and were against any one mandatory even in the future, when the posibility of an intervention might be envisaged.[3] This was indeed a deadlock and the French, who felt rather impatient with this inaction reacted rather strongly. Though they did not show previously any special initiative in this matter, they were now prepared to do anything to create a military diversion in the Far East.

Throughout February 1918 the British and French governments were seeking a way out of the impasse. While the British were still keen on seeing Japan actively in the war they were, nevertheless, opposed to having them in the war at any price. First they tried to convince the French that Japanese intervention was impossible without American support. But the French remained unconvinced. They now impatiently pressed for a Japanese drive through Siberia up to the Urals and saw no complication in it provided that no territorial annexations were contemplated. But it was the question of guarantees which complicated the Japanese drive as far as the Russians and Americans were concerned. Anyway the British thought such a drive militarily impossible.

The French then decided to push the other allies into some kind of

[1] Balfour to Pichon, 26 January 1918; Sir William Wiseman to Colonel House, 30 January 1918; Balfour to Pichon, 31 January 1918.

[2] Italian Foreign Ministry to Foreign Office, 6 February 1918.

[3] Wiseman to Balfour, 1 February 1918.

decision. They suddenly started their own negotiations with the Japanese; their aim was a limited joint action in Siberia. This joint drive should secure the foodstuffs and other stores in the area against possible German seizure. The French even went as far as to float a rumour to alarm the other allies. According to it Japan was contemplating seceding from the alliance in order to procure for herself a free hand in the Far East. Then the Japanese would occupy the Far Eastern Russian province up to Irkutsk.[1]

But the rumour failed to alarm the other Allies, for it was hardly credible. In the meantime the Italians changed their minds and accepted Balfour's 'mandatory idea' but it was not the result of the French-inspired rumour. American opposition in any case killed the idea and events in the Far East suddenly made Japanese intervention less urgent. Ataman Semenov at long last showed some promise by scoring several local successes against the bolsheviks.[2]

Evidently all depended on the Americans and their change of mind. At first President Wilson seemed to agree to the 'mandatory idea'. He drafted a letter to the Japanese Ambassador in which he cautiously approved of the idea. The draft of the letter was shown to the Allied governments and everyone was hopeful. But then suddenly the President re-drafted the letter and in the end the Japanese received a very discouraging missive. Colonel House, the President's right hand man, also remained strongly opposed to an unilateral action.[3] However, this American obdurance seems to have finally decided the Japanese. If they were going to intervene alone they were going to do it on their own terms.

In London ways were still being explored how to make an unilateral action by Japan more palatable to the other allies. On 4 March 1918 it was suggested that the Japanese should guarantee the Russian Siberian provinces against the Germans and act as Allied mandatories up to Chelyabinsk, or at least up to Omsk.[4] But this idea did not really solve anything. The declaration was hardly a suitable replacement for solemn guarantees; and the Germans still had to be found in the area which Japan was to occupy.

[1] Jusserand to Lansing, 8 January 1918; Lansing to Jusserand, 16 January 1918; Sharp (Paris) to Lansing, 28 February 1918; Balfour to Cambon, 12 February 1918; Cambon to Balfour, 16 February 1918; Greene to Balfour, 23 February 1918 (Regnault's conversation with Motono).

[2] Lord Rodd to Balfour, 16 February 1918; Jordan to Balfour, 4 March 1918.

[3] Wiseman to Balfour, 4 and 5 March 1918.

[4] Balfour to Greene, 4 March 1918.

By March 1918, however, the situation had substantially changed. Up to then Japan was asked to join in the war against Germany and act in the Far East. But on 15 March 1918 the bolsheviks finally ratified the Peace of Brest-Litovsk and thus became in Allied eyes if not an ally of Germany at least its helpers. The Allies began more and more to think of bolsheviks as German agents or puppets and consequently Japan could now move against them, even despite American opposition. On 4 March 1918 Sir Robert Bruce Lockhart was instructed to warn the bolsheviks that an agreement with Germany meant Japanese intervention.[1] This open move was calculated to precipitate a crisis, one or the other way, the other way being an agreement between the Allies and bolsheviks. But Trotsky probably knew of American opposition to Japanese intervention. Thus he responded rather enigmatically: the bolsheviks were prepared to go down fighting the Germans rather than having the Japanese as allies intervening on their behalf in Russia. France and Britain could not use Japan to threaten the bolsheviks. On 14 March 1918 President Wilson finally took care of this diplomatic weapon. He declared that Russia had no need to fear a Japanese intervention as long as he was President.[2]

In March 1918 the fear in the west was that the Germans would gradually occupy the whole of Russia. Desperate plans were hatched to prevent this from happening. It was still thought that a Japanese intervention against the Germans in Russia was imperative, despite bolshevik objections. Last efforts in this sense were made by Balfour on the same day on which President Wilson rejected so decisively Japanese intervention. In the House of Commons Balfour declared that Russia would not gather the fruit of her revolution if she was occupied by the Germans. He therefore publicly urged the bolsheviks to invite the Allies to intervene in Russia via Siberia at this fatal hour. Lockhart, who was given the draft of the statement prior to the House, tried his best but failed to procure the necessary bolshevik invitation. But the invitation continued to figure in Allied-bolshevik negotiations henceforth for some considerable time.[3] But then the peace treaty was signed, German advance stopped and the bolsheviks remained in power in the unoccupied territory.

On 15 March 1918 the European Allies met in London and dis-

---

[1] Balfour to Lockhart, 4 March 1918.

[2] Lockhart to Balfour, 14 March 1918; Wiseman to War Office, 14 March 1918.

[3] Balfour to Lockhart, 17 March 1918.

cussed among other things the dangerous situation in Russia. The conference was unanimous on one point: only Japan could save the situation there by a direct intervention. It was decided that concerted pressure should be put on the American President to sanction, if not join, the intervention via Siberia.[1] But once again the Americans rejected the idea outright. Through Admiral Knight at Vladivostok they declared that the idea of a direct intervention was premature, and in any case it would have to be a joint venture.[2]

The war situation during the month of March 1918 continued to deteriorate for the Allies in all the war theatres. The Japanese became very restless; they also came to identify the bolsheviks as German puppets and launched their own pressure campaign for an intervention. In Washington they asked the President for the reasons for his 'friendliness' towards the bolsheviks. France was next attacked for maintaining official representatives with the bolsheviks and Allied inability to come to an agreement on intervention came under fire. There was really no sense in this campaign: it only created further confusion. The issue now was straight: would Japan accept to act in Siberia as an Allied mandatory, and would the United States help the intervening Japanese at least financially?[3]

On 21 March 1918 the British War Cabinet took its final decisions: Japan was to intervene and American support would somehow be obtained. It was also decided that if Japanese intervention were to take place at all, it would have to be a substantial effort.[4] Colonel House was immediately approached and told of the British views. He was impressed by the British case: the German offensive in France was in full swing and served as the most compelling argument for a diversionary action elsewhere. But the Colonel was utterly unimpressed by the Japanese, who were to provide the diversion. He asked very pertinent questions: have they sufficient troops? how much financial aid would they require from the United States? The Colonel also insisted on a joint action, if the United States decided for an intervention. He added a rider: Lockhart would have to obtain an invitation for it from the bolsheviks.[5]

This latest reaction of Colonel House to Allied proposals was

[1] Balfour to Lord Reading, 16 March 1918.
[2] Wiseman to Balfour, 29 March 1918.
[3] Greene to Balfour, 19 March 1918.
[4] Balfour to Wiseman, 26 March 1918.
[5] Wiseman to Balfour, 29 March 1918.

interpreted as American softening up. But the President still remained adamant: nothing could be done in Russia at present. Unlike Colonel House he simply refused to discuss intervention. But the French and British were prepared for the final assault on the President. The Allied general staffs were given orders to draw up special military memoranda for the President arguing for the necessity of an Allied intervention in Russia. On 15 April 1918 Colonel Robins and Lockhart were asked to obtain bolshevik invitations.[1] All contingencies were considered and no excuse would be left to the Americans to object.

But these manoeuvres and delays disturbed the Japanese. They also put pressure on the Americans to decide either way; in any case they were ready to act unilaterally. When their intentions became known to the bolsheviks Trotsky suddenly announced his invitation to the Allies to intervene. The Allies were puzzled but pleased. However, soon the purpose of the invitation became clear: it was to delay and check the Japanese. The invitation was followed by orders from Lenin to remove all the war stores from Vladivostok and subsequently by a request from Trotsky for *Allied proposals* for the intervention.[2]

Though the move failed to prevent the Japanese to land a small force in Vladivostok it did succeed in driving it out of the city. During March 1918 the chaos in Vladivostok increased and general lawlessness prevailed in the city. When several Japanese citizens were attacked and one killed Admiral Kato landed some marines to protect the lives of the Japanese in the city. A small British force was also landed possibly to give the action the appearance of an Allied effort, possibly also to keep an eye on the Japanese. But the choice of the moment for the landing could not have been worse. With strong American opposition and the bolshevik invitation in the air the action was doomed. Within a month the marines and sailors were withdrawn, the Japanese foreign minister, Motono, who was the driving force behind the landing, dismissed and the question of Allied intervention unresolved.

One small difference was apparent in the situation after the Japanese withdrawal. The bolsheviks, if really pressed, were willing to strike a bargain. When Trotsky saw that the Japanese landing was no bluff he tried hard to bargain. His 'invitation' was still troubling

[1] Balfour to Reading, 29 March and 15 April 1918.
[2] Lockhart to Balfour, 13 April 1918; Balfour to Lockhart, 15 April 1918.

Allied statesmen. When the invitation reached Washington the President declared that 'it changed everything'.[1] On 26 April 1918 Lord Reading reported that both the President and the Secretary of State were very pleased with the invitation.[2] But both avoided a final decision. Still it was obvious that American attitude towards intervention was changing if it had not changed already. On 1 May 1918 President Wilson saw the Japanese Ambassador, Ishii, who tried to find out when the intervention would start. He told the President that Japan was ready to intervene when this became absolutely necessary.[3] On 7 May the Americans replied that the intervention was not yet necessary. The delay in decision was obviously occasioned by Trotsky's apparent willingness to have the Allies intervene on the bolsheviks' behalf.

The invitation had other and quite unforeseen effects. The Japanese were completely confused by it. They were at that moment helping Ataman Semenov in what was clearly an anti-bolshevik struggle. The Japanese were now prepared to drop this ally in order to get invited to intervene.[4] But before an irrevocable decision could be made regarding Semenov the invitation bubble burst.

The British unofficial agent with the bolsheviks, Lockhart, worked hard to obtain clarifications about the invitation. Shortly after his invitation announcement Trotsky had raised the question of Allied guarantees. These were never specified. On 4 May 1918 the bolsheviks made it clear that they never intended to invite the Allies to intervene on a large scale. They were prepared to tolerate Allied troops if they were landed at Murmansk, Archangel and the Far East provided the Allies gave guarantees that the troops were not to be used for the destruction of the bolsheviks. This was obviously a manoeuvre to delay something that the bolsheviks thought inevitable. It became clear that this was so on 18 May 1918 when Trotsky declared that he had been waiting for concrete Allied proposals over a month. He accused the Allies of not being serious about the bolshevik offer or at least being unreliable.[5] Trotsky made an obvious effort to shift the blame for the withdrawal of his invitation from himself on to the Allies.

[1] Reading to Balfour, 23 April 1918.
[2] Reading to Balfour, 26 April 1918.
[3] Reading to Balfour, 1 May 1918.
[4] Greene to Balfour, 16 May 1918; Goto to Balfour, 22 May 1918.
[5] Lockhart to Balfour, 13 April and 18 May 1918.

Thus at last it became clear that there would be no intervention by invitation. But these clever manoeuvres of Trotsky did achieve something that the European Allies had been striving for for so long. Whether or not the President saw through Trotsky's machinations he now made a decision. While still rejecting the Siberian enterprise he consented to a direct Allied action at Murmansk and Archangel to protect these ports and the war stores against German danger.[1] However, his opposition to the intervention in Russia was crumbling and his European Allies were preparing a *coup de grâce*.

The British issued orders to the Captain of HMS Suffolk in Vladivostok to assist the Japanese if they landed troops to protect the war stores still left in the city. General Bridges suggested that General Foch should declare the intervention in Russia as indispensable for the final victory.[2] Clemenceau pressed the British, if pressure they needed, to act without the bolshevik invitation pointing out their duplicity.[3] Even Lockhart who had for so long opposed the intervention without bolshevik consent came out for it, and with the zeal of a new convert urged the government to prepare secretly a large scale action for 20 June 1918. In his opinion this would be a resounding answer to the Germans. He even drafted an Allied proclamation to be issued to the Russian people upon landing.[4]

The British Cabinet needed no special persuasion. On 29 May 1918 it was decided to wrench the President's sanction 'by all means'. Lord Cecil suggested that General Knox should be sent to Washington to speak to the President in person. Though this visit was ultimately cancelled other arguments and circumstances forced Wilson to modify his position. On 3 June 1918 the Americans agreed to send troops to the north of Russia, if General Foch wished it.[5] On the same day the Japanese at long last agreed to a joint intervention. All that was now needed was the action itself.

By May 1918 the military situation both in Russia and on the western front was reaching a climax. Everybody now, the Allies, bolshevik and White Russians were convinced that a massive intervention was imminent. Though the intervention depended entirely on the President's decision, the decision now seemed to be only a

[1] Reading to Balfour, 24 May 1918.
[2] General Bridges to War Office, 24 May 1918.
[3] Clemenceau to Lavergne, 22 May 1918 (copy to Cambon).
[4] Lockhart to Balfour, 27 May 1918.
[5] Reading to Balfour, 3 June 1918 – two telegrams.

question of time. On 12 May Lord Reading reported that the President still made a great distinction between the intervention in the north and in Siberia.[1] But the British, for all practical purposes, refused to recognize this distinction. In any case they were planning a two-pronged intervention. According to Captain Garstin, Lockhart's Intelligence Officer, two Allied divisions would be sufficient to secure the north. A considerably larger Allied force should shortly afterwards join them via Siberia. On 24 May 1918 the joint thrust into Russia by massive intervention forces was the subject of a secret operational directive by the War Office.[2]

In turn Japanese pressure on the Allies reached its pitch in May 1918. After several months of inter-Allied consultations and disagreements on the Japanese rôle in the intervention Japan had finally decided to clear up the issue. The new Foreign Minister, Baron Goto, instructed his London Ambassador to approach the British to clinch off the bargain, namely the Allied approval for an intervention by Japan. No other ally was approached but this move seemed natural, for the British had exerted themselves on Japan's behalf for several months. Viscount Chinda dealt with Lord Cecil: his note contained two major points: the Japanese wanted to know what had happened to the bolshevik invitation which Lockhart was still procuring; and what happened to Siberia – was Semenov to be dropped in preference to the bolsheviks?

Lord Cecil found himself in a difficult position. Both the idea of a Japanese intervention and the bolshevik invitation were the results of British initiative. But at that moment Britain was not able either to sanction the former or to obtain the latter. The Americans were the key to the intervention. While he had Japanese consent in principle to a joint intervention he had none from the United States. Without the latter Baron Goto's personal commitment to thrust the Japanese up to the Urals was of no avail. Nevertheless, in anticipation of American consent, Cecil told Chinda that Japan would have to act without the bolshevik invitation and act decisively, right up to Chelyabinsk. The outcome of the war depended on their thrust through Siberia.[3] This dramatic plea sounds less dramatic now. But at that moment the Germans were some 37 miles from Paris and the

[1] Reading to Balfour, 12 May 1918.

[2] Lockhart to Balfour, 10 May 1918; The Director of Allied Military Operations in the North of Russia, 24 May 1918.

[3] Chinda to Cecil, 22 May 1918; Greene to Balfour, 21 May 1918.

loss of the French capital would probably have meant the end of the war.

At this desperate juncture the Allied military command turned on President Wilson and practically bombarded him with memoranda. On 9 June Major General Knox came out strongly for Siberian intervention. The northern landing, according to him, was insufficient.[1] But there were signs now indicating that the northern operation would soon be realized; obviously Siberia would come next. On 3 June 1918 the Allies finally agreed to land troops at Murmansk and Archangel. The combined forces were to be placed under the command of General Poole. On 11 June President Wilson was asked for three infantry battalions. The battalions, after some delay caused by the United States Army objections to be under British command, were sent to Northern Russia.[2]

On the same day Balfour sent an important telegram to impatient Lockhart in Moscow. This telegram shows clearly how far were the Allies from actually carrying out an intervention in Russia in June 1918. After the long months of diplomatic and political preparation Lockhart was told that the intervention was not subject to any changes of opinion by the Allies. If anything the rapidly changing situation in Russia and elsewhere, was to blame for what to him seemed changes. Delays in the intervention were not the result of Allied indecision but rather of the variance in Allied decisions. What was needed was an agreement among the Allies, not a decision by the Allies. France, Italy and Great Britain were for the intervention, but the United States opposed it. Japan would do nothing until asked by the Allies. Britain still hoped for an Allied agreement, but it was sure that with the United States in opposition nothing decisive could be expected in Siberia. If the intervention came too late it was not Britain's fault. The British were trying their best and would probably ultimately succeed in persuading the Americans to drop their opposition and join in in the intervention in Russia.[3]

The telegram reveals another fact: the complete dependence of the other Allies on the United States. But in the desperate situation the Allies turned once again directly to Japan. On 7 June 1918 a combined note was delivered at the Japanese Foreign Ministry on behalf of Great Britain, France and Italy. It urged the Japanese to intervene

---

[1] *Knox Memorandum*, cf. Chapter I.
[2] Balfour to Reading, 11 June 1918; War Council Meeting, 3 June 1918.
[3] Balfour to Lockhart, 11 and 13 June 1918.

in Russia on the following conditions: (i) to respect the territorial integrity of Russia, (ii) not to interfere in internal Russian affairs and (iii) to push as far west as possible. These conditions were nothing new and Japan had already agreed to them in principle. But the third condition needed clarification. Ambassador Chinda immediately asked how far west the Japanese would have to advance in order to comply with this condition and was told that at least to Omsk and possibly to Chelyabinsk.[1]

The third condition was troublesome indeed, and again delayed the final Japanese decision. Chinda told Cecil, when handed the note, that the Japanese would advance no further than Eastern Siberia. On 3 July Goto confirmed this decision. While it was important from the Allied point of view that the Japanese intervened decisively, at this moment it was even more important they intervened at all. The third point was therefore ignored. It was thought that once the intervention started its limits would be determined on the spot later. But the Japanese made their position quite clear: they still hesitated about going into Siberia without the United States, but were absolutely certain in their refusal to discuss any limits of the eventual intervention.[2]

In June 1918 the Americans began to modify rapidly their ideas on the intervention. President Wilson finally dropped his idea of a civilian commission for Russia and began to think in military terms. On 20 June a War Office memorandum claimed that there would be no victory without a Japanese intervention in Siberia. General Foch, Supreme Allied Commander, also wrote to the President in rather forceful language a few days later. On 2 July the Supreme War Council approved the British proposal to call on the President to intervene in the Far East. This appeal contained all the old arguments, which had so far proved ineffective. The only new one proved decisive: the Czechs who had recently revolted against the bolsheviks had to be helped.[3]

On 27 May 1918 fighting broke out between the Czechoslovak Corps and the bolsheviks. The Corps was officially a part of the French Army and was *en route* to Vladivostok and France from European Russia. Early in July 1918 the Allies had little or unreliable

[1] Balfour to Chinda, 7 June 1918.

[2] Chinda to Cecil, 24 June 1918.

[3] War Office Memorandum, 20 June 1918; Foch to Wilson, 27 June 1918; Supreme War Council Resolution, 2 July 1918.

news as to its whereabouts and it was even thought in Paris and London that the combined forces of the bolsheviks and the German prisoners of war fighting in the Red Army, could annihilate the Corps. On 4 July Lansing was under a similar impression when he told the President that the Czech involvement had completely changed the situation. Two days later the President expressed his views on the altered circumstances in an important memorandum. He did this without the slightest consultation with his European allies: he appealed directly to Japan for a joint intervention to help the Czechs. He was still unconvinced that the intervention should go farther than Irkutsk; and he set an upper limit on the forces to be deployed.[1]

However much desirable this seemed a strange initiative. But the other Allies were beyond caring about susceptibilities and subtleties. The French and the Italians, when told, simply acknowledged the fact that the United States were going to intervene in the Far East. In any case the French were too busy making their own arrangements in the Far East to be offended. The British, after a discussion, agreed to ignore this 'insult' and concentrated on getting as much as possible out of this *volte-face*. They immediately raised their objection to the upper limit: an intervention with such a limit would be utterly inadequate. They further argued that the Czech Corps would counterbalance any Japanese forces sent to Siberia in excess of President Wilson's 12,000 limit.[2]

On 10 July 1918 the British, in order to stimulate the Americans, announced publicly that they would shortly transfer the 25th Battalion of the Middlesex Regiment from Hong Kong to Vladivostok.[3] But the Americans moved slowly; only about a week after the British announcement the President released an *Aide Mémoire* explaining the Siberian venture. On 22 July the British Cabinet sent the official reply to the *Aide Mémoire*. It welcomed this American step: only some reservations were voiced about the size of the expedition.[4]

It was now the turn of the Japanese to enter the arena. President Wilson addressed himself directly to them ignoring all the previous arrangements between Japan and the European Allies. When Wilson's

[1] Lansing to Wilson, 4 July 1918; President's Memorandum on Russia, 6 July 1918.

[2] Lloyd George to Reading, 10 July 1918.

[3] Balfour to Reading, 10 July 1918.

[4] Reading to Lansing, 30 July 1918.

terms became known in Japan they were violently discussed and practically all rejected. First, Ishii, Japanese Ambassador in Washington, rejected bluntly all the limitations on the troops. But then he promised that Japan would not send to Siberia more than 12,000 men. On 31 July the Japanese made it clear to the British that there would be no compromise on this point. In the end the Japanese agreed to all the points of the *Aide Mémoire*, except the last one.[1] After this last consultation with their Allies Japan seized the initiative.

On 2 August 1918 Japan issued its own declaration on the intervention. This was done without the slightest consultation with the other Allies, though the declaration did contain points previously agreed to with them. Two new points, however, were added: the Japanese did not propose to create a new eastern front by intervening in Siberia and they repeated their objection to any upper limit in the forces employed in this operation.[2] Next day the 12th Infantry Division disembarked at Vladivostok. Within a week the Japanese were actively helping the hard pressed Czechs in the Ussury and Amur regions.

The Americans landed on 10 August 1918 and remained in Vladivostok without pressing on to aid the Czechs. The decisions to land troops in the Far East were taken rapidly. The swiftness with which they had been carried out was obviously the result of the hard fought diplomatic battle and political pressure within the alliance. But the reasons for which the intervention was finally launched were substantially different from those advanced during the discussion stage.

III

It is curious that France which did not exhibit any special political or diplomatic initiative *vis-à-vis* Japan should have caused it to intervene. It was, nevertheless, the French factor, in the form the Czechoslovak Army Corps, which ultimately forced the issue. Throughout 1917-18 France in fact had no real Far Eastern policy. Her relations with Japan were of minor importance and of matter of fact character.

It is certain that the French government was from time to time confidentially informed about British intentions in the Far East, but apart from occasional support of the British, France remained pas-

[1] Ishii to Polk, 24 July 1918.
[2] Japanese Declaration, 2 August 1918.

sive.[1] This passivity could possibly be explained by the lack of national interests in the area. But after the Brest-Litovsk Peace the circumstances changed. The majority of the prisoners of war of Central Powers were interned in the camps in Siberia and it was of vital importance to France that they should not reach Germany. Siberia also abounded in foodstuffs: it was equally imperative that these should not reach the Central Powers.[2] In contrast to the British who had formulated a policy and employed deliberate and subtle tactics to achieve the aim France had none of these. But she shared the aim with the British: Japan's entry in the war.

French passivity was relative, only when compared to British activity, but it was no inaction. In fact too many rather clumsy moves did take place and their resoluteness far exceeded the British. Thus when in January 1918 Balfour floated his mandatory idea, the French immediately supported him, and instantly showed their own initiative. The French Ambassador in Tokyo, Regnault, asked the Japanese government to set up a joint commission to study problems connected with the protection of the Trans Siberian Railway.[3] This initiative proved rather typical of the French approach to the Japanese: no great enterprise, no real diplomatic plan nor a subtle political move, but rather a minor point, concrete proposal with the simple aim of dragging the Japanese into the business of war whether they wanted it or not.

Shortly afterwards the French made another determined little effort. When the British switched their pressure from Japan to the United States thinking that the American involvement would facilitate Japanese intervention, the French showed their impatience with this delay by vehemently starting new discussions with the Japanese. This time it was to be a joint military action in Siberia which was to secure Siberian foodstuffs and war stores from the Germans.[4]

This initiative probably ended as badly as the previous one remaining just another diplomatic proposal. The French had no forces in the Far East and consequently any discussion of joint actions sounded rather hypothetical. But then suddenly 'French' forces began to arrive. On 21 March 1918 while the Ukraine was overrun by the

[1] e.g. Panouse to Clemenceau, 28 March 1918; Panouse to Clemenceau, 2 April 1918; etc.
[2] Panouse to Clemenceau, 5 January and 2 February 1918.
[3] Cambon to Balfour, 16 February 1918.
[4] Regnault to Pichon, 23 February 1918.

Germans General Foch gave his final order to the Czechoslovak Corps transferring it from the invaded territory to Vladivostok or Dalny (Darein).[1] On 22 March 1918 the French opened official negotiations with the Japanese for shipping which would take the Czechs from Vladivostok to France.[2] However, the negotiations proved abortive; the Japanese had no ships available for these purposes. The Americans and British could not help either, therefore new dispositions had to be made about the Czechs.

By 7 April 1918 the French General Staff could clearly see that the Czechs would have to stay in the Far East for some considerable time, unless suddenly ships were found. In the meantime discussions were opened about their deployment in that area. Ultimately it was thought that once the Czechs actually arrived in Vladivostok they could be used for two purposes: either to support the Semenov forces or the Japanese. It was obvious that the French preferred the second alternative.[3]

The second proposal received a fillip during April 1918 when the Japanese landed in Vladivostok, but was almost killed by Trotsky reacting against the landing: he stopped all the Czech trains *en route* to the Far East. Thus on 11 April it was not sure at all whether the Czechs would ever arrive in Vladivostok. But the preparations for their arrival and their eventual departure to France went on. The French asked the Japanese not only for the ships but also for supplies.[4] Clemenceau ordered the formation of a special commission headed by the Military Attaché in Tokyo and consisting of French officers serving with the Legion or on other duties in the Far East. The commission's main task was to screen the arriving Czechs and Poles and sort out all the unreliable elements. The commission asked for Japanese cooperation and for this purposes appointed a special liaison officer.[5] On 26 April 1918 Clemenceau sent a special telegram to Ambassador Regnault exhorting him to act with urgency.[6]

It can be deduced from a French GHQ Memorandum of 22 April 1918 that Regnault had previously approached the Japanese about the possible use of the Czech Corps in the Far East. The terms of this

---

[1] Foch to Lavergne, 21 March 1918.
[2] General Granat's Memorandum for French GHQ, 22 March 1918.
[3] Clemenceau to Panouse, 7 April 1918.
[4] Clemenceau to Pichon, 20 April 1918.
[5] Clemenceau to Military Attaché, Tokio, 26 April 1918.
[6] Clemenceau to Regnault, 26 April 1918.

proposal are still obscure, but they seem to have run along the following lines: if the Czechs and the Japanese agreed, a Far Eastern centre of resistance against German penetration into Siberia should be established in the Maritime province. It would then be up to the Japanese and the Czechs to conduct hostile operations against the Germans or their agents. However, the Ambassador insisted that the Czechs' consent for this contingency would have to be obtained first. If the Czechs refused to cooperate shipping would have to be found for them and they would depart for France as originally planned.[1]

In the meantime the Czech troops continued to arrive in Vladivostok, for Trotsky, as soon as the Japanese withdrew from the city, rescinded his order stopping their trains. But it is clear from the proposals presented to the Japanese by Ambassador Regnault that Franco-Japanese negotiations and plans in the Far East had not advanced much: they were in fact in a very initial stage. However, with Czech troops actually in the Far East and in particular in Vladivostok, both sides, whatever their ultimate intentions might have been, were forced to deal with the actual situation jointly and seriously.

The French Ambassador asked now concretely for credits to purchase from the Japanese medical supplies and linen for the Czechs. He also asked for orders from Paris for the dispatch of French officers serving in Tokio to Vladivostok so that they could start the screening of the arriving Czechs conforming thus to the decisions previously taken.[2] The screening would obviously facilitate further decisions about the Corps: whether it could be used on the spot or whether it would have to be sent on to France.

The second alternative, however, seemed to have been least envisaged. On 26 April Pichon sent an explanatory telegram to Regnault in which he repeated the two alternatives known already to the Ambassador. This telegram stressed much more the possibility of the Czechs continuing their journey to France rather than staying in the Far East. The Ambassador was in fact requested to take the necessary steps with the Japanese to provide their cooperation with the transportation of the Czechs to France.[3] From this last request it is obvious that all the previous French *démarches* had come to nothing and negotiations and pressure had to be renewed.

[1] Clemenceau to Regnault, 26 April 1918 – second telegram.
[2] Regnault to Pichon, 16 April 1918.
[3] Clemenceau to Regnault, 26 April 1918.

On 28 April the French Consul in Vladivostok reported to Paris that General Dieterichs, in command of the Corps, and some 2,000 Czech soldiers arrived with the first train to reach the city. Dieterichs immediately called on the Consul and asked for instructions. The Consul had none but the general had some useful information for the Consul: according to him the ultimate number of the Czechs would be in the region of 70,000, for another recruitment drive had been launched and Czech prisoners of war in Siberian camps were joining up. The Consul calculated that the required shipping for the transfer of 70,000 men and equipment would amount to some 150,000 tons.[1]

The transportation problem the French had to face was serious, for they themselves had no ships available. When this was definitely found out the French GHQ produced a special memorandum dealing with the shipping difficulty and the consequences it would have on the Czechs in the Far East. First of all, the events and decisions leading up to the formations of the Corps were recapitulated. Franco-British negotiations about the use of the Corps in the Far East were then singled out and reasons for abandoning this idea enumerated. In conclusion Japanese cooperation in shipping was advocated and concrete proposals as to its extent were laid down. The memorandum was intended for all the Allies involved in this operation and certainly constituted another form of pressure on the Japanese and possibly also on the Americans.[2]

Unfortunately it had very little effect on either. On 10 May 1918 Colonel Lapomarede reported from Tokio that some 8,000 Czechs were ready to board any ship available to take them to France.[3] But as far as can be ascertained there was no reply to this telegram from Paris. On 22 May Clemenceau sent an important telegram to Colonel Lavergne in Moscow dealing with the Czech problem and making no mention of Japanese ships.[4] As Lavergne was still nominally in charge of the Czech Corps he would have been the first to be informed about any favourable development in the transportation crisis. Since no mention of it was made it seems clear that the Japanese refused to cooperate.

The reasons for the Japanese refusal are not known yet. It is possible that the French were secretly negotiating with the Japanese about

[1] Regnault to Pichon, 28 April 1918.
[2] French GHQ Memorandum, 29 April 1918.
[3] Regnault to Pichon, 16 May 1918.
[4] Clemenceau to Lavergne, 22 May 1918.

the use of the Corps in the Far East, but in view of the subsequent Japanese decisions and unilateral actions, this seems unlikely. There is a slight indication of some Franco-Japanese talks in progress in a telegram from Lavergne to Clemenceau on 1 June 1918. In it Lavergne observed that the Czech Corps was strung out along the Trans Siberian and as a soldier he pointed out to Clemenceau the strategic advantage of such a situation. He urged the Prime Minister to make use of it and start a massive intervention against the Germans and bolsheviks from the Far East.[1] But whether such secret negotiations were going on or not they certainly had no effect on the Czechs, who, without prior consultation with Lavergne, Clemenceau or the Japanese started their own action against the bolsheviks whom they now considered as German agents.

The Czech revolt, of course, immediately solved the shipping problem. It also solved the problem of employment of the Corps in the Far East. But it created new and unplanned problems. First it exploded the idea of the massive Allied intervention, so long discussed and prepared. In fact the operation became much less massive than anticipated and assumed the form of a rescue action rather than intervention. It was only on 2 July 1918 that the French GHQ found out a little about the military position of the Czechs. It was certain that the fighting isolated substantial Czech forces in Western Siberia. To save them a massive drive from the Far East was required and only the Japanese could effect it. It was therefore urgently proposed that the Allies ask officially and jointly for a massive Japanese intervention.[2] To give this operation a truly Allied character it was suggested that a special force be formed consisting of the Vladivostok Czechs, Semenovite Russians, Italians (some 1,000 from the Pekin-Tien Tsin area), British 25th Battalion (Hong Kong), French Colonial Battalion (Indochina) and American marines from *USN Brooklyn*. This scratch force suitably supported by Japanese divisions would break out of the Maritime province into Siberia thus saving the 2nd Czech division from destruction. These troops would also act as a covering force for a real landing and intervention by the Japanese which would follow shortly afterwards. The French GHQ then urged the Allies to recognize the situation in Russia as highly critical and therefore force the Japanese to act decisively.[3]

[1] Lavergne to Clemenceau, 1 June 1918.
[2] French GHQ Memorandum, 2 July 1918.
[3] French GHQ Memorandum, 29 April 1918.

Both the new situation and possibly also this memorandum forced finally the Japanese to decide and intervene. In one sense this decision was indeed forced on them by the unexpected revolt, but the French went out of their way to facilitate it. On 5 July all transport arrangement for the transfer of the Czechs to France were officially cancelled. On 7 July the French reached an agreement with the Japanese according to which the Japanese immediately supplied the Czechs in Vladivostok with 20 machine guns, 2 million rounds of ammunition, 6 heavy guns and 100 rounds of ammunition.[1] Shortly afterwards the Japanese recognized the Czechs as soldiers of the French Army.

Faced with these new developments in Siberia the Japanese made their decisions and began to land their forces responding thus to the French pressure to rescue the Czechs. But it is obvious that the final decisions were also the result of the careful British diplomatic preparation. However, the abruptness with which the Japanese acted and the lack of consultation boded ill for the future of the intervention in Siberia. After so many months of inter-Allied negotiations more unity and less rivalry should have been the result. However, from the very beginning of the intervention it was obvious that there was no common policy *vis-à-vis* Russia. There were only common points of interest, both short-termed: the action was launched to destroy the bolsheviks and their upholders in Siberia, the German prisoners of war and thus rescue the hard pressed Allied troops, the Czechoslovak Corps. But as soon as the intervention was started the question arose: were the prisoners of war really upholders of the bolsheviks; and was the Czech Corps really in need of the Allied rescue operation?

---

[1] Panouse to Clemenceau, 5 July 1918; Clemenceau to Military Attaché, Tokyo, 7 July 1918.

CHAPTER THREE

PRISONERS OF WAR
IN SIBERIA

I

On 5 June 1918 the unofficial British agent in Moscow, R. H. Bruce Lockhart, sent off to London his appreciation of the Czech revolt against the bolsheviks. The day before he had joined the American, French and Italian colleagues in protest against bolshevik hostility and threats to the Czech Corps. He summarized his views on the revolt: the Czech Corps impatient at the delays *en route* to Vladivostok and France was finally so enraged by *German provocations* that it started the revolt.[1] Though undoubtedly the causes of the revolt were more complex than Lockhart's summary indicated, all the same it was very much to the point. He singled out German provocations as the decisive factor which sparked off the revolt and this view, however mistaken, was shared not only by his Allied colleagues but also by the Czechs themselves.

It should be stressed that from the very emergence the bolsheviks were thought by both the Allied representatives in Russia and their Russian opponents, as somehow connected with Germany; many of them were suspected to be paid agents of Germany. The circumstances of Lenin's return to Russia did not help to clear up these suspicions. Then shortly after Lenin's return the bolshevik-inspired riots in Petrograd coincided with the July offensive of the Provisional Government which only increased suspicions. When on 7 November the bolsheviks finally succeeded in overthrowing the pro-Allied Provisional Government the *coup d'état* was almost automatically attributed to German influence and aid. These general impressions were confirmed by persistent reports from Allied undercover agents: several reports had it that the Red Guards which figured so prominently in the Petrograd uprising were led by a German army lieutenant, Bauer. General impressions and grave suspicions became a certainty when on 8 November 1917 the bolsheviks publicly appealed to all the combatants in the war to conclude an armistice and start peace negotiations.

[1] Lockhart to Balfour, 6 June 1918.

48

Thus in 1917 the overwhelming majority of Allied representatives in Russia considered the bolsheviks German puppets. On 2 December 1917 the British Ambassador reported that German staff officers were definitely behind the recent *coup d'état*; apparently they directed actual operations from the Smolny Institute, bolshevik headquarters in Petrograd. The Ambassador went as far as giving six German names of officers concerned.[1] The Ambassador had no doubt that his sources of information were absolutely reliable and was convinced that German agents were behind all bolshevik ventures. While his attitude was typical it was not always correct. It is probable that the bolsheviks received German aid, but Lenin and his associates were agents of their own cause and no one else's. Many of them had German names and this helped to create mistakes and wrong impressions; thus again rather typically the Czechs made a mistake in May 1918 when they thought that the Russian adjutant, General von Rauch, who signed an order stopping their trains in Siberia was in fact a German staff officer.

Apart from these often mistaken identifications German influence in Russia haunted the Allies throughout the war and the suspicions became acute after the bolshevik coup. Thus in December 1917 the Germans were seen as being behind the riots in Helsinki and Tsaritsyn.[2] The Allies had also numerous reports of German presence in many Russian cities and especially in Moscow and Petrograd, which were 'literally swarming with German prisoners of war and German civilians[3].' These reports were probably exaggerated and the explanation of German presence in Russian cities was probably much simpler than the excited informants would admit. On 14 December 1917 the British Ambassador sent another report on the Germans which largely explained their omnipresence: the bolsheviks had completely lost control over the PoW camps and German prisoners were fleeing *en masse* from the camps to the cities. But the Ambassador added an important rider: he had heard rumours that the bolsheviks were arming these prisoners.[4] It is true that he tried to point out that the rumour was spread by the Russian opposition, and therefore possibly exaggerated, but by December 1917 the Allies would have been surprised by nothing and the rumour was widely believed.

[1] Buchanan to Balfour, 2 December 1917.
[2] Buchanan to Balfour, 19 December 1917.
[3] Buchanan to Balfour, 23 November 1917.
[4] Buchanan to Balfour, 14 December 1917.

The Ambassador left Russia shortly afterwards. His successor F. Lindley (later Sir F. Lindley), then Chargé d'Affaires in Russia, confirmed the previous reports on 21 January. Lindley stressed again the complete loss of control by the bolsheviks over the PoW camps; he described the situation as 'complete anarchy'. But he also repeated the rumour, now as a fact, namely that the bolsheviks were organizing and arming large groups of prisoners of war, especially in eastern Siberia.[1]

This last report was accurate, especially in shifting the centre of bolshevik organizational efforts to Siberia. After all it was mainly in Siberia that enemy prisoners were concentrated. At the same time Lindley's dispatch remained for almost two months the only Anglo-French report on the subject. It may be that in the meantime the bolsheviks succeeded in controlling the Allied observers more efficiently, hence the lack of reports. But it seems more probable that Anglo-French attention was diverted to the Ukraine thus leaving Siberia to the Americans who in turn proved quite active.

The best informed and most reliable American source in Siberia was the Vladivostok Consul, Caldwell. His reports substantially confirmed Anglo-French observations. On 22 December 1917 Caldwell reported that owing to general chaos no one really controlled the PoW camps and prisoners were escaping in large numbers.[2] Then came the dramatic days at Irkutsk on 27 and 28 December 1917: the bolsheviks though a minority in the city seized power and in doing so killed the French consular agent and two French officers. It was widely rumoured that the *coup de force* was only made possible by employing German PoWs which the bolsheviks did indeed do. Caldwell had further confirmation on 1 January: he quoted local Russians as saying that German prisoners kept them in check thus enabling the bolsheviks to triumph.[3]

The Irkutsk episode naturally upset the Allies, especially the French, who for a time threatened to send there a punitive expedition, but finally dropped the idea when the British and Japanese refused to respond to this wrathful declaration. The Americans simply ignored the French outburst. They were firmly opposed to any Allied interference in Siberia, though they diligently collected any evidence of German influence and efforts in the area. During the latter part of

[1] Lindley to Balfour, 21 January 1918.
[2] Caldwell to Lansing, 22 December 1917.
[3] Caldwell to Lansing, 30 December 1917.

February 1918 Major Drysdale, the American Military Attaché in Pekin, set out on a fact-finding journey through the Russian Far East. Everywhere he went he found German influence on the increase. On 21 February his reports were confirmed by another source from Irkutsk: German prisoners there were prepared to mobilize as soon as they received orders from Petrograd. This presumably meant that the bolsheviks could count on PoW support in case of trouble. In the same report the Siberian bolsheviks were declared pro-German, and the Whites pro-Japanese.[1]

We know now that all these reports were rather inaccurate. While the bolsheviks were willing to exploit the proletarian consciousness of the PoWs and thus also use them in their manoeuvres with the Germans, they were not particularly enthusiastic about the latter. However, the reports rather typically reflected the confused situation in Siberia. After the signing of the Brest-Litovsk Peace confusion increased; German influence was detected everywhere. During March 1918 grossly exaggerated reports of armed German PoWs in Siberia reached western capitals. Thus on 6 March the Americans claimed that they had confirmation of previous reports that there were 2,000 armed German PoWs at Irkutsk.[2] On 16 March Drysdale reported that at Nikolsk prisoners were almost free fraternizing with the bolsheviks.[3]

These persistent reports of chaotic conditions, of the break-up of prisoner camps and of the recruitment and arming of the prisoners alarmed the Allies. It was decided that a formal protest against these happenings should be made and Allied representatives in Moscow delivered a joint note. Both the protest and explanations, however, were bluntly rejected by the bolsheviks. Trotsky came out with a strong statement, although this time he was contradicted even by his friend and admirer, Colonel Robins. The Allies received several definite reports from Red Cross representatives in Siberia and the British officer *en route* to Irkutsk, Captain Webster, confirmed the validity of Allied protests. Major Drysdale, the travelling Military Attaché, sent in another report according to which Chita was full of armed PoWs and the camps were under no guard or supervision.[4]

Thus there was no end to alarming reports. It is probable that the

---

[1] Caldwell to Lansing, 1 January 1918.
[2] Spencer, Chargé d'affaires, Pekin to Lansing, 6 March 1918.
[3] Drysdale to Lansing, 16 March 1918.
[4] Drysdale (via Spencer) to Lansing, 26 March 1918.

rumours and increased activity of the bolsheviks among the PoWs influenced the Japanese in deciding to land in Vladivostok; during the two weeks preceding the landing the reports became very numerous. On 29 March the French Consul in Irkutsk observed a close cooperation between the bolsheviks and Austrian prisoners who were joining the Red Guards.[1] On 30 March the Allies had a long report on the activity of Hungarian PoWs at Omsk. The Hungarians had joined the Red Guards in great numbers and were now on their way to the Far East as bolshevik reinforcements.[2] Then on 2 April the American Ambassador in China, Reinsch, confirmed their presence in the area: the bolsheviks officially admitted their presence there and claimed that they were arming the PoWs against Ataman Semenov.[3]

On 5 April, when a Japanese force landed in Vladivostok, the Allies had additional reasons for being alarmed. On landing, the marines captured a German commercial mission; its agents were all over Siberia trying to negotiate large-scale purchases of Siberian grain. This seems to have been the last straw for Allied patience; for the Japanese it was an additional excuse for landing their marines. But while the Allies were resolved to act on these rumours and suspicions they were not sure of the ultimate intentions of the bolsheviks, for it was also rumoured that they were increasingly becoming pliant tools of the Germans and this made no sense. For the Allies the arming of the PoWs by the bolsheviks for internal purposes was not such a terrifying deed; however if this led to a German take-over in Siberia it was terrifying, indeed. But on this point Allied intelligence was far from unanimous. Thus on 10 April Lansing came to believe Summers' and Drysdale's reports: the bolsheviks were indeed arming PoWs and they could easily get out of control.[4] However, on the same day Ambassador Reinsch reported that the British observer in the Far East, Major Fitzwilliam, told him that there existed no concerted German plan to control Siberia by means of the prisoners of war. In any case the Major thought that the reports of arming the prisoners were exaggerated.[5] However, only on 12 April Lansing asked for confirmation of reports from other sources which had it that a

[1] Bourgeois to Pichon, 29 March 1918.
[2] Caldwell to Lansing, 30 March 1918; Greene to Balfour, 26 March 1918.
[3] Reinsch to Lansing, 2 April 1918.
[4] Lansing to Francis, 10 April 1918.
[5] Reinsch to Lansing, 10 April 1918.

German General (von Rauch), two German Colonels and thirty-four German officers were in Irkutsk on a special mission charged with the organization and arming of prisoners of war.[1]

The alarm obviously reached a stage when the bolsheviks would have to be tackled directly. With the Japanese in Vladivostok the latter were in no position to reject a protest or request for an enquiry. Trotsky was formally approached and proved most obliging. He promised to help in any way he could the *ad hoc* investigation commission which the Allies proposed to set up. To everybody's surprise he carried out his promises: he provided Allied officers with special *laissez-passés* and instructed Soviet authorities, especially in Siberia, to aid the investigators. Trotsky had nothing to fear from this investigation. To him it was obvious that the Allies were looking for the wrong thing. The bulk of his armed prisoners was in European Russia; any way the Allies were looking for some links with the German army. It would be difficult to find them since they did not exist in this area.

Thus after these camouflage manoeuvres by Trotsky, Captains Hicks, Webster, Macgowan and Colonel Thompson, Consuls Jenkins and Thomson were 'let loose' on Siberia and soon their contradictory reports began to reach Allied capitals. Macgowan's reports were contradicted by Hicks' and Webster's; Ambassador Francis did not trust Webster's judgement and on the whole thought that the 'commission' was hoodwinked. But the lack of positive evidence was strangely confirmed by Professor Masaryk, whose Czechs were soon going to use the German and PoW questions as a pretext for their revolt. On arriving in Tokio from Siberia Masaryk left a special memorandum with the American Ambassador, Morris, in which he denied the existence of any German master plan for the control of Siberia; neither did he observe any large-scale arming of prisoners nor did he detect any evidence of PoW plots.[2]

After this inconclusive enquiry and contradictory reports the Allies simply dropped the subject. It is true that most of them retained their previous suspicions, but it was clear that nothing could be done about these suspicions. But Allied agitations did achieve one great result: they drew the attention of the already suspicious Czechs to this problem. For the Allies Trotsky's enlistment of some 1,000 detected prisoners was insignificant. When Trotsky declared that they were all

[1] Morris to Lansing, 13 April 1918.
[2] Francis to Lansing, 13 April 1918.

Soviet citizens the Allies decided that it was not even worth a protest. But it was of great importance to the Czech Corps in Siberia. When in April the bolsheviks made concrete moves to enlist prisoners in that region and made them Soviet citizens the Czechs became convinced that this was part of a bolshevik-German conspiracy against them.

II

The Czechs were quite wrong about this German–Soviet conspiracy. The German and Austro-Hungarian governments had nothing to do with bolshevik recruitment; in fact both governments strongly resented it. They had always kept an eye on the prisoners and were most indignant to see them serving in the Red Army.

On 4 March 1918 the Director of the Austrian Intelligence Service circulated an interesting report on the conduct (or better, misconduct) of Austrian PoWs of Czech origin. The report was compiled by Captain Kopřiva and Dr Turba, both Austrian Counter-Espionage experts of Czech descent, and it summarized succinctly the difficulties the Czech PoWs had to face in PoW camps and subsequently in the Czechoslovak Corps, since the Corps was so obviously anti-bolshevik. The sources for this report were Ukrainian deserters and captured Czechs who put the strength of the Legion (Corps) at 50,000 men.[1] From the Austrian point of view the Czech Legion was much more alarming than the other (bolsheviks) 'International Legion', of which existence they also knew.

In May 1918, just before the Czechs revolted against the bolsheviks, the other Legion replaced the Czech Corps as a dangerous organization in Austrian eyes. The intelligence service produced another report on the 'International Legion 1918'. The report spoke of a large bolshevik international organization which was engaged in recruiting politically and otherwise sympathetic prisoners into the Red Army. The appeal of the Executive Committee of 'International Red Guards' was launched on 4 March; it claimed that returning PoWs were badly received at home and were quickly sent to the front again by the imperialist masters. The prisoners were bidden to avoid this fate and "join us as free citizens" now, while they could. The recruitment centres were listed on the appeal.

Next the report described a large PoW meeting in Moscow organ-

[1] Referat über das Verhalten der čechoslowakischen Kriegsgefangenen in Russland, erstattet auf Grund von Aussagen aus Russland zurückgekehrten Angehörigen der ö.u. Wehrmacht sowie auf Grund von ausländischen Pressenachrichten.

ized by German communist prisoners; the meeting was addressed by the Hungarian, Bela Kuhn, and the Czech communist, Toman. Though the meeting was attended mainly by prisoners, some were noticed wearing Red Army uniforms. On 1 May 1918 the Omsk PoW paper "Die Wahrheit" stated that about 400 prisoners had difficulties in getting home; the authorities at home were obviously not keen on having them back. About a week later the Moscow PoW paper "Die Weltrevolution" reported that the Omsk international communist party was founded in December 1917. It had now some 6,000 members and was sending out some 10,000 propaganda sheets in German and Hungarian all over Siberia. The paper also claimed that by then (May 1918) *three volunteer battalions* had been sent east of Omsk. It added that the Samara (Kuybyshev) organization consisted of 1,300 members, the Red Guard of 200.

The assembly point for the "Austrian Red Army" was Kineshma on the Volga. The Hungarians were centered on Novonikolayevsk where they formed the 1st Proletarian Red Army. The last document produced in this report was another appeal to the PoWs published in the (bolshevik) *Pravda* on 9 May 1918. It called on all the proletarians to join the Red International Legion to fight for freedom and world revolution. The commanding officer of the Chinese International Battalion signed this appeal. The Austrian evaluation of this evidence was interesting: to them it was clear that the reasons for joining the Red Army were the hunger and miserable conditions in the PoW camps. They practically discounted any political motivation and pointed out that the bolshevik recruiting drive concentrated on technical and artillery experts.[1]

The Germans were perhaps less systematic but nonetheless well informed about their prisoners in Russia. However, the number of German war prisoners was comparatively small; above all there were many dependable officers among them. Thus the German reports on the 'internationalists' in Siberia emanated mainly from the latter source. But similarly to the Allied reports they were often contradictory. On 20 May 1918 the German General HQ received a report from Siberia which said that the White movement in Irkutsk was relying on PoW support to overthrow the bolsheviks.[2] The Allies had very different reports on Irkutsk, but Lieutenant Balogh's report summed up the Siberian situation: "prisoners suffer from utter

[1] International Legion, 1918.
[2] Trauttmansdorf to Burian, 20 May 1918.

55

confusion; that is why some of them go over to the Reds but the majority remain loyal".[1]

Though on 22 April the Germans protested to the bolsheviks against any forcible recruitment of prisoners and demanded the separation of the German and Austro-Hungarian prisoners, they were far from worried. In July 1918 they had a detailed report on all the international units in the Red Army and from their point of view they were entirely satisfied. They saw the international units as an Austro-Hungarian headache; on 20 Feburary the 150–200 delegates at the PoW meeting in Petrograd were mainly Hungarians. The Saratov and Samara centres were also Hungarian dominated: the Hungarians, Dr Gubor and Kiscz were the proclaimed leaders of the internationalists though they published a German as well as Hungarian papers. What concerned the Germans most were reports on the conditions in the Siberian camps. The Danish Red Cross Mission said they were miserable; from the Turkestan reports spoke of hunger and epidemics in these camps. But nothing could be done about conditions in the camps and the Germans concentrated on speaking very forcefully to the bolsheviks on forcible recruitment.[2] As soon as they found out that at Omsk the bolsheviks coerced some PoWs to fight against the Czechs they protested most vehemently. On 16 July joint German-Austro-Hungarian protests were delivered to the Soviet Foreign Ministry.[3]

It is obvious that while the Germans did not take the PoW question seriously the Austrians had to do so. Their investigating commission, as compared to the Allied one, issued its report in July 1918. The most conservative estimate of the engaged internationalists in the Red Army was 40,000 to 50,000. Thus in Karelia there were, according to the commission report, 3 battalions of the 4th International Regiment (4,000 men) while in Petrograd itself there were the Karl Liebknecht Regiment and 2nd Communist F. Adler Battalion. The 1st International Battalion in Moscow was probably the largest in the country; apart from it there was the Chinese Regiment and two Revolutionary Polish Regiments in the city. Then there were the 1st and 2nd Iron Communist Regiments at Yaroslavl, 3rd International Regiment at Voronezh, Karl Marx Battalion at Kazan and the International Unit at Saratov.

While the report is very detailed when dealing with European

[1] Trauttmansdorf to Burian, 21 May 1918 (copy).
[2] Danish Embassy to Ministry of Foreign Affairs, 3 April 1918.
[3] Von de Potere to Chicherin, 16 July 1918 and 25 July 1918.

Russia it is unfortunately incomplete on Siberia, which was so crucial to the Czech Corps. It stated that there was the Karl Marx Regiment at Novonikolayevsk, but its strength was unknown. Some 2,400 bolsheviks and prisoners were armed at Omsk. Two Internationalist Companies were at Irkutsk and one International Battalion at Krasnoyarsk. The Far East was left out of the report completely; no information was available.[1] Thus it seemed clear that the Allied investigators had been hoodwinked, indeed, and that Czech fears were certainly justified.

III

Though the question of PoW recruitment appeared to the Germans relatively unimportant the bolsheviks took it very seriously. They were prepared to risk both Allied suspicions and German anger to enlist these prisoners. When in March 1918 the bolsheviks decided to build a new army, the Red Army, they had two reasons for wishing to have these soldiers join them. First of all, they were starting from scratch and needed organizational advice; then also they needed to stiffen up the cadres and units with experienced soldiers and politically conscious elements. All this could be expected from the suitable prisoners of war.

However, the recruitment of foreign officers and troops was in the Russian military tradition, and Trotsky was not really creating a precedent. Even in 1904 in the Japanese war there was a Chinese Regiment fighting on the Russian side. Above all the Czechoslovak Corps itself was the result of similar recruitment, for similar reasons: the Czechs were to take over the conquered territory and administer it on Russia's behalf. The bolsheviks thinking in terms of a world revolution certainly could not ignore this particular Russian experience.

The more immediate reason for recruiting foreign soldiers into the Red Army were their own spontaneous requests. Shortly after the November rising Chinese labourers and various underprivileged nationals joined spontaneously the Red Guards. Thus on 16 November the Rumanians living in Odessa declared themselves pro-bolshevik and joined en masse the Red Guard there. On 24 November 1917 the Petrograd Poles voted for the solidarity with Soviet struggle; on 3 December the Czech left-wing socialists had joined the Poles and then appealed to the Czech soldiers to leave the Legion for the Red Guards.

[1] Kriegsgefangene der russischen Roten Armee, Ende Juli 1918.

The plausibility of the idea of 'foreign troops' was stressed still further after the four Latvian regiments decided to join the bolsheviks *en masse*. They soon became the decisive military factor in preserving bolshevik power. However, they were in a special position: the Germans occupied Latvia in August 1917 and the Latvians retreated from their native country with other units of the Russian 12th Army north. After the November coup they did not disband, as many regiments did, neither did they go over to the enemy, nor back home as most of the Russians did. Instead they maintained cohesion and their officers, above all Colonel Vatsetis, the future Commander-in-Chief of the Red Army, offered their allegiance to the bolsheviks. How reluctant were the bolsheviks to accept this offer is not known, but soon after, towards the end of November 1917 the Latvians were already proving their worth: the 6th Tukum Regiment was transferred to Petrograd from the northern front and held the city for them. By the end of December some 40,000 Latvian Rifles were in bolshevik service: they garrisoned Petrograd, guarded the Kremlin in Moscow, fought General Kaledin's troops in the south, and later the Czech Corps in the east. They suppressed the Moscow and Yaroslavl uprisings by the social revolutionaries and proved invaluable in maintaining bolshevik power.

The Latvian Rifles were usefully supplemented by the smaller units formed from the Chinese labourers who were used in Russia for wartime civil constructions such as the Murmansk Railway line. The Chinese joined the bolsheviks spontaneously after the November uprising: a few of them even took part in the storming of the Winter Palace on 7 November 1917. They proved the most loyal troops and were massively employed at Odessa, Petrograd, Moscow, Perm, Vladikavkaz and Petrozavodsk, always as shock troops or internal security units.

For internal purposes a Red Army based on the Latvian Regiments and Chinese Battalions seemed more than sufficient. Nevertheless, the bolsheviks had tried to gain all foreigners, even the Czechoslovak Corps to their side, but failed with the latter. They had obviously other reasons for forming new units and organizing a large Red Army: the reason appears to be exclusively ideological. From the very beginning the bolsheviks came to believe that the imperialist powers would turn against them and destroy their régime as soon as they could: both sides, the Central Powers and the Allies (Entente) were suspected of these intentions. This was why in order to protect themselves the bolsheviks launched a two-pronged attack: first they increased to the maximum revolutionary propaganda in both imperialist camps and then started to recruit Allied citizens and German and Austro-Hungarian prisoners in the Red Army.

The latter move was considered particularly astute. This recruitment was thought to weaken both camps: Germany, as it would deprive it of additional soldiers and after suitable training and political indoctrination would make of the recruits proletarian fighters in a German revolution. On the other hand it was reasoned that the recruits would be most willing to fight against their former enemy, the western Allies, if the Allies decided to intervene against the bolsheviks in Russia.

Similary to the Chinese, German prisoners of war had joined the Red Guards shortly after the November coup. But their numbers were small despite the misery, hunger, epidemics and chaos in the camps. They were, however, recognized by the bolsheviks as potentially useful soldiers, especially as officers, sappers, engineers and artillery experts, in the newly established Red Army.

First bolshevik appeals to the prisoners were made on the political basis: they were bidden to examine their proletarian consciences and then join the bolsheviks in their proletarian struggle. One of the first appeals appeared in the *Pravda* on 2 December 1917; another in the *Izvestiya* three days later. The latter appeal was more reasoned and promising: the conscious proletarian soldiers were promised immediate and future rewards. However, the actual organization of the prisoners was started only in February 1918.

It undoubtedly took a month or two to train political agitators and emissaries after the original appeals had been launched. Agitators addressed prisoners in their camps, told them to organize themselves and send their representatives to various meetings. During February a series of PoW meetings took place: on 10th at Omsk, 13th in Moscow, 19th in Petrograd. The last one seemed particularly fruitful, for it decided to set up a new Red prisoners of war organization and send out additional agitators to camps so far untouched: Borovsk, Novgorod, Yaroslavl, Tver and Moscow.

In March 1918 the appeals stressed another aspect of the proletarian revolution: they no longer concerned themselves with proletarian consciences – the task now was to *defend* the proletarian revolution. It was not specified against whom the revolution was to be defended, but this was deliberate: every one could choose the enemy.

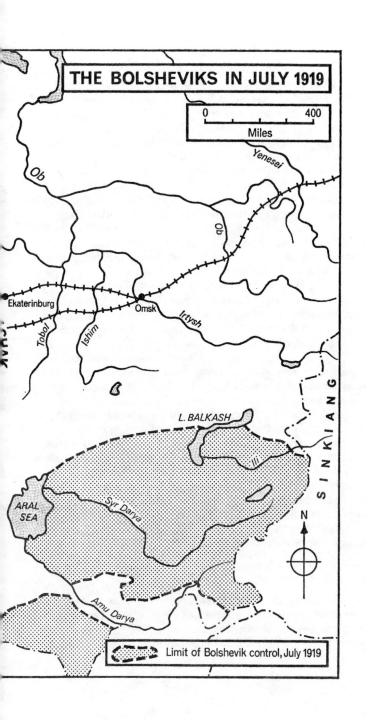

THE BOLSHEVIKS IN JULY 1919

0   400

Miles

Ob

Yenesei

Ob

Ekaterinburg   Omsk

Tobol   Ishim   Irtysh

L. BALKASH

S I N K I A N G

Ili

Syr Darya

ARAL
SEA

N

Amu Darya

Limit of Bolshevik control, July 1919

On 10 March the Hungarians at Omsk were asked to join the Red Army in defence of the revolution; on 20th other prisoners in the Kineshma and Kostroma provinces. The Samara prisoners heard a similar appeal on 23rd. In the same month the Moscow Revolutionary Committee formally decided to organize international units consisting of foreign communists in Russia.

From the available communist evidence it is clear that recruitment campaigns began to bear fruit in April 1918, i.e. at the time when the Allies became suspicious and were allowed to investigate. The recruitment drives were particularly successful in the Turkestan camps as well as the Volga region (Samara, Saratov, Penza and Ufa), Chelyabinsk, Ekaterinburg, Omsk and Tomsk. But the success did not mean that the organization and formation of these new soldiers was completed. In May 1918, when the Czech Corps finally rebelled, there was still a lot of tidying up to be done. The Central Federation of the Foreign Groups of the Russian Communist Party (bolsheviks) was only just established and held its first conferences and congress. In fact the formal decision of this organization to form "Communist International Units" was only taken on 12 July 1918 and was rather the result than the cause of the Czech revolt. This decision concerned more separate national units rather than individual soldiers and officers already in the Red Army. Ultimately these foreign units consisted of some 12 nationalities and amounted to 182,000 men.

Although the large-scale organization of PoWs was effected late in 1918 and early 1919 the initial agitation and arming of the PoWs had the most unexpected effect on the Czech Corps. When the Czechs noticed that while moving east to Vladivostok they were gradually disarmed by their erstwhile camp companions, they came to the conclusion that there had to be some connexion between the Germans and bolsheviks. Furthermore the Czechs knew of rumours, however unjustified, that Germany was preparing to take over Siberia. This was their final justification of the revolt against the bolsheviks to the incredulous Allies.

IV

When considering the Czech revolt one of the most fundamental factors in bringing it about was without any doubt the all-pervading fear of the German Army. The Legion soldiers had experienced German hostility in the PoW camps and again, more recently, during their retreat from the Ukraine. With the delays and in the isolation of Siberia their fears became unreasonable. But it should be remembered that these fears were shared by many Russian and Allied personnel in Russia. The decisive factor in revolting against the bolsheviks was the identification of the bolsheviks with the Germans, the persistent bolshevik arming of PoWs and the planned German take-over of Siberia.

Within the context of events Czech fears, however exaggerated, were not completely groundless. During the war the German Supreme Headquarters and the *Auswärtiges Amt* had consistently evinced interest in Siberia, Turkestan and the Volga region, all of which contained large German minorities or PoW camps. Necessarily this interest remained largely on paper and owing to wartime difficulties and distances even intelligence proved insufficient and sketchy. All the same, reports of Siberian revolts aided by PoWs reached the *Auswärtiges Amt* as early as 1916.[1] In September 1917 the Germans learned about the Siberian Assembly at Tomsk, while in December 1917 G. Hellenius, a Red Cross representative, submitted to them a report on the situation at Irkutsk. According to him the officer-cadets were beaten by the Reds after a bloody fight in the town and there was fear for the safety of the PoWs in the region.[2]

After the Brest–Litovsk Treaty had been signed and PoWs began to be evacuated reports became more numerous. Thus on 19 March 1918 the German War Ministry received a curious appeal of the Siberian Central District Committee at Krasnoyarsk for help in building up a 'free republic'. In April 1918 Lieutenant E. Scholz, who had just returned from Siberian captivity, urged the German government to take steps to increase its influence in Siberia. He claimed that there were some 80,000 Germans willing to support such efforts.[3] For the moment it seemed that the German government, however, was more concerned with the bolshevik moves to organize internationalist units, especially in Siberia, rather than with the penetration of Siberia.[4] Significantly, in May 1918 Count Mirbach asked the Foreign Ministry to recall the Consuls at Rostov, Nizhny Novgorod and perhaps also Astrakhan and appoint consuls at Saratov, Omsk and Irkutsk: '. . . da Sibirien besonders wichtig und ohne konsularen

---

[1] Bernstorff, Washington to Auswärtiges Amt, 22 December 1916.
[2] G. Helenius to A.A., 28 December 1917.
[3] Kriegsministerium, 19 March 1918; Scholz to A.A., 5 April 1918.
[4] Major Henning to A.A., 21 May 1918.

Vorposten Politik Entwicklung sich unserem Urteil und Einfluss enthielt . . .'[1]

While the Germans were passively considering the extension of their influence in Siberia they were preparing rather actively another military operation. After a series of alarmist telegrams from the German representatives in Russia the German High Command began to plan another offensive made possible by the utter military weakness of the bolsheviks.[2] The aim of this offensive was the destruction of the latter, but also the consolidation of the military and political situation in Russia.[3] It is true that this offensive was never carried out but its discussions and plans were very much advanced. In the chaos of Russia the offensive seemed imminent.

Thus in May 1918 the bolsheviks continued to arm German prisoners, the German Foreign Office continued to speak of German interests in Siberia and elsewhere in Russia, the German High Command actively discussed and prepared plans for offensives; and the alarmed Czechs continued to move towards Vladivostok and henceforth to France. Then suddenly on 25 May 1918 Trotsky ordered them to be disarmed. Combining all these, often contradictory, factors the Czechs decided, even against Allied opposition, to revolt against the bolsheviks and try and get to France on their own.

---

[1] Mirbach to Hintze, 18 May 1918.
[2] Berckheim to Hintze, 28 May 1918; Berckheim to A.A., 24 April 1918.
[3] Berckheim to Hintze, 22 June 1918; Lersner to Hintze, 18 July 1918.

CHAPTER FOUR

THE ALLIES AND THE
CZECH REVOLT
I

On 14 June 1918, in his speech to the executive committee of the
Moscow Soviet, Lenin stated that the Czechoslovaks (who had been
actively fighting the Soviets for over a month) had been bought by
Franco-British imperialism for 15 million rubles and induced to rebel
against the Soviets. In computing this sum he quoted Czech communist sources, which were remarkably well informed. The Legion
communists knew that the British in the Ukraine gave the Legion
£80,000. They did not know that General Tabouis gave it some
400,000 rubles when the Allied representatives had to leave Kiev in
February 1918. But they had details of sums of money paid by the
French Consul in Moscow to the Czech representative Šíp and
Čermák which seem accurate, although Lenin never quoted the sum of
1,100,000 rubles which the French Ministry of War allocated to Czech
recruitment and organization in Russia as far back as July 1917.

To clarify this accusation it seems best to recount the struggle for
the Czechoslovak army in Russia as it appears from official French
documents. From the very beginning of their struggle against Habs-
burg rule it was obvious to both Professor T. G. Masaryk and his
younger colleague Dr E. Beneš that without an armed force at their
disposal they would never achieve their aim, the independence of the
Czech lands. So long as war was being waged, they had to work
through the Allied governments to achieve their aims. Thus as early
as 1916 Major Štefánik, another Czechoslovak fighting the Habs-
burgs, set out on missions to Russia and Rumania on behalf of the
French government. Štefánik was charged with the task of organizing
Czechoslovak prisoners of war in these two countries for eventual
use against the Central Powers. In 1917 Masaryk was sent by the
British War Office to Russia to organize the Czechs for the same
purpose on behalf of the British government. In this way the Czech
leaders active in Russia were of necessity 'paid agents' of the Allied
governments. But this did not mean that they were pliable tools
without their own objectives and aims.

Beneš and Štefánik at first remained in France after Masaryk had left for Russia. They continued to press for the recognition of an autonomous Czech army by the Allied governments, while Masaryk did the actual organizing. In June and July 1917 Masaryk reached several agreements with the French and Russian High Command on the recruitment and formation of the Czech prisoners of war in Russia. It was now that the French advanced to the Czechs their first credit of 1,100,000 rubles. While Masaryk concerned himself with the Czechs in Russia, Štefánik went to the United States and tried to organize the Czechs there. Some 20,000 of them volunteered but only 235 ever reached France. Beneš went to Italy on a similar mission. There were some 15,000 Czech prisoners of war in that country, but the Italian government was by no means eager that they should be organized and his mission failed.

In the meantime the Russians formed the 1st Czechoslovak Army Corps. On 7 November 1917 the bolsheviks seized power; their *coup d'état* accelerated French recognition of the Czech Corps, and *ipso facto* recognition of an autonomous Czech army as well. On 11 November the French Prime Minister informed the Quai d'Orsay that the recruitment of the Czechs was under way and requested it to draft a decree regulating their position. On 4 December S. Pichon, the new Foreign Minister, signed the decree which established an autonomous Czech army fighting alongside the French army. On 16 December 1917 President Poincaré countersigned the decree, which then became law. However, an *instruction générale* still had to be worked out translating this law into practice. Such an instruction was finally issued on 7 February 1918. The Czech army comprised the units organized in Russia, the United States and Italy. It was modelled on the French army and was to be used by the French High Command as an autonomous group ('est employée par le commandement français en groupement autonome . . .'). But even at this late stage the French government does not seem to have done much to finance the Czech army, for it was still waiting for parliament to vote the proposed credits for this purpose.[1]

It is well known that until March 1918 the Czechs subsisted in the Ukraine on Russian and Ukrainian credits. Only when the Germans invaded these territories did the Allied representative on the spot give them any money. By the end of March 1918 the French Consul in Moscow, Grenard, had received instructions to pay out credits in Russian rubles. He thereupon did so, as Lenin rightly claimed.[1] In

[1] Armée tchécoslovaque: circulaire de principes, 1917–19.

the meantime the Czech Army Corps (or Legion, as it was subsequently called) was in the Kursk province making its way to Siberia. It is obvious that despite Grenard's action it still had to depend on Soviet provisioning and finance, for it took some time for the money to filter down to 'echelon' level. In fact the Czech soldiers received hardly any pay while *en route* – a point that was fittingly exploited by Czech communist propagandists. It is still a mystery how the funds paid out to the Czech representatives in Moscow reached the Corps on its way to Vladivostok, if indeed they ever did.

It is also established that Šíp, the principal Czech representative, who cashed most of the money paid out by the French, dealt with Siberian co-operative representatives in Moscow, from whom he bought large quantities of wheat and other foodstuffs. Before the revolt Šíp then made his way from Moscow to Siberia, presumably with the money. But it is far from clear how the financial arrangements worked. On· 19 April 1918 the American Consul in Vladivostok, Caldwell, claimed that the French Consul there had been told some three weeks previously by Professor Masaryk (who was then passing through the city) that some forty to fifty thousand Czechs would arrive within ten days. The Consul had no official instructions, billets or supplies, and asked for Allied assistance. Caldwell himself was able to improvise some help, but not for long. A fortnight later he reported that some 6,000 Czechs had in fact arrived, and that the local Soviet was looking after them.[2] By 1 May 1918 Major Pichon had reached Vladivostok, where he began to take steps to billet and provision the Czechs. Even then the whole undertaking was precarious, for it was still uncertain whether all the Czechs would indeed come there. Some were apparently destined for Archangel.[3] Consequently Major Pichon encountered great difficulties, and the Czechs were left almost entirely without provisions or money. Perhaps the most conclusive proof that the French 'purchased' the Czechs can be found in Clemenceau's telegram to General Lavergne, chief French military representative in Moscow, on 22 May 1918, a day or two before the Czech Legion decided to revolt. In this message Clemenceau told Lavergne of a report from the French Military Attaché in Tokyo that the Czechs in Vladivostok had enough money to keep the units in the city paid and provisioned for two months.

[1] Niessel to Clemenceau, 18 February 1918.
[2] Caldwell to Lansing, 19 April 1918.
[3] Sharp to Lansing, 1 May 1918.

Clemenceau then asked Lavergne about the units still in European Russia and authorized him to grant them credits, if this should prove necessary.[1] It is obvious from this telegram that the French (and other Allied) governments had only vague ideas about the actual state of the Czechs' finances and supplies. It is equally obvious that their representatives on the spot knew even less and in any case could do little to relieve the situation, as they were far removed from the territory through which the Legion was advancing.

It therefore seems clear that, far from being 'bought' by the Allies, the Czechs had less support from them than from the Soviets. The small credits paid to them were usually those which threatened to fall into 'enemy' (i.e. German or bolshevik) hands. On the whole the Czechs depended for supplies and food on the Soviets and were consequently reluctant, especially in Vladivostok, to undertake any move against them. It is also clear that the Allies had little control over the money paid to the Czechs; in fact they had little control over the Czechs and their movement at all. Thus when in May 1918 the Allies finally informed the Czechs that they were to proceed elsewhere, they were at first disbelieved and then openly defied.

II

The French attitude to the Czechs at the outbreak of the revolt was ably summarized by Captain Sadoul, who had negotiated with Trotsky their free departure from Russia to France, and so was close to events. In his view the Czechs were keen to fight the Germans and no one else. They had previously refused to join Generals Kaledin, Alekseyev and the bourgeois Rada against the bolsheviks, and he saw no reason why they should start fighting the bolsheviks for ideological reasons. The causes of the revolt were the endless delays in transporting them to Vladivostok, incitement by the remaining White officers, agitation by Czech communists and the bolshevik reputation of being German puppets. French officers, he thought, were in no way responsible for the revolt. When told by Trotsky that the revolt was the dress rehearsal for Japanese intervention, an Allied plot directed by the French, he stated categorically: 'Je suis tout à fait sûr qu'il se trompe.

Though Sadoul subsequently had second thoughts on the subject and blamed Allied intelligence agents, he never really withdrew his original assessment of the Czech revolt. The matter was more com-

[1] Clemenceau to Lavergne, 22 May 1918.

plex than he suspected, but his analysis was broadly speaking correct. The French were short of troops for the western front, which in their eyes was of paramount importance, and they sincerely wanted the Czechs in France. Masaryk's agreement with General Tabouis and Berthelot that the Czechs should be evacuated to France via Vladivostok (as had already been done with a Serbian brigade) was approved and upheld by the French Government.[1]

But the French attitude was more complicated than they cared to admit. Between March and May 1918, during the German offensive on the western front, the French could undoubtedly have used the Czechs in France. But they were equally preoccupied with Russia's position in the war, and still hoped that some sort of eastern front could be re-established. To their minds the Japanese were the most suitably placed to launch such a venture, but they were willing to support anybody who would undertake it, even the bolsheviks. This plan was never realized, and ironically enough it was the Czechs who were responsible. This was so, not because the Allies instructed the Czechs to act in this way, for they did not even discuss their plans with them, but because of Allied delays and vacillation. On 18 March 1918, while the Czechs were slowly making their way to Vladivostok Major-General Knox, the British military expert on Russia, felt compelled to circulate his memorandum 'Delay in the East', for which he blamed Bruce Lockhart and Colonel Robins.[2]

Discussions continued to be held, especially in military circles, about intervention by the Japanese (and eventually by the Allies) in Russia *against the Germans*. Thus when Lieutenant-Colonel Lavergne (General *en mission*), who after General Niessel's departure (Niessel was the head of the French Military Mission in Russia which was withdrawn after the peace of Brest-Litovsk) became the senior Allied officer there, reported to the War Ministry in Paris that the Czechs were on their way to Vladivostok, and urged it to warn French Consuls along the route and to provide shipping for them, he was answered by General Foch.[3] Foch was preoccupied, as were the British, with the bolshevik moves which indicated that the bolsheviks might ask the Allies to help them against the Germans. Consequently Foch first answered an earlier telegram from Lavergne in which he had stated that the bolsheviks showed interest in retaining the

[1] André to Pichon, 6 April 1918.
[2] Major-General Knox Memorandum, 18 March 1918.
[3] Lavergne to Clemenceau, 18 March 1918.

Czechs in Russia and making them the nucleus of the new Russian army. (This sentiment developed especially after an engagement at Bakhmach, when the Czechs together with bolshevik detachments temporarily halted a German advance.) Foch agreed with this bolshevik plan and suggested that the transportation problem might not be so urgent, since the Czechs could be used on the spot.[1] But the real reason why he was anxious to keep the Czechs in Russia as long as possible emerges from a memorandum which his staff prepared on the following day: if the Czechs could not be used on the spot, they should be transported to Vladivostok via the Trans-Siberian; Franco-Japanese negotiations were under way for the evacuation of the unreliable Russian forces at Salonika; if successful, the Japanese ships could first take the Czechs from Vladivostok to Europe and then bring back the Russian troops. However, as it would take some time before these negotiations were concluded it was thought inopportune to concentrate all the Czechs in the Far East.[2]

Lavergne was in due course informed of these negotiations and suggestions, but he himself was full of initiative in any case. His readiness to take independent action undoubtedly sprang from his equivocal position in Russia. He was originally a Military Attaché, and consequently under Ambassador Noulens's close supervision. However with the Ambassador far away in Vologda and the military mission withdrawn, steps were taken to put him in charge of all military matters and make him less dependent on the distant Ambassador. Lavergne obviously knew of these developments and even before the final sanction arrived began to negotiate without reference to the Ambassador. Thus he conducted political negotiations with the Czechoslovak Council in Moscow. When Trotsky asked him (probably via Ṣadoul) whether he would be capable of stopping the movement of the Czechs to the Far East if the Germans launched another offensive against the bolsheviks, Lavergne set out to investigate. He saw Čermák, the Czech representative in Moscow, and reported the result in the following terms: (i) the 1st Czech Corps was definitely going to France and any return to the west through Siberia would undermine its morale; (ii) the 2nd Corps which was still being formed at Omsk could be used on the Russian front. Lavergne consequently suggested that the 1st Corps be evacuated: 'It would be very difficult to re-route the 1st Corps to Vologda to defend there the Allied

---

[1] Foch to Lavergne, 21 March 1918.
[2] Note for GHQ, Paris, 22 March 1918.

embassies against the (bolshevik) Russians alongside whom it has just fought'. The 2nd Corps could be used in Russia but with the proviso that it was not relied on to engage in very much fighting against the (bolshevik) Russians.[1] Trotsky undoubtedly received a modified answer: he then asked the French representative about the possibility of the Czechs aiding the bolsheviks in case of another German attack.

Two important points, however, emerge from this report. One is the suggestion that the Czechs be used to protect Allied embassies in the north even against the bolsheviks, and the other is the warning not to rely on them to fight the latter. This warning was emphasized a day later by the chief of the French military mission at Murmansk, who was asked by Paris whether it would be possible to have the Czechs re-routed and shipped via Murmansk and Archangel (obviously the negotiations with Japan were not progressing). He was against this plan, pointing out that even if the bolsheviks allowed the Corps to be re-routed, which was improbable, it could not be used successfully against the Germans if they decided to attack the northern ports in strength. If the Czechs were not shipped west, the bolsheviks would certainly undermine their morale. The Corps could not be considered as absolutely reliable in all circumstances.[2] This report on the political reliability of the Czech Corps (as well as of some smaller Polish units that it was planned to ship to France) was taken very seriously in Paris. On 7 April 1918 the Military Attaché in Peking passed on orders to the French military personnel in Russia to screen all the Czechs (and Poles) before embarkation and notify Paris of all unreliable elements.[3]

But the situation was further complicated by an unexpected British initiative. So far only the French had worried about the Czechs. They wanted to have the Czechs in the west, but were not sure whether they could not be better used on the spot. If they could not be used and therefore had to be transported to France, would they be sufficiently reliable to fight there? Britain had no such reservation *vis-à-vis* the Czech Corps. The Foreign Office had throughout March 1918 been bombarded by Lockhart's telegrams indicating that the bolsheviks were about to turn against the Germans and fight them with Allied

[1] Clemenceau to Lavergne, 19 April 1918; Lavergne to Clemenceau, 23 March 1918.

[2] Chief of the Military Mission, Murmansk to Clemenceau, 24 March 1918.

[3] General Alby to Military Attaché, Peking, Tokyo, Russia, 7 April 1918.

aid.[1] On 21 March Lockhart told Balfour, the Foreign Secretary, that Trotsky had asked for British instructors for his new army and on 28 March Lockhart spoke of a dramatic *volte-face*: the bolsheviks were ready to start fighting the Germans alongside the Allies.[2] It seems clear that Lockhart was listened to carefully, for the Foreign Office passed on to him Major-General Knox's confidential memorandum 'Delay in the East', which spoke so discourteously of Lockhart and his promptings. Lockhart commented on the memorandum in kind and continued to urge the Foreign Office to advocate British aid in the reorganization of the Russian army.[3]

Under the impact of Lockhart's representations, and doubtless for other reasons that have yet to be clarified, on 21 March the Foreign Office prepared a memorandum for the War Office on the rôle and usefulness of the Czech Corps in Russia. Whatever additional reasons there may have been for this memorandum, the War Office was in no hurry to react to it. All the same the French Military Attaché in London, General Panouse, was notified when the reply was finally forthcoming on 1 April. First of all the War Office felt obliged to correct certain inaccuracies in the Foreign Office memorandum. It was very doubtful whether there were 70,000 Czechs organized in the Legion in Russia; there had been some 42,000 in Kiev before the bolsheviks took the city. At that stage an attempt had been made to send them under French officer-instructors to the Rumanian front, but this move had failed. Now it was almost certain that the French officers had left the Legion, and according to the latest information the Legion was moving from Kursk to Samara. In view of transport difficulties, the Legion was probably without artillery and ammunition. At the same time the War Office pointed out that Trotsky had asked the Legion to become the nucleus of the Russian army and that this had been refused by the Czechs. The Legion was making its way to Vladivostok and thence to France. But it was impossible to find shipping for it, and the troops' morale was uncertain; for these reasons they would have to be kept in Russia for some time. The War Office suggested that while they were waiting, the Czechs could be used in one of three different ways: (i) they could be concentrated around Omsk; (ii) they could be re-routed to Archangel; (iii) they could be concentrated in the Trans-Baykal region for possible aid to Ataman

[1] Lockhart to Balfour, 25 February, 2 March, 12 March 1918.
[2] Lockhart to Balfour, 21 March 1918.
[3] Lockhart to Balfour, 31 March 1918.

Semenov. General MacDonogh, Director of Operations at the War Office, wished to know their real military value before any decision was taken. In his view the first proposition was the most attractive, as they would then be able to block any action by German prisoners of war in Siberia.[1]

If the motives for the Foreign Office initiative still remain rather obscure, the attitude of the War Office towards the Czechs was one of guarded suspicion. The Czechs were not forgiven for their 'disobedience' of Allied orders to move to Rumania while Rumania was still a partner in the war. On the whole they seemed to have little military value. It was thought that, if they were to be used in Russia at all, it would be in a passive way: to prevent any moves by German prisoners of war. The alternative plan, that they should assist Ataman Semenov was not even argued out. From the Foreign Office memorandum and the War Office reply one thing at least is clear: the British were far from being scheming 'imperialists' bent on destroying the Soviets by every means at their disposal, as some communist historians have maintained. In this case the evidence indicates that they were most reluctant to use this 'unreliable' Czech force against the bolsheviks.

Nevertheless, the British initiative did ultimately result in the revolt of the Czechs against the bolsheviks. The extent to which this was intentional will become apparent from a consideration of the various Anglo-French deals concerning the Czechs which followed, after the Foreign Office memorandum had been circulated and discussed in authoritative Allied circles. It seems probable that the memorandum was in fact another aspect of British policy planning towards Russia. To all appearances the British government was much less preoccupied with the western front than the French. It believed in fighting the Central Powers anywhere, and especially in the east, where the British empire had vital interests. The British, like the French, were ready to use any troops or forces available for this purpose. But in contrast to the French the British wanted to keep the Japanese out of the Russian Far East, especially if the United States refused to intervene, since they distrusted them. This distrust was partly based on very practical considerations: it was hoped that the threat of the Japanese intervention would force the bolsheviks to turn against the Germans themselves and invite a direct Allied intervention.[2] These broad objectives were reflected in various delaying

[1] Panouse to Clemenceau, 1 April and 2 April 1918.
[2] Panouse to Clemenceau, 2 April 1918.

actions taken by the British at this time. It is true that no cabinet decision setting out this policy is yet known but indications of such a decision are clear. From Moscow Lockhart continued to bombard the Foreign Office with telegrams in which he demanded that Japanese intervention be delayed.[1] His advice was obviously heeded, while no attention was paid in London to the views of Major-General Knox, who advocated immediate action in the east without bolshevik consent. On 17 March 1918 Knox told Panouse that he would shortly be leaving for the Far East: intervention was imminent.[2] But on 21 March he complained to Panouse that President Wilson was responsible for the failure of his Far Eastern plans. He was clearly under the influence of Robins, and also of Lockhart, who only echoed the former.[3] Yet on 2 April Panouse was informed of plans for the Far East worked out by the Deputy Director of Military Intelligence: evidently the War Office at least was taking Knox seriously.[4] But before these plans could even be discussed the Japanese landed in Vladivostok on 4 April. The British immediately followed suit.

This landing was an unexpected unilateral act of the Japanese. In Moscow Trotsky expressed himself very strongly to Lockhart about British 'perfidy' in allowing the Japanese landing. Lockhart may even have sympathized with this view.[5] But the move had clearly not been sanctioned by the British or the Allies. Knox was still in London, and he was to stay there until July 1918, which was a sure sign that the British were not considering any further military action.[6] The French were informed of these developments in some detail on 8 April.[7] By 12 April even Moscow came to view the landing differently. Trotsky thought that the British had landed so promptly in order to paralyse the Japanese, and in this he was probably correct.[8] In any event the British stock went up in Moscow and Lockhart soon had Trotsky's ear again. A fortnight later there were no British troops in Vladivostok, and shortly afterwards the Japanese also withdrew.

[1] Lockhart to Balfour, 31 March and 8 April 1918; Panouse to Clemenceau 12 March 1918.

[2] Panouse to Clemenceau, 17 March 1918.

[3] Panouse to Clemenceau, 21 March 1918.

[4] Panouse to Clemenceau, 2 April 1918.

[5] Lockhart to Balfour, 5 April 1918.

[6] Panouse to Clemenceau, 9 July 1918.

[7] Panouse to Clemenceau, 8 April 1918.

[8] Lockhart to Balfour, 12 April 1918.

It is plain that by now all the other Allies had come round to the British point of view, namely that it was more convenient to be invited to intervene by the bolsheviks than to do so against their will.[1] However, since the Japanese had been so rudely checked and no other ally could provide and land troops in Russia within a reasonable period of time, the unfortunate Czechs came up for discussion again. There followed a sort of seesaw contest between the British and French whether the Czechs should or should not be withdrawn from Russia.

The question of using the Czechs in Russia had previously been raised in the Foreign Office memorandum to the War Office of 21 March 1918, before the Japanese landing. On 1 April Panouse sent to Paris the first indication of this new British approach, and on the following day he enclosed a translation of the War Office reply to the Foreign Office memorandum. The gist of the War Office memorandum as we have seen, was that the Czechs should be used in Siberia. But the French were in no mood to agree to this reasonable suggestion, for they were badly in need of fresh troops; encouraging reports were received from Russia that the Czechs were indeed on the move and that their morale was excellent. Consul André even asked for instructions how he should deal with the Czechs when they arrived.[2] On 7 April 1918, three days after the Japanese surprise landing, the French General Staff had a reply ready for the British, which Panouse handed to the War Office. This was very cautious in tone – as one might expect in view of the fact that the French depended completely on British shipping. It did not reject the British suggestion outright but contained a compromise proposal. The French still insisted that the Czechs should be shipped to France and not used in Russia, but conceded that they might possibly help Semenov while waiting for British ships to arrive for them. The final decision would only be taken when the Czechs were actually concentrated at Vladivostok.[3]

This French 'softness' only complicated the situation. The British became convinced that the French would yield and employ the Czechs in Russia if a reasonable pretext could be found. On 8 April, at a meeting of the permanent military representatives of the Supreme War Council at Versailles, the French were imprudent enough to

[1] Lockhart to Balfour, 8 April 1918.
[2] André to Pichon, 6 April 1918.
[3] Clemenceau to Panouse, 7 April 1918.

vote for the use of the Czechs in the future Allied force in Siberia, if this force should come into being.[1] This vote for a hypothetical contingency did not signify a change in the French attitude. Lockhart reported from Moscow that Lavergne vehemently opposed an intervention by force in Russia, and his views still commanded much sympathy in Paris. On 9 April, however, Lavergne unwittingly complicated the Czechs' position still further by suggesting that, since their movement to Vladivostok had in any case been stopped by Trotsky on account of the Japanese landing they should be re-routed to Archangel.[2]

This was indeed a dangerous suggestion, but Lavergne probably never realized that he was playing into the hands of the British. By now the Japanese had refused to ship the Czechs, and if this suggestion were to be acted upon the ships would have to be provided by the British. On 11 April Lavergne repeated his proposal, and reported that Czech morale was excellent. This confirmed his government in its desire to have the Czechs transferred to France as quickly as possible.[3] On 16 April the French General Staff once again took the matter up with the British and suggested another compromise. If the British would consent to evacuate the Czechs to France by way of Archangel and Murmansk, the Czechs could in the meantime be used to guard the northern ports.[4] This was possibly what the British were waiting for. Their direct commitment to ship the Czechs to France would in any case give them much more power to decide the fate of the Czechs in Russia.

On 20 April 1918 Lockhart received instructions from the Cabinet regarding the Czech Corps. The British government saw the Czechs as the only force in Russia willing to fight the Germans. They were to be re-routed from Siberia to Archangel and Murmansk and then transported to France. To help Lockhart in his negotiations with the bolsheviks on this matter he was given ideological guidance: the Czechs were said to have declared themselves in sympathy with the Russian peasants.[5] This instruction was certainly sent with the French government's approval, for on the same day Clemenceau instructed Lavergne in a similar vein, although using slightly more

[1] Military Representatives, 25th Meeting, 8 April 1918.
[2] Lavergne to Clemenceau, 9 April 1918.
[3] Lavergne to Clemenceau, 11 April 1918.
[4] General Spears to War Office, 16 April 1918.
[5] Balfour to Lockhart, 20 April 1918.

sophisticated terms.[1] Clemenceau made his intentions still more plain in a memorandum which he sent simultaneously to the Quai d'Orsay: from Lavergne's reports he had heard that the Czechs were in excellent fighting condition, and it was therefore imperative to move them to France quickly.[2]

It is difficult to discover how serious the British were about bringing the Czechs from Russia to France, but there can be no doubt concerning the French position. They immediately entered into talks with the British about the details of their transportation. One week after the policy declaration Lavergne received another telegram from the War Ministry: the French were having difficulties with the British. Thus even if the Czechs were re-routed to Archangel, and the bolsheviks would agree to this, there would still be no British ships to take them to France. The British, obviously with the object of delaying the operation were making additional demands: French officers were to be put in charge of the Czech contingents going via Archangel and bolshevik elements were to be excluded from the Legion.[3] On 26 April 1918 Clemenceau repeated these directions to the Quai d'Orsay and requested that the Ambassador in Tokyo be notified; he should also try and get Japanese help.[4] To make sure that the Czechs reached France, the French took steps to commit formally all the other allies, however remotely connected with the transaction they might be. Upon their initiative the permanent military representatives of the Supreme War Council at Versailles solemnly approved the decisions so far reached on the Czechs.[5]

All these preliminary negotiations and preparations had been conducted in a vacuum, far away in Paris, London, Tokyo or Washington. The Czechs were *en route* through Russia, and no one knew their exact whereabouts. However, on 28 April Consul André reported from Vladivostok the arrival of the first Czech 'echelon'.[6] Something very concrete had to be done.

On 29 April 1918, probably as a reaction to the Consul's report, the French General Staff circulated a memorandum on the Czechs in Russia. It contained a summary of previous developments. At first it

[1] Clemenceau to Lavergne, 20 April 1918.
[2] Clemenceau to Pichon, 20 April 1918.
[3] Clemenceau to Lavergne, 26 April 1918.
[4] Clemenceau to Military Attaché, Tokyo, 26 April 1918.
[5] Supreme War Council Meeting, 26 April 1918.
[6] André to Pichon, 28 April 1918.

had been intended that the Czechs should be used on the spot, especially in view of their supposed deal with the bolsheviks; at that stage no other solution had been possible in any case, since no shipping was available. But then, because the Czechs had refused to come to an agreement with the bolsheviks, and because of their combat value, it had been decided to transfer them to France. On 14 April Lavergne had suggested Archangel as an alternative and speedier route for the Czechs. Since the British were expected to agree to this idea more readily, the suggestion had been taken up and explored in London, Moscow and Washington. However, no reply had been received from the Americans to the request for shipping, and London and Moscow had shown tentative interest. Then Ambassador Regnault had reported from Tokio that the Czechs were moving on, and Lavergne had asked for instructions about shipping and about his idea of routing the Czechs via Archangel. Thereupon the French Cabinet took firm steps to remove the Czechs. At Versailles the military representatives had approved their move north and requested the British government to negotiate this re-routing with the bolsheviks.[1] On 2 May the Czechs figured prominently on the agenda when the Supreme War Council's political and military representatives met at Abbeville. Both the French and British Cabinet ministers solemnly agreed to implement a formal resolution, which the conference passed, to remove the Czechs from Russia to France.[2]

It is not clear who, if any, of the French liaison officers with the Czechs in Russia was ever consulted about the re-routing idea. On 3 May the French Consul at Irkutsk, Bourgeois, passed on a telegram to Paris in which Colonel Paris, who was the French liaison officer with the 1st Czech division, urged the War Ministry to have ships ready for this division by 15 May. He also confirmed that the 2nd division under Colonel Vergé could proceed to France via Vologda.[3] Obviously the plan was broached to some of the French officers and approved by them. However, not all of them were consulted or even told about it. In any case the bolshevik agreement to the plan was not negotiated until 5 May, and even then their approval was only given 'in principle'. Both Lockhart and Lavergne reported to their governments that a provisional agreement had been reached with the bolsheviks. According to Lavergne, however, it was doubt-

[1] GSHQ, Paris, 29 April 1918.
[2] Supreme War Council, 5th session, 2 May 1918.
[3] Bourgeois to Pichon, 3 May 1918.

ful whether the re-routing project could be carried out. He also urged his government to keep these negotiations secret. The reason for this secrecy was that he did not wish to embarrass the bolsheviks by revealing that Trotsky had consented to hand over to the Czechs when they arrived in Archangel, some of the Allied stores in the city.[1]

In the meantime further reports reached the Allies that the Czechs arriving in Vladivostok were in excellent fighting condition. At the same time the British reported that they were finding it difficult to provide shipping. The position of the British and French *vis-à-vis* the Czechs appeared irreconcilable. Perhaps the British never really wanted the Czechs in Europe, for as well as procrastinating they claimed that by allocating shipping to the Czechs they would jeopardize their own interests in Mesopotamia and India.[2] This consideration probably only strengthened British determination to keep the Czechs where they were, based on the view that their contribution in the west would be trivial in any case.

On 11 May 1918 Clemenceau put further pressure on the British by reiterating his position: the French were responsible for removing the Czechs to the point of embarkation, while the British were to provide the transport.[3] Whether this forceful statement by Clemenceau was realistic or not remains problematic. There are many indications that he was genuinely concerned to bring the Czechs to France. He was under pressure for more troops in France itself. He was also under pressure from local French representatives abroad, who were clamouring for ships. To all appearances therefore he did not want to use the Czechs in Russia. However, the situation was complicated by the fact that in the meantime Franco–British discussions had started on large-scale intervention in Russia. On 18 May 1918 Lord Cecil wrote to Clemenceau very frankly that, since no ships were available for the Czechs, the latter should be used in Vladivostok. He argued that both governments wanted to force the United States and Japan to intervene as well, and the Czechs could serve as an excellent pretext to bring this about.[4] However, Clemenceau would have none of this. On 22 May 1918 Clemenceau, still unaware that the Czechs had taken their final decision to revolt against the bolsheviks at the Chelyabinsk conference, protested to Cecil that his propositions

[1] Lavergne to Clemenceau, 5 May 1918.
[2] L. S. Amery to Shipping Minister, 9 May 1918.
[3] Note on the Command of Czechs and Serbs in the Archangel and Murmansk Region, 22 May 1918.
[4] Cecil to Clemenceau, 18 May 1918.

violated the Abbeville agreement: the British could not deprive France of Czech troops which were badly needed.[1] At the same time Clemenceau sent a long telegram to Lavergne instructing him to start re-routing the Czechs to Archangel even against bolshevik wishes. Negotiations with them were useless and there was no need for a written statement by Trotsky. He added that the British and French Cabinets were actively studying the question of the northern ports and their protection.[2]

These were the last instructions by the French Prime Minister to the local representative in Russia before the outbreak of the Czech revolt. It is not quite certain what instructions the British government sent to Lockhart, but they were probably very similar. For Lockhart left Moscow for Vologda to see the Allied ambassadors there, and thereupon changed his mind about the merits of Allied intervention. On his return to Moscow he found the Czechs in full revolt, whether he or Lavergne wished it or not. The revolt may have been a godsend to them, but it was certainly not their work.[3]

III

The question of the rôle of the Czech leaders in the preparation of the revolt is easily resolved. For understandable reasons the Czechs were not kept informed about inter-Allied squabbles and changes of plan. It is true that Beneš was consulted from time to time. First the British asked the French to find out whether he would agree to the Czechs being used in Siberia.[4] But Beneš was opposed to this idea and to any delay in getting the Czechs to France. He wanted the troops in Europe, and as the French also needed them there, he was on safe ground. But then the Czech 'echelons' were stopped by Trotsky and Lavergne reported that their release was uncertain. This must have influenced Beneš's decision to agree to their re-routing to Archangel. But again Beneš only thought of speeding the Czechs' departure from Russia and could not know what complications the re-routing order would cause among the Czechs.

After the war, when he was Foreign Minister of Czechoslovakia, Beneš resolutely denied that the Allies had ever asked him or the Czechs to intervene in Russia. He obviously meant an intervention

[1] Clemenceau to Cecil, 22 May 1918.
[2] Clemenceau to Lavergne, 22 May 1918.
[3] Lockhart to Balfour, 5 June 1918.
[4] Panouse to Clemenceau, 1 April 1918.

against the bolsheviks. For the Allies, and above all the British, did ask him several times about an Allied intervention in which the Czechs would take part. But this intervention was intended to be directed against the Germans, not against the bolsheviks, who it was thought might even invite them to take such action. On 14 May 1918 Beneš committed himself to an agreement with the War Office by which he consented to the use of Czech troops in western Russia as part of a massive Allied intervention against the Germans, provided that there was no interference in Russian internal affairs and that at least half of the 70,000 Czechs were transported to France.[1]

It may be argued that this agreement was naïve, and was bound to be misconstrued as it actually was. However, it did reflect Czech thinking on the problem, for almost at the same time the Czechs in Russia decided to revolt against the bolsheviks and force their way to Vladivostok but at the same time not to interfere in internal Russian affairs. The Russian Czechs, and Beneš never consented to a Czech intervention against the bolsheviks and never in any way prepared the revolt. When it came, Beneš did not welcome it enthusiastically, but later he was to exploit it very skilfully.

If the Czech leaders in the west did not prepare the revolt, it must be attributed to the Czechs on the spot. It was a revolt by resolute young men against their timid local leaders, who can also be absolved of responsibility for its preparation. The revolt was a sudden and spontaneous affair which surprised everybody foe and friend alike. When considering it the following main factors need great emphasis: the inexperience of the Czech leadership, both political and military; the muddle into which the leaders and Allies got themselves by negotiating clumsily with the bolsheviks; the morbid fear of the Germans, which was felt by both leaders and the rank and file; the unprincipled and purposeless adventurism of the young Czech officers; the lack of political foresight by the Czechs generally, when the revolt was sparked off; and the misleading optimism of the junior Allied personnel when tolerating and supporting the revolt.

IV

Professor Masaryk, the leader and organizer of the Czech Corps, departed from European Russia on 7 March 1918 leaving behind a number of plenipotentiaries and vague instructions: 'the Czechs were

[1] L. S. Amery, Note on a Conversation with Dr Beneš, 14 May 1918.

to execute the evacuation agreement which he concluded with the French Military Mission in Russia on 18 February 1918. They were to travel to France via Vladivostok and while doing so remain neutral i.e. avoid interfering in internal Russian affairs.' However, Masaryk was foreseeing enough to have ordered the Czechoslovak Legion to *defend itself energetically*, if attacked by any Slavonic force in Russia or Siberia. He evidently foresaw difficulties ahead, but nevertheless considered his departure more important than staying on with the Legion and extricating it from the quicksands of the Russian revolution.

Masaryk left in charge of Czech affairs in Russia J. Klecanda and P. Maxa; the former, an exceedingly young secretary-administrator whose only recommendation was that he spoke good Russian and that he carried out instructions faithfully; the latter a youthful PoW representative, ex-politician and ex-schoolmaster, with plenty of cunning but otherwise with an excessive regard for his own life which he had just normalized after a prolonged period in Turkestan camps. These were then the two key political figures who were to accomplish the tremendous task of steering the Czechoslovak Army Corps from European Russia to Vladivostok and thence to France.

Apart from their personal disabilities and lack of experience, the circumstances in which the task was to be carried out would have defeated even much stronger and more experienced men than Klecanda and Maxa. On 17 February 1918, shortly before his departure, Masaryk held a conference with his C-in-C, General Shokorov, and the C-of-S General Dieterichs; both Klecanda and Maxa attended. On the agenda there was only one item: 'the moral decay of the Legion'. The generals were pessimistic. It was not only external (revolutionary) influences which were undermining morale but also internal influences. Both officers and men, according to the generals, did not understand their duties properly and were in need of re-education. Two days after this conference a member of the Czechoslovak National Council in Russia, the political organization whose chairman Masaryk was, Ježek, hazarded the opinion that some 80 per cent of the Czech soldiers were dissatisfied with their service in the Legion. Though Ježek's estimate was undoubtedly exaggerated the Legion was far from happy during the period of inaction in the Ukraine.

If the soldiers were dissatisfied the political conditions in the Czechoslovak movement were equally depressing. With the bolshevik occupation of Kiev and under pressure from the representatives of the PoW section, who happened to be left-wing social democrats, Masaryk was forced to accept the resignation of two right-wing members (Hess and Eisenberg) of the National Council. But the left went even further: on 24 February 1918 it attempted a *coup de force* against the National Council in Masaryk's name. But Masaryk resolutely disowned the coup and before he could deal with this challenge any further the Germans invaded the Ukraine and thus solved the Czech internal problems, at least for the time being. On 20 February 1918 orders were sent out for the evacuation of the Legion from the Ukraine to France.

The evacuation was in fact an improvised retreat before the Germans and this retreat proved most important for the further development of the Legion in Russia. Ultimately the evacuation brought about a change in the Czech leadership. During the evacuation the politicians showed themselves increasingly more incompetent while the officers, only recently appointed, gradually regained their courage and self-confidence. On the retreat the 1st Division, which was on the western bank of the Dnieper, had to march east. While doing so it was involved in several skirmishes with the advancing Germans. These skirmishes, though militarily insignificant, were of great psychological value. The 1st Division's retreat was only vaguely planned and the Czech officers were thus able to prove their mettle in 'organizing' the retreat. In Kiev, as well as at the 'battle' of Bakhmach where the units of the 2nd Division defended the trains for the 1st Division, the Czechs managed to beat off the insufficient German forces which were threatening to cut off Czech retreat lines by advancing too fast. While soldiers were 'victorious' on these occasions, the political representatives, when trying to secure an armistice with the Germans, were unsuccessful. Gajda later wrote contemptuously about these efforts: 'they were extremely ridiculous; veterinary surgeons, musical band conductors were members of armistice delegations, but there were no soldiers on them.' The failures in negotiations and German arrogance towards the delegates also had a great effect on the Czech soldiers. The Legion could see for the first time quite explicitly that there would be no mercy from the Germans. This realization, confirmed later by actual executions of captured Czechs, became the most potent factor in holding the Legion together.

At Bakhmach the Czechs also had their first experience in fighting side by side with the bolsheviks, who joined them during the engagement. On this occasion the Czechs saw undisciplined 'Red youth', embarrassingly heavily armed, but ready to fly as soon as a sustained attack was pressed upon them. At the moment when the soldiers' self-confidence and contempt for the bolsheviks were on the increase the politicians began to negotiate with the latter the precise terms of the previously agreed evacuation to Vladivostok.

V

The Legion had concluded a number of local armistice agreements with the bolsheviks. The most important one was signed with Colonel Muravyov, C-in-C of the Soviet forces in the Ukraine, on 10 February 1918. On 16 February 1918 Muravyov confirmed this agreement in person and also expressed his consent to the eventual evacuation of the Legion to France. Since the Legion now actually withdrew from the Ukraine new agreements had to be negotiated. In Masaryk's absence the talks were badly tackled from the very beginning. To make doubly sure negotiations were started locally with the Southern Front C-in-C, Antonov-Ovseyenko, and centrally with the Sovnarkom. Klecanda was in Petrograd and then in Moscow for this purpose with a few other members of the National Council. But he was isolated from the Legion. Surprisingly he was very success-ful. The central bolsheviks, anxious to avoid complications with the Germans and also probably fearing the nearness of this 'disciplined' Army Corps with its Tsarist officers, were more than willing to permit the Czechs to move from the danger areas, the Ukraine and the Don territory, into the 'wilderness' of Siberia. On 15 March 1918, after negotiating with Aralov and Stalin, Klecanda was given the Sovnarkom's permission to evacuate freely via Siberia. As these nego-tiations were proceeding in Moscow, Maxa was conducting his own at Kursk. The Kursk bolsheviks reasoned differently from the centre. They saw a retreating Czech Corps, necessarily suffering from chaotic arrangements and lack of supplies. They also argued with the Czechs, reproaching them for abandoning the German Front and leaving them, badly armed as they were, to oppose their own national enemy. Maxa proved receptive to these arguments. Unable to consult with his Moscow colleagues he signed a local agreement on 16 March 1918, one day after the central bolsheviks had conceded a practically unmolested evacuation. The terms of this local agreement were un-favourable to the Czechs and so vaguely defined as to cause disagree-ments in the future. In accordance with it, all the 'excessive' artillery, machine guns and also armoured cars were surrendered to the bolsheviks, who issued a festive proclamation thanking the Czechoslovaks for their 'brotherly gifts'.

In Klecanda's report on his negotiations with Stalin there was unbounded optimism. According to it the bolsheviks trusted the Czechs and would even help them as much as possible with the formation of the second Army Corps, for which the Czechs hoped to recruit Czech PoWs in Siberia. What possibly cheered Klecanda most was Stalin's permission for the National Council of Moscow to remove to Omsk. Perhaps Stalin and the bolsheviks were quite genuine *vis-à-vis* the Czechs at this stage. But the situation was rapidly changing. Soon Klecanda became convinced that the bolsheviks were hatching a secret plot against the Czechs. Still, on 21 March 1918 Maxa wrote hopefully: 'For the time being we ride on ... It is almost a miracle.' The ride was truly only for the time being and in a sense it was a miracle. The miracle came to an abrupt end on 22 March, when the chairman of the Penza Soviet, Kurayev, issued an order by which all Czech trains were stopped and the Czechs were to be disarmed completely. Klecanda heard of this difficulty in Moscow and had several interviews with Trotsky, who in the meantime had become Commissar of War. He found him distrustful of Czech intentions in the Far East, where Essaul Semenov was actively anti-Soviet. Klecanda soon lost his temper and had several quarrels with the Commissar, but was no match for him. In any case it is doubtful that Trotsky caused this stoppage. As far as Kurayev was concerned the immediate cause was Antonov-Ovseyenko's telegram from Kursk alleging the violation of the local agreement by the Czechs. Kurayev also had several reasons of his own: the Czechs were behaving provocatively towards Russian civilians and Soviet representatives. The slowness of evacuation irritated the Legion soldiers. On 24 March 1918 with the trains standing still, General Podgayevsky, Commander of the 2nd Division and one of the few Russians remaining with the Legion, even marched into Kurayev's office with an armed escort to tell him that he would hang him if he would not release the trains.

Thus tension and suspicions increased on both sides. Each side started to threaten the other. In Moscow Klecanda dared to threaten Trotsky without an armed escort. At Penza Maxa disagreed with General Podgayevsky's action. On 25 March 1918 Maxa, backed by General Dieterichs, another Russian general, but with Pavlů dissenting, proposed to Kurayev the surrender of most of the Legion's arms in return for his permission to let it proceed to Vladivostok. On 26 March 1918 Kurayev telegraphed these proposals to Moscow. Stalin then replied with the famous telegram in which he accepted Maxa's proposals and imposed a few further conditions, such as the dismissal of 'reactionary' officers. Trotsky then called Klecanda's bluff and the latter in disgust left Moscow to investigate on the spot the incredible news of capitulation. Soon afterwards he died of pneumonia and was thus saved from witnessing the complete collapse of the political leadership which proved so unsuccessful in the face of the bolsheviks.

So far it was the various armistice and disarmament agreements which were the cause of the slowing and stoppages of Czech trains. In April 1918 another factor began to aggravate the relations between the Legion and the Soviets. On 5 April 1918 the official journal of the Czechoslovak movement, *Československý deník*, announced that a group of Czech communist agitators had arrived at Penza and Samara to launch a recruitment drive for the Red Army. Since Penza had become the key point for the further movement of the Legion a party branch was founded and the 1st Czech International Regiment was formed there. The party activity did not consist of newspaper propaganda only (two Czech communist papers were distributed free among the Legion] soldiers, the *Průkopník svobody*, with a circulation of some 10,000 and the *Československá Rudá armáda* with 3,500), but also of direct contacts with the Czech soldiers. At the Penza station the party had at its disposal a special propaganda-recruitment coach, and public meetings were organized from which officers were excluded and the men were addressed by communist agitators. Though the effect of this activity was not remarkable the National Council felt itself threatened enough to order the Legion soldiers not to leave their trains at Penza. The agitators were then debarred from the Czech trains.

The greatest pressure exerted by the Czech communists on the Legion was through the local and central Soviet authorities, and especially through the Arms Control Commission, whose members they were, and whose decisions meant either good speed or delays for the Czech trains. On 3 April 1918 Štrombach, CO of the Czech International Regiment at Penza, wrote to the Moscow Czech centre that he had asked Kurayev to hold up the Czech trains as much as possible and permit agitators to undermine the Legion from within.

Though Kurayev disliked this request he acquiesced in it, especially when the Czech comrades produced some results. But these results were grossly misleading: apart from a few soldiers the most encouraging success was the 'desertion' of two members of the National Council and four regimental delegates to the projected Czech army congress. After 26 April, when this success was scored, the Penza communists became over-optimistic. They became convinced that by these artificial delays the Legion would be unnerved and ultimately become so disgusted with its journey to France that it would revolt against its 'reactionary' political and military leadership and join the Soviets. Great hopes were centred on the coming congress which it was thought would unleash this revolt.

Even the communist historian Vávra admits that Czech communist tactics at Penza were naïve and that the campaign misfired psychologically. The leadership, if it existed in the real sense, was not blamed for the delays. The soldiers were turning against the Soviets whom they clearly recognized as the cause of the delay. While the men waited endlessly in godforsaken village stations they were preoccupied with two thoughts: to put between themselves and the Germans as many miles as possible and to reach Vladivostok as well armed as possible, for the journey through Siberia – whence many had come – meant passing by many PoW camps full of hostile Germans and Hungarians. During the intermittent periods of waiting they also saw local Soviets arming these very same PoWs. The Internationalist Units seemed to them the cover for the recruitment of their national enemies and increased their doubts as to the real intentions of the bolsheviks towards them. The Czech communist propaganda left them very sceptical. They saw the communists escaping from the Legion when it was in difficulties for the better conditions in the Red Army. They saw the Arms Commission Control twice dissolved when its members became too friendly with the Legion by accepting bribes and conniving at concealed arms. The men asked themselves what was behind the Soviet demands for arms: Penza asked for the agreed arms, Samara for as many more to defend itself against some Cossacks; Omsk asked for machine guns permitted by Penza, while on arrival at Irkutsk the last remaining rifles were requested as a condition for the trains being let through.

As delays multiplied and tension mounted the Legion's nerves became edgy and discipline was getting out of hand. Incidents were occurring which should have warned the Penza communists as well as the bolsheviks in Moscow that the Legion might get out of control. On 26 April 1918 Lieutenant Bajer, whose regiment had been immobilized before Penza for some considerable time, marched on the town with a strong escort to 'purge it'. The unfortunate National Council had to exert great efforts to dissuade Bajer from the purge and calm the whole regiment. But the Czech communists blundered still further: they 'skilfully' released such alarming rumours as that they were now the only recognized representatives of the Czechoslovaks in Russia and that the National Council and its documents were unrecognized and its identity papers invalid. Other rumours had it that the complete disarming of the Czech Corps was imminent and its repatriation to Austria-Hungary assured.

The Czechs in the Legion were forced to act in defence. The National Council released counter-rumours. The bolsheviks were labelled as German puppets and there were talks about their dark plans. Certain officers began to propagate plans for every and any contingency'. But nothing substantial was done, no agreement reached, even though it was becoming increasingly evident that a final showdown with the Soviets was probable. Senior officers agreed with Generals Shokorov and Dieterichs that peaceful passage to Vladivostok was imperative under any conditions the bolsheviks might impose. Others thought the right moment for shooting one's way to Vladivostok had not come yet. Only 'Captain' Gajda, CO of the 7th Regiment (under investigation for fraudulently assuming his rank), whose contempt for the bolsheviks was boundless, was serious about taking action against them if they tried to block his way to Vladivostok. He ordered his C-of-C, Captain Kadlec, the only Czech officer with staff experience, to prepare plans for such a contingency. In the 1st Division such plans were prepared by General Kolomensky and Colonel Dorman but they made them under protest as they had no faith in armed action against the Soviets. But tension was rising. On 13 April 1918 at Kirsanov all the officers of the 1st Division, which had been most delayed, held a conference and passed unanimously a resolution in which they not only refused to surrender any more arms, but on the contrary demanded from the National Council fresh equipment and arms.

The resolution was absurd. The National Council had no arms or equipment and in any case favoured negotiations with the bolsheviks rather than a showdown. But this paradoxical demand clearly points to the unreality of the situation in which the Czechs found themselves.

Isolated as they were they saw in the delays and disarming a bolshevik plot to hand them over to the Germans. The opinion in the Legion for strong action was hardening. Men egged on their officers who in turn put pressure on the senior officers and the political leadership. Plans began to be hatched without the slightest regard for political implications of such actions and with no thought for the far-away Allies.

The latter, though accused by Soviet historians, sparked off the revolt without real intention, and if at all consciously then prematurely. In France Dr Beneš who was most active, was willing to make the Legion a docile tool of the Allies. The Allies were tentatively interested; several times they brought up the matter at their meetings; decisions were even taken, but there was no way of implementing these decisions without bolshevik consent. Though there were French liaison officers with the Legion, for all practical purposes the Czechs were cut off, left to their own devices. In the meantime the Allies decided that since they had not enough ships in the Far East they would re-route the Czechs to Archangel. Obviously the Czechs would also be useful near the northern bases. General Lavergne and Lockhart were therefore charged with negotiating with Trotsky the Legion's re-routing. On 21 April, when the negotiations were successfully concluded, Chicherin telegraphed to stop the slowly rolling trains again. The Czechs west of Omsk were to go to Archangel. This new order surprised everybody, the Corps as well as the National Council. The Allies acted over the heads of the Czechs, thinking that as an Allied army unit they would obey their orders whether they made sense or not. They were soon undeceived. In the prevalent psychosis in the Legion the German name of the Russian adjutant who signed the telegram meant that the order was a German-bolshevik trap to divide the Czechs in order to destroy. Gajda's idea of shooting one's way to the east became popular.

By now the confusion was inextricable. On 9 May 1918 the hesitant Maxa was rushed to Moscow to get a clarification of Chicherin's telegram, which everybody refused to obey. To his surprise he found on arrival in Moscow that the re-routing order did come from the Allies and had Trotsky's blessing. But by then Maxa was also cut off from the Legion, as much as the Supreme Allied Council, the various military and diplomatic missions in Russia and the central bolsheviks. A series of misunderstandings and incidents, in an atmosphere in which everyone suspected everyone else, led to the final break.

On 12 May 1918 Lieutenant Syrový, the future C-in-C of the

Czechoslovak forces in Russia, wrote a situation report on his regiment. In it he succinctly summed up the desperate muddle the Czechs were in: '. . . no one wants to go to Archangel . . . as soon as this (change of direction to Vladivostok) became known the soldiers began to grumble . . . they grumbled for several reasons . . . (they feared) hunger, danger from the Germans and the sea with the German U-boats . . . intrigues of the Germans and Russians alike and the stupidity of our leadership . . . they would rather run away and go independently to Vladivostok . . .' Lieutenant-Colonel Voytsekhovsky, the future White C-in-C in Siberia, similarly summed up the mood of his regiment. On 6 May 1918, facing semi-mutiny, the National Council – or what was left of it – decided to convoke the military congress for which the election had already been carried out. Thus it prepared for itself a *coup de grâce* with typical nonchalance. The Czech communists, who also convoked a party conference in Moscow for 20–21 May, were to be equally surprised by the outcome of the long expected congress.

On 14 May 1918 an incident occurred at Chelyabinsk where the precongress conference of the 1st Division was to take place. During a stop at the station a Czech soldier was wounded by a piece of iron thrown out of a train repatriating some Hungarian PoWs. The train was stopped and the culprit lynched. Tempers rose. Czech reinforcements marched into the town and freed the imprisoned soldiers arrested by Soviet forces after the lynching. At the same time arms were seized from the town arsenal.

Incidents were taking place all along the Trans-Siberian between the Czechs and the Soviets, but this particular one shocked Moscow into action. It seems obvious that the patience of Moscow bolsheviks ran out. While they allowed these extremely suspect 'Allied' troops to remove to Vladivostok, they were having nothing but trouble with them. The permission in any case was given against the wishes of Siberian Soviets. Now there was Semenov raiding Soviet territory, the Allies were plotting 'something' and the White opponents were still powerful, especially in the provinces and above all in Siberia. The Czechs who had reached Vladivostok were accumulating in the town and no ships were in sight. The Chelyabinsk incident was the last straw; while the Czechs were partially disarmed the Soviets would have an advantage in a showdown. On 21 May 1918 Maxa and Čermák, who were still in Moscow, were abruptly arrested and forced to sign an appeal to the Czech Legion to surrender all its arms to the Soviets. At the same time telegrams went out bidding the local Soviets to disarm the Legion forcibly if it refused Maxa's appeal.

In the meantime at Chelyabinsk the pre-congress conference was in session. The discussion centred on the re-routing order which was disbelieved and on continuing the journey to Vladivostok even against the will of the Soviets. There was still some hesitation. Above all the junior French officers advised against such an action. On 23 May 1918 the Chelyabinsk conference read an intercepted telegram by Aralov ordering the Soviets to disarm the Czechs. It was obvious that the bolsheviks meant business and the Czechs were forced into a decision. On 25 May 1918 Trotsky's telegram ordering the Soviets to disarm the Czechs or shoot them was read by various regimental commanders after the conference at Chelyabinsk had dispersed for action. When on the same day the weak forces of the Maryanovka Soviet actually tried to execute Trotsky's order, Gajda started the revolt in his· section of the Trans-Siberian and the rest of the commanders and forces had to follow suit.

It does not seem an exaggeration to say that without the pre-congress no revolt would have taken place. In the first instance the conference overthrew the irresolute and incapable political leadership left behind by T. G. Masaryk. By voting unanimously for the resolution: 'To Vladivostok armed and even against the will of the Soviets' the conference in fact handed over unlimited power to the military commanders who at this stage were mainly young Czech officers. Though many delegates and the chairman, Zmrhal, were socialists, they were powerless to oppose the violent action the conference proposed to take against the Soviets. It was a vain gesture of political inexperience to send a socialist member to Moscow to explain the 'violent' decisions of the conference.

A new 'provisional' leadership was elected at Chelyabinsk while the old was declared deposed. The radical, impulsive Pan-Slav Pavlů, who always objected to Maxa's conciliatory attitude to the bolsheviks, achieved his ambition for which he had had to wait for almost four years. He became the chairman of the new executive. But with all his Pan-Slavism and right-wing views he was forced to declare only limited aims of the new executive: threatened by German-bolsheviks and 'betrayed' by the old leaders the Legion would take into its own hands the continuation of its journey to Vladivostok. The Chelyabinsk elections and decisions were then unanimously approved by the final congress at Omsk in June 1918. But the real

91

power slipped out of Pavlů's hands as soon as he had completed his declaration.

In the Legion the command was also deposed and purged, but there were no public declarations. In effect the officer-delegates, Čeček, Gajda and Voytsekhovsky, were given full command of all the troops in their respective areas. All the hesitant Russian officers were dismissed or even arrested. Some ran away at the inception of the revolt. Czech officers took their places. The charges of White encouragement or collusion are exaggerated. The Czech officers needed no encouragement from that quarter. They achieved their dream: they were given a free hand to get the Corps to Vladivostok. If their handling proved a success new vistas would open. There were no Russian generals left and the new 'provisional' leadership controlled promotions. But even at Chelyabinsk while some delegates enjoyed their new powers and others dreamed of future rewards, there was no agreement on a united action aginst the bolsheviks. Perhaps this did not matter so much as the young officers preferred improvisation. All the same, by failing to make concrete plans and to define the purpose and limits of the action, the conference unwittingly completed the anarchy in the Legion which by now was nothing more than a desperate panicky crowd of men in uniforms. In these unfavourable conditions, with the bolsheviks thundering from afar but impotent on the spot, with the Allies far away and with the political and military leadership deposed, the new young men took their chance and sparked off the revolt which they considered the only way out of the predicament in which the Legion found itself.

VI

However much Gajda and some other officers might have talked tough the revolt would have been impossible without their men's wholehearted consent. The men were in a state of high excitement with the one great fear of being divided into smaller groups, disarmed and handed over to the Germans by their 'bolshevik agents'. The lynching of the Hungarian PoW at Chelyabinsk was a clear indication of this obsessive hatred and nervousness, but also of indiscipline. In many places soldiers forced their officers to act. Voytsekhovsky's diary entries for these days show how reluctant he was to start fighting. He and Čeček also opposed Gajda's energetic 'shooting one's way through' and proposed different courses for action.

As for Gajda he was animated by a blind hatred of the Germans hardened by the years of war and heightened by the present condition. He sensed instinctively that his men felt like himself and he therefore decided to act on his own. At Novonikolayevsk he was the least threatened, but it was he who started the revolt. Throughout the initial phase he saw Germans everywhere; they spied on the Czechs and he had them mercilessly shot without trial. They officered the Internationalist Units and he spread among his men the idea that fighting the bolsheviks meant fighting the Germans. He said: 'It is the old game, as in the war.'

While fighting he raided German PoW trains and prevented the evacuees from returning home. He had his men 'clean up' the PoW camps, summarily executed PoWs who opposed him with or without arms, and kept the camps under Czech control. He liquidated Lavrov's Hungarians, wrought vengeance on the Baikal bolsheviks, for they had captured, tortured and killed his friend Colonel Ushakov. Throughout the fighting, he proudly remarked in 1921, no prisoners were taken. He was cold about the fate of the Imperial family, for he was told that the Tsar was being taken to sign the Brest-Litovsk Treaty, and he believed it. Thus, fighting in bands with no special discipline and nevertheless winning easily, he and his men reached Vladivostok. When they turned back to the Urals again it was the beginning of the end of the Czechoslovak Legion.

The seed of anarchy and decomposition sprouted as soon as the revolt flared up. A momentary cohesion was achieved by means of fear and the *idée fixe*, Vladivostok. The cohesion collapsed as soon as Vladivostok was reached. There were no other aims, there was no common plan, no appreciation of political implications of the revolt, no anticipation of the next step. The revolt brought about the inevitable: interference in Russian internal affairs and with it complications and divisions and further demoralization. As could be anticipated, military necessity forced the Czechs to seek White support. Gajda became first involved. His grandiose plans dispersed his weak forces in the drive east and west and the effort to secure his flank to the south. His forces were insufficient for such a task; he therefore sought the support of the Novonikolayevsk Officers' Association even before the revolt. But the two sides seemed incompatible allies; subsequent enmity showed that both were interested in short-term advantages. On 4 May 1918 the Novonikolayevsk Soviet arrested Gajda. This probably discouraged the Whites from

committing themselves to such a weak ally and nothing really was
arranged. When the revolt started Gajda had to take all the Siberian
cities. Only Tayga and Tomsk were seized by the Whites—after
being abandoned by the panic-stricken bolsheviks under the impression of Czech victories elsewhere. Many other 'liberation' attempts
by the Whites were easily suppressed by the local Soviets and Gajda
had to disperse his precious Czechs still further for his weak allies.
To bolster up his units he was forced to employ from the beginning

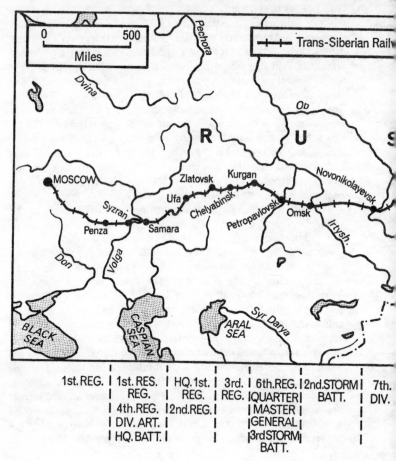

1st. REG.	1st. RES. REG.	HQ.1st. REG.	3rd. REG.	6th. REG.	2nd. STORM BATT.	7th. DIV.
	4th. REG.	2nd. REG.		QUARTER MASTER GENERAL		
	DIV. ART.			3rd STORM BATT.		
	HQ. BATT.					

Russian auxiliaries. It was these Russians who fought the most important and bloody engagements in the Trans-Baikal region.

While the fighting was on Russian military aid was accepted and no political implications were thought of. Gajda's western advance was completed on 9 June 1918 when he made contact with the Voytsekhovsky group, but his eastern drive reached the Vladivostok forces only on 31 August 1918. The other groups naturally also became involved in Russian affairs, though both preceded their revolt

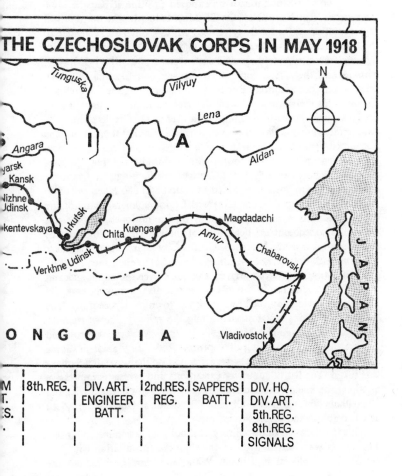

THE CZECHOSLOVAK CORPS IN MAY 1918

M	8th. REG.	DIV. ART.	2nd. RES.	SAPPERS	DIV. HQ.
T.		ENGINEER	REG.	BATT.	DIV. ART.
S.		BATT.			5th. REG.
					8th. REG.
					SIGNALS

with declarations of 'neutrality'. Voytsekhovsky made his declaration on 19 May and on 27 May occupied Chelyabinsk, developing his operations east and west rather slowly. Obviously he lacked Gajda's enthusiasm and as a Russian he probably saw more clearly the political implications of the revolt. He made contact with Čeček and his group on 6 July 1918.

Though the most exposed, the Čeček group seems to have been the last to revolt. But because of its exposed position it became most involved in Russian affairs. On 26 May 1918 Medek, the political representative at Penza, flatly refused Maxa's order to surrender to the bolsheviks. But while on 27 May Gajda and Voytsekhovsky were fighting, the Czech soldiers at Penza were addressed by Kurayev, Minkin and the Czech communist Raušer at a meeting to which officers were not admitted. But even without officers the men refused to surrender their arms. All were determined rather to fight it out. On 28 May the Penza station was taken over by the Czechs peacefully. On the morning of 29 May, after declaring again that the 'action' was not aimed against the Soviets, Lieutenant Švec, in Čeček's absence, led his men on Penza and took it after sporadic fighting. As previously at Zborov in July 1917, Czechs were fighting Czechs. Some 150 Czech communists were killed in action and 250 taken prisoner. As could be expected of the unnerved Legion soldiers, many of the captured Czechs were shot and many others 'disappeared'; the rest were imprisoned. But the behaviour of the exasperated soldiers was also tough towards the Russians. The SR City Duma which took over the administration begged the officers to discipline their men.

By 30 May 1918 Čeček arrived and took over the command and on 31 May Czech trains began to evacuate Penza moving east. On 2 June the Soviets returned and took the town over peacefully. The 'sacking' of Penza was repeated along the railway line *en route* to Samara. There even the Menshevik journal, *Nash golos*, protested against the illegal shooting of captured Red Army soldiers. Some 2,304 bolsheviks and suspects were arrested on the same day Samara was taken. The list of summary executions and arrests is impressive all along the line of Czech advance: at Petropavlovsk the Soviet and 20 civilians (among them 3 Czechs) shot dead; at Omsk some 1,500; at Chelyabinsk the whole Soviet, etc.

With the fighting, both military and political discipline collapsed. The revolt was started without the slightest consultation with any senior Allied official in Russia. While Lavergne declared all the

Czechs who disobeyed his orders to surrender to be traitors, Major Guinet wrote in the *Československý deník*, the Legion newspaper, that the order to go to Archangel must be obeyed and that the Allies would provide protection for the Czechs. In the meantime Colonel Vergé, another liaison officer, arranged an armistice at Irkutsk and was never forgiven by Gajda for 'disrupting' his operations. In the supreme moment of panic the Czechs obeyed no one and Gajda was quite willing to arrest the French, if they interfered, on the spot. In all fairness, the Allies in a sense deserved this treatment. They recognized Czechs as their own units, promised substantial help and protection, but right up to the moment of the revolt the Czechs depended almost entirely on the supplies provided by the Soviets, and Allied protection amounted in Czech eyes to surrender to the bolsheviks. Also the Allies had a natural tendency to make decisions concerning the Legion without the slightest consultation with it, although it was a volunteer body and had by now a long tradition of being consulted in advance of a decision. Naturally in the revolutionary conditions these misunderstandings were aggravated by the lack of contact. But the basic difference between Allied and Czech thinking was that the former might have wanted the Legion to revolt against the bolsheviks and stay in Russia, while the Czechs revolted in order to get out of Russia. In the initial stage of the revolt the Czechs were only willing to use the Allies locally to gain military advantage. It was a different matter when the objective of the revolt was achieved.

It was at Samara that Allied influence and interference began to make itself felt on the Czechs at long last. Čeček took the town on 8 June and continued east taking Buguruslan on 23 June and Ufa on 4 July and then joined the Voytsekhovsky group. Samara, however, was not evacuated as Penza had been. In taking Samara the Czechs were assisted by SR insurgents who staged a diversionary uprising in the country round Samara. Čeček handed the city over to them as a reward and left a small garrison to aid them. But in Samara there were several active Allied Consuls with contacts in Moscow, in other words with responsible Allied personnel. Čeček at least realized that the fighting was not just for its own sake; under the impression of his victories, SR aid and lack of Allied shipping in Vladivostok, it dawned on him that perhaps something else could be done than just reach Vladivostok.

On 9 June, one day after his capture of Samara, Čeček went to see the American Consul, C. W. Williams. He handed him some papers with the request to have them passed on to Ambassador Francis. He wanted to explain the revolt and get instructions as to the next step. Williams had no direct contact with Vologda, but only with the Moscow Consul, Poole. Both these junior diplomats began to take risky and unauthorized initiative with the inexperienced Czech commander in search of a purpose. At the same time the French began to stir. The revolt, however surprising, was a fact and it deserved to be taken advantage of. On 20 June Major Guinet had General Lavergne's telegram sanctioning the revolt. On 22 June Guinet conveyed Ambassador Noulens' thanks to the Czechs for their revolt. With the sanctioning of the revolt by the Allies, which in any case was neither surprising nor useful, the aimless Czechs were going to be given an aim – as they all wanted. On 24 June 1918 the *Československý deník* spoke of the Czech Legion as the *avant-garde* of the Allies. They were to re-constitute the Eastern front on the Volga against the Germans and an Allied army from Vyatka would come to their aid.[1]

These announcements were taken extremely seriously by the Czechs and no one questioned their feasibility. Williams, Captain Bordes and Guinet, the Allied representatives on the spot were simply trusted, and on the whole the subsequent deception was not a question of their bad faith. While the Czechs proved such pessimists *vis-à-vis* the bolsheviks, they proved incurable optimists about the Allies. So the planless, desultory fighting of the Legion continued with the new aim in view and with the firm expectation of a relieving force.

VII

Apart from the diplomats the two key figures responsible for generating excessive optimism and subsequent disillusionment of the Czechs were Major Guinet and Captain Bordes. While the Czech officers tended to distrust the diplomats they saw no reason to distrust their brother-officers. They reasoned that the two Frenchmen were acting on the orders of their government and it somehow never entered their heads that the two isolated officers, while ostensibly acting on orders from France, were in a sense interpreters of these orders. In the light of subsequent knowledge they could be described more accurately as misinterpreters, but undoubtedly very convincing

[1] Poole to Lansing, 31 May 1918; Poole to Lansing, 2 June, 9 June, 17 June 1918.

ones, since only bitter failure undeceived the Czechs. Bordes especially proved an arch-intriguer with plenty of unauthorized initiative and unjustified optimism. His diary, which he compiled for the Ministry of War when threatened with a court martial, gives the picture of a soldier of fortune in the Russian revolution and perhaps also helps to explain the confused French policy towards the bolsheviks.[1]

First Bordes was sent on a special mission to the Don by General Berthelot from Rumania. Soon afterwards he was in touch with the Czechs and his initiative and interference made itself felt. On arriving at Samara his enquiries about war material led him to General Orlov, the city commander, who calmly declared that all war supplies would be handed over to the Germans, if they arrived at Samara. Bordes was outraged and consequently began to take steps to prevent this from happening. He had already, on his way to Samara, spoken to the Czechs on their way to Vladivostok; he had a long talk with them at Rtishchevo. Now at Samara he came across more evidence that the Czechs and bolsheviks were having disagreements. When collecting his own telegrams he stole Trotsky's telegraphic order to the Samara Soviet bidding it to enrol PoWs against the Czechs. Then Jannot, 'French Consul', told him of Maxa's and Čermák's arrest in Moscow. Bordes soon had a telegram on the Chelyabinsk incident and managed to read another telegram from Trotsky ordering the Czechs to be disarmed. Bordes then ventured to organize what seems to have been the first Allied plot with the Czechs. In his railway carriage he gathered Jannot, Dr Fischer whom he called C-in-C of Czech troops in the West Volga region, a Russian SR named Bogolyubov who allegedly controlled some 1,500 men and a Cossack Colonel Shoroshkin (?). He told them of the conflict between the Czechs and the bolsheviks and urged them to overthrow the Samara Soviet. After this conference Bordes took Jannot's wife and daughter and left for Moscow. Nothing happened at Samara and it is not known whether Lieutenant Čeček, the actual C-in-C of the Czech forces in the region, benefited from Fischer's contacts with Bordes and the Samara underground.

In Moscow Bordes contacted Colonel Hurstel who was in charge of the training mission for the Red Army. Vologda was asked for instructions and when Trotsky called Major Lelong to send some French officers to Samara to calm the revolting Czechs, Bordes was

[1] Dossier Bordes; also Clemenceau to Janin, 22 December 1918; Janin to Clemenceau, 25 January 1919.

sent out again. At Syzran he was joined by Maxa, who had been released by Trotsky on signing the declaration to the Czechs to surrender. Maxa sadly realized that the Czechs would not obey him. Bordes added that they would rather kill him than obey him. Colonel Hurstel also arrived and after seeing the telegrams from Lenin and Trotsky ordering the disarming of the Czechs, he wondered at their 'perfidy'; undoubtedly he saw his mission coming to an abrupt end.

By now the Czechs refused to listen to the French and nothing further could be done. Bordes learned of Noulens' instructions not to surrender, so he left for Moscow for new orders. There at a dinner at General Lavergne's Bordes described to Noulens the Czechs and their army. Noulens seemed exceedingly impressed by Bordes' report and the upshot of this dinner was the Allied declaration the following day making the Czechs an Allied *avant-garde*. In the meantime the indefatigable Captain Bordes set out from Moscow to join the Czechs and still further complicate their sufficiently confused situation.

Bordes left on 4 July 1918 and reached Kazan on the 8th. At Kazan he witnessed rioting. He was quickly in the thick of events. The left SRs persuaded the Red Army C-in-C, Colonel Muravyov, to order the Red troops to stop fighting the Czechs at Simbirsk. According to Bordes this ex-French soldier (allegedly paid by Colonel Arquier at Odessa) took some 30 Serbs and after convincing the garrison at Kazan went to Simbirsk to ask the soldiers there to join him and the Czechs and turn the fighting against the Germans instead. At Simbirsk he was again successful with the garrison, but after this success he abandoned prudence. As he went to inform the Revkom of the decision taken by the garrison, accompanied only by one of his Serbian soldiers, he was killed by Revkom members after killing two of their number. By 11 July 1918 fear of arrest compelled Bordes to move on. He left behind Major Blagotić and his 350 men and 30 officers. While at Kazan he also made contact with the White Russian underground, organized by General Romanovsky, Captain Gurken, Kalinin (Savinkov's representative) and Colonel Galkin. By 16 July the situation at Kazan became dangerous and Bordes had to run. Eventually he reached Nurlat where the Czechs arrived on 18 July. Bordes immediately sent a courier to General Lavergne with the report on the line of communication to be followed in order to reach the Czechs. On the same day he met Lieutenant Švec, the Czech CO, and was greatly impressed by him. From Nurlat Bordes went to

Simbirsk where he found Fortunatov, Galin and Lebedieff in power. He analysed the situation: 'The call for volunteers came too late, by then people feared reprisals. At the same time workers were left with arms, remaining bolsheviks under the influence of the German and Jewish agents.'

By 25 July he had news of the bolsheviks evacuating Kazan. The gold reserve was shipped to an unknown destination. The prospect of capturing 650 million rubles in gold excited Bordes and he hurried by plane to Samara to persuade Čeček to take Kazan. Before leaving Simbirsk he sent another courier to Lavergne and on 26 July he sent further reports to Moscow and to Blagotić (at least one courier was caught and hanged by the bolsheviks). On 27 July he had Lavergne's instructions: he was to inform General Alekseyev at Tikhoretskaya that the Serbs at Tsaritsyn were ready to take the town when required; he was also ordered to require Švec and Stepanov to take Kazan. Thus it seems probable that this higher order overruled Čeček's prohibition of the raid. Bordes did not wait to clear up this matter with Čeček. Next he was at Tetyuchi with 400 guns and 10 machine guns for Blagotić's Serbs who had to retreat from Kazan after Bordes' departure. On 5 August Bordes flew over Kazan dropping leaflets. On the way to Kazan the Serbs overtook the Czechs who got lost using inaccurate maps. The bolsheviks were leaving the town in panic. On taking Kazan various medical missions were arrested (and disposed of), millions of rubles' worth of material were seized, and also Trotsky's codes. The decoded telegrams from Lenin were encouraging: Lenin apparently sounded desperate. On 6 August Bordes was busy repairing planes captured at Kazan and bombing Trotsky's train at Svyazhsk after pilot Storm and Captain Campatanjano crossed the front and told him of the train's position. Bordes also supervised the evacuation of the gold reserve: 1,733,000 francs in gold, 500,000 in platinum and 900 millions in silver. Then Lebedieff tried to spoil Bordes' deal with some Cossacks who came to Kazan to get arms. With the help of General Romanovsky they were given arms all the same. On 10 August enormous crowds attended the funeral of the seven Serbian officers killed in the battle for the city. The same day Savinkov arrived from Moscow. He had allegedly modified his political views considerably. He was not so 'left' and came to some kind of arrangement with Lavergne in Moscow.

The Czechs were popular with the population who showered presents on them. Bordes had time to remark that Williams, the United

States Consul from Samara, also visited Kazan, but according to him Williams was interested in neither politics nor war but in commercial transactions and old furniture. After describing the quarrel between Čeček and Stepanov, the local Russian commander who had previously commanded the 1st Czech Regiment, he left for Samara to ask Čeček for troops to defend Kazan. On 2 September the workers of Kazan revolted but were suppressed. By now the Czechs quarrelled bitterly with the Whites, especially when Colonel Kappel's raid had been beaten off by the Reds: the Whites accused the Czechs of being responsible for the failure. The Serbs were also demoralized by Blagotić's death and by the Czech recognition of Premuzić as the Serbian representative. Bordes could see that Kazan was surely lost and set out for Ufa to meet Major Guinet whom he considered as his superior officer. However, Guinet had also left by then and Bordes made his way to Chelyabinsk and Vladivostok, leaving behind all the confusion he had helped to create.

From Bordes' account it is obvious how individual French officers took advantage of the confusion created by the Russian revolution and the Czech revolt. General Lavergne was conducting military operations from Moscow while Bordes interfered on the spot. But Guinet caused far greater confusion.

Guinet was attached to one of the Czech 'echelons' when the revolt started. At first he was reluctant to sanction the revolt. His superior officer, then Colonel Paris, was in Vladivostok and Guinet was cut off from him between May and September 1918. According to Colonel Paris Guinet began to consider himself the chief representative of the French Military Mission at Samara and Chelyabinsk during this period. But he completely exceeded even such powers and authorization. He made certain commercial transactions with Jannot at Samara for which Jannot was later arrested by the White authorities. Guinet was in occasional touch with Lavergne and Noulens and undoubtedly conveyed their instructions to the Czechs. However, when Paris reached Ufa on 18 September he found this self-appointed chief immersed in Russian politics, solving Russian internal problems. He was unfavourably impressed by Guinet's self-importance and optimism in promising everybody everything. Paris left Colonel Menu as the mission representative at Ufa and himself left to inspect the front. During his tour he noticed trains with the inscription *Mission Militaire Française*, and became suspicious. On his return Paris dealt summarily with Jannot whom he sent back to France; Guinet was reprimanded, made supply officer and forbidden to meddle in politics. Before leaving for Vladivostok Paris appointed Major Pichon as CO in the rear area, which made Guinet resentful. But the latter was soon recalled to France where he was denied the Légion d'Honneur.[1]

It is often pointed out that the Allies lacked a defined policy towards the bolsheviks. But it is obvious that even if they had one, in order to make it effective the interpreters on the spot would have had to be of different calibre. Even in purely military terms both Bordes and Guinet created nothing but confusion. The one caused the Czechs to over-extend themselves to Ekaterinburg and Kazan by promising a relief Vyatka army. The other made the Czechs believe in this and other Allied armies so that an anti-German front be re-constituted. In addition to these military blunders Guinet created a political precedent. During his isolation he dictated to the White Russians what he conceived to be the Allied policy. He was largely responsible for the artificial unity at the Ufa conference; by threatening an Allied boycott he foisted onto the White movement leaders acceptable to himself but not so much to them. But no German arrived to oppose the Czechs, no Allied army appeared to relieve them; instead the Czechs noticed they were fighting Russians, while those Russians whom they were now 'helping' were systematically weakened instead of being strengthened and made useful in military operations by Guinet's interference and their own political instability.

VIII

By the end of August 1918 it must have become evident to every Czech that even the new aim, namely the continuation of the struggle against the Germans in Russia, was illusory. No Allied troops were coming and military operations were in a mess. There were no fronts. There were raids, pursuits and unexpected victories. Ček and some Komuch (Constitutional Assembly) leaders at first thought that a junction should be effected with the South, the Urals Cossacks and even with Krasnov's Don and General Denikin's Volunteers. But many SRs were against this move; some officers feared an influx of generals from the south. Thus only the 4th Czech Regiment and a few other units were sent south.

On 27 August 1918 the bolsheviks reached an agreement with the

[1] General Paris to General Janin, 17 July 1919.

Germans on freeing the Soviet forces facing the latter. They could transfer them east. Trotsky, exaggerating the gravity of the situation and perhaps also ignorant of Czech weakness, took command in person and ruthlessly restored discipline in the Red Army facing the Czechs and Whites at Kazan. While the Czechs and the Komuch troops continued to roam the countryside he built up his forces and reorganized the front. In the first days of September he struck. On 12 September Kazan fell without much fighting; the Czechs withdrew to avoid encirclement. Real fronts began to take shape and real military operations started. Kazan was a turning point.[1]

In the south the 4th Regiment suffered heavy losses on taking Niko-layevsk on 20 August, and abandoned the town the same day. A crisis was reached and was felt even by the insensitive Czechs. On 28 August the non-existent fronts were reorganized. Lieutenant Syrový, who in the three months of fighting was made Colonel, now became General and C-in-C of all the Czech and Russian forces. On 2 September Čeček and Gajda earned their rewards for their part in the revolt; both were named generals commanding the dispersed and demoralized 1st and 2nd Divisions. These youthful generals (Gajda 26, Čeček and Syrový 32 and 33), supported by the experienced Dieterichs, Voytsekhovsky and Bogoslovsky, were to stem the bolshevik advance. But the troops were neither reorganized nor relieved and since they were offered no comparable inducements the advance was not stemmed.

A new stage of development was reached; a chasm now opened between the military leaders and their soldiers. It was the generals' fight, not the men's. The impact of the Red offensive was devastating. Simbirsk fell on 12 September, Volsk on the 15th, Syzran on 4 October and Samara on 8th. On 20 October the heavily mauled 4th Regiment mutinied. On 24 October the 1st Regiment joined the 4th in mutiny. The 2nd and 3rd Regiments were on the verge of mutiny. The 1st Division collapsed. On 19 October, when the inevitability of mutinies became obvious even to the political leadership, General Čeček was relieved of his command and sent to Vladivostok. On 25 October his successor, Colonel Švec, committed suicide when his troops refused to obey his orders.

In the 2nd Division, which returned from the Far East to the Urals, the situation was not much better. Though Gajda did not hesitate to apply severe measures to restore discipline, lack of supplies, the

[1] Trotsky to Lenin, 7 to 9 July 1918.

Siberian winter, bolshevik resistance and the high casualties undermined Czech morale. By now the Czechs were told that they were fighting for democracy in Russia – a new aim after the illusory anti-German front. But the Czechs were depressed. They had started a revolt to get out of Russia and instead they were now upholding Russian democracy for the Russians and the Allies. Neither seemed in a hurry to uphold democracy themselves. As a fighting force the Czechs were finished and after the armistice in the West and the formation of their own independent republic, they became obsessed with one idea only: to get out of Russia and return home. But that took them much longer than they ever thought possible.

CHAPTER FIVE

SIBERIAN INTERVENTION

I

Whatever plans France and Britain, the Supreme Allied Council, the French High Command or the Japanese High Command had prepared for Russia, they had to be scrapped or completely altered after the unexpected revolt of the Czech Corps (or the Legion). Up to June 1918 all planning was hinged to the Czech Corps and the northern bases at Murmansk and Archangel were considered the best position for its use in Russia. The Corps would form the nucleus of the Allied intervention force and when Allied reinforcements strengthened it it would strike out into Russia against both the Germans and the bolsheviks. But the revolt brought the Czechs to the Volga, so the northern plan had to be abandoned. Only one feature of it was retained: Allied reinforcements which were already on the way would try and break out of Murmansk and Archangel to Kotlas to link up with the Czechs. This was really a hopeless objective, but in Paris and London it seemed possible that Allied units could march over some 500 miles of territory without proper supplies and reach the more powerful Czechs without bolshevik opposition. Allied forces under General Poole landed in Archangel on 2 August 1918 and though they tried hard to break out, they never succeeded in getting anywhere near the Czech Corps. After being literally frozen in during the winter 1918–19 they were finally evacuated in the autumn of 1919.

But this northern link-up was unimportant; neither the Czechs nor the Allies in the north could benefit decisively from it, and it caused tactical difficulties only. However, the Volga-Vladivostok link-up was of vital importance, and here the Japanese might have helped. One day after the Japanese actually began to land their forces to help the Czechs, General Sir Henry Wilson urgently requested additional 8 Allied battalions to clear the way from Vladivostok to Irkutsk.[1] But this appeal was directed more at the Americans than the Japanese. On 19 August 1918 the Americans did respond to combined Anglo–French pressure and the more discreet influence exercised in Washington by Professor T. G. Masaryk, the Czech leader. The news of the American landing in Vladivostok injected

[1] General Sir Henry Wilson Memorandum, 9 August 1918.

new enthusiasm into the fighting Czechs, and above all into their political leaders. All the same the effect was purely psychological and did not add one soldier, not to mention a division, to the military strength of the hard pressed Czechs. Soon Masaryk sent to his compatriots in Siberia a solemn warning not to expect too much from the Americans. On 22 August 1918 President Wilson confirmed publicly Masaryk's warning: the Americans were sent to Vladivostok to help the Czechs in that area and not to get entangled in the Allied project of re-constituting an eastern front against Germany. Though Wilson's declaration clearly stated what the Americans would not do, it did not define sufficiently how they would help the Czechs. The Czechs, who were ten times as numerous as the American contingent, had been sufficiently helped by the Japanese to achieve their primary objective: on 31 August they effected the junction between the three fighting groups, the Čeček, Gajda and Vladivostok forces. They thus controlled the whole of the Trans-Siberian Railway from the Volga to Vladivostok and in Russia they were extending their operations in the southern and northern direction.

August 1918 was a crucial month for the Allies and their plans in Russia. Had the Japanese and Americans been willing to intervene really and push on to Irkutsk or even further, the Czechs thus freed might have made a decisive difference to the operations launched by them in Russia without consulation with the Allies. But the Japanese failed to react to Czech and Allied exhortations to push on. The Americans proved even more disappointing: they came ashore and remained passively in Vladivostok until new instructions would reach them. Somehow these instructions failed to arrive and the Americans stayed put for practically the whole period of the civil war in Siberia at Vladivostok. Only a few small units branched out of the city; American intervention consisted mainly of interference in economic matters.

II

As it became obvious that the Americans and Japanese would do next to nothing in Siberia, France and Britian were forced to make their own decisions. On 24 August the French government appointed General Janin C-in-C of all Allied forces in Russia.[1] However, many months would elapse before Janin would actually take up his

[1] Clemenceau to Janin, 24 August 1918.

appointment. The British government appointed General Sir Alfred Knox as head of the British Military Mission to Siberia. Knox had been ready to depart for some time and arrived in Vladivostok well in advance of Janin. But there was not much to do in Vladivostok. The situation in the Far East was obscure and the situation of the Czechs even more so. Thus both the British and French first engaged in collecting accurate intelligence about the Czechs and their struggle.

The information that both governments possessed on the subject was scanty, indeed. This was possibly the reason for Janin's delayed departure. Thus it was important to establish communication lines first. Knox sent some of his officers to European Russia soon after his arrival. Colonel Paris was ordered to return to Russia from Tokio and report on the military situation. But it was to take another month before these officers could arrive in the war zone. In the meantime even the small French contingent at Archangel was anxious to find out when the Czechs would turn up there. It bombarded Paris with requests as to the situation in the Far East and the heroic Czechs.[1] It is obvious that the morale of these French troops was not outstanding and that they hoped to be relieved by the Czechs in the very near future. But the garbled reports they received from Paris proved disappointing; they indicated that not only would they not be relieved but also that the French government itself did not know much about the Czechs.[2]

On 8 September President Wilson made it painfully clear to those who still doubted him that the Czechs would only get American aid in the Far East and not in western Siberia. Soon after this statement the Allies finally received their first authoritative reports about the military situation. The reports made it clear that Wilson's declaration was the death-blow to the Czech military effort. General Paris who had just completed his tour of the 'front' reported on 18 September 1918 that the Czechs could not hold on much longer without substantial Allied relief force.[3] The British government knew about the desperate situation of the Czechs from a report by General Knox a week before the French.[4]

It seems clear that everybody realized the seriousness of the situation and after American disappointment all hopes were now pinned

[1] Colonel Donop to Clemenceau, 29 August 1918.
[2] Clemenceau to Donop, 8 September 1918.
[3] Paris to Clemenceau, 18 September 1918.
[4] Knox to Milner, 12 September 1918.

to Japan. On 16 September 1918 by some strange coincidence both General Knox and Clemenceau made their separate urgent appeals for a massive Japanese intervention. The former rightly thought that the Czechs were in their last gasp and saw the Allies' last chance in two Japanese divisions which would restore the front in eastern Russia.[1] Clemenceau sent his instructions to General Janin, who was on his way to Tokyo. On Paris's advice he requested Janin to ask the Japanese government for urgent help; he wanted them to push on as far as Omsk and thus consolidate the Czech rear. Czech retreat would anyway be halted when General Gajda finally reached them with his division from the Far East.[2]

The Japanese were slow to move. General Paris who in the meantime reached Tokyo had to stand in for General Janin who was still crossing the Pacific from the United States. He undoubtedly put pressure in the right quarter, but with no more success than the French or the British Ambassadors. At the same time the instructions he received for General Janin from Paris sounded unduly optimistic. Janin was ordered to proceed immediately on arriving to Chelyabinsk in order to assume command there and coordinate military operations. The telegram also promised reinforcements via Archangel: the northern group would press on to Kotlas.[3]

The telegram, of course, spoke in terms of operational plans and not of reality. The aid from the north was a distant prospect indeed. In the meantime Japanese aid and support were much more important and the Allies were prepared to go a long way to obtain it. Thus they agreed to subordinate their own generals to the supreme command of General Otani, and silently tolerated the latter's activity in Siberia though they strongly disagreed with it. Otani, for example, appointed Ataman Semenov Commander-in-Chief of the Transbaykal region; the high sounding title in fact signified nothing militarily and politically complicated the situation. Both Knox and Janin thought that Semenov was quite unsuitable for such an appointment, but had to swallow their objections to maintain Allied unity, i.e. not to discourage the Japanese. As late as September 1918 the Allies hoped that the Japanese 'would intervene decisively'.

As before the British conducted final negotiations about this

[1] Knox to Milner, 16 September 1918; Clemenceau to Janin, 16 September 1918.

[2] Clemenceau to Janin, 16 September 1918.

[3] Clemenceau to Janin, 20 September 1918.

'decisive intervention'. Sir Cunnyngham Greene delivered a note on the subject on 16 October 1918: it only reiterated the British government's position, namely that the Japanese were to push on to Omsk at least. A clear statement of Japanese intentions was also demanded.[1] The Japanese statement of intentions was clear and killed completely any further idea of decisive intervention. On 23 October the reply stated that Japan was not interested in restoring Russia as a great power that it had its own interests to pursue in Siberia and that it would not act according to Allied wishes.[2]

With the American and Japanese refusals to act in Siberia France and Britain were forced to deal directly with Siberian problems. Both countries did so rather reluctantly, but had no real choice. The common interest in Siberia was the Czechoslovak Army Corps; the intervention was on its behalf. But as the French had much more control over the Czechs than the British rivalry soon developed between the representatives of the two Allied powers which finally resulted in the British backing various White Russian régimes and the French exclusively occupied by the Czech Corps.

In a sense this was a natural development, for the British from the beginning thought of re-establishing the Whites in Siberia; the Czechs after all would have to go home at some stage leaving behind a power vacuum. But what was certainly undesirable was mutual recriminations and hostility which gradually replaced the *entente cordiale*. Sir Charles Eliot, the British High Commissioner, arrived at Omsk on 5 October 1918 with a set of instructions from the Foreign Secretary, Lord Balfour. Sir Charles' first task was to convey to the Russians the shock the Allies felt at seeing the disunity in the White movement. He was charged with investigating the possibility of a stronger Russian government: a temporary dictatorship seemed an obvious remedy for political disunity. But the Foreign Secretary was not sure that there was a suitable dictator in Russia, so he urged Sir Charles to place all the weight of Britain behind General Alekseyev, who was at least known to the British.[3] But Alekseyev was far away in the south of Russia, in Siberia there were no military men of similar stature and Sir Charles was more impressed by the Czechs than the Russians. To him the Russian military meddled in politics and were no good in either. On 24 September General Boldyrev, one of the

[1] Curzon to Greene, 16 October 1918.
[2] Greene to Curzon, 23 October 1918.
[3] Balfour to Elliot, 5 October 1918.

White Generals-Leaders, patched up an agreement with the Czechs which made him the Supreme Commander. Czech Generals Syrový and Gajda remained in command of the Volga and northern fronts so that apart from the empty title the Russians and Boldyrev gained nothing. When soon after his arrival Sir Charles pointed this out to Boldyrev the latter was surprised; when Sir Charles expressed his doubts saying that the subordination of the Czechs had been premature, Boldyrev was offended.

Though Sir Charles undoubtedly saw the necessity of maintaining the Czech Corps in Siberia in support of the White Russians and thought in terms of a gradual hand-over of power by the Czechs, the French plans were quite different. They saw the struggle in Siberia as conducted by the Czechs aided by the Allies with the ultimate aim of destroying the bolsheviks. The Whites hardly figured in French plans; they were there only to carry out auxiliary tasks. Thus on 12 October the French political representative in Siberia, after the inspection of the front, telegraphed General Janin to speed up his arrival to the front; his presence there was of utmost importance. The fronts were in a chaotic state mainly thanks to the refusal of the Russians to obey the Czech officers. Only Janin's prestige would impress these recalcitrant Russians who in any case were incapable of planning military operations.[1]

On 21 October Sir Alfred Knox arrived from Vladivostok at Omsk and made Allied intentions known to the Russians. Acting in conjunction with the French he negotiated with the Supreme Commander, General Boldyrev, an agreement which made it clear that the Czechs and Janin were the basis of any settlement in Siberia. Thus on 24 October 1918 Boldyrev signed off his supreme title to General Janin, who accordingly became the Commander-in-Chief of all Allied and Russian forces. For this the Allies promised the Whites material and technical aid and advice with the formation of a new Russian Army without committees and with good discipline.

The agreement at first sight appeared as a great political and military achievement. But it seems that Boldyrev concluded it only because he knew of his own and White weakness; utter disunity prevented the Russians from achieving anything except quarrel among themselves and question each other's and everybody else's authority. But he threw away responsibility rather lightly and in turn the Allies were saddled with a paper agreement and empty titles. The

[1] Regnault to Janin, 12 October 1918.

111

C-in-C was not even in Russia and unified command brought neither Russian obedience nor Allied reinforcements to the front. Though perhaps of some importance for the future the agreement's immediate result was the complete collapse of the Czech Corps. It not only failed to discipline the Russian units fighting alongside the Czechs, but also failed to restore Czech morale: they were now tired of fighting and simply opted out by withdrawing from the front.

The indications of the Czech collapse had been known to Boldyrev when he signed the agreement. It was obvious that the Czechs would soon cease to be 'the cornerstone of Allied action' in Siberia. The Whites were the only alternative, but the question was which faction would be chosen as the alternative. Supreme Commander Boldyrev represented the Directory, which was based on the members of the Constitutional Assembly and claimed to be the Provisional Government of all the Russias. At Omsk there was the Siberian government which supposedly was subordinated to the Directory. Both 'governments' were dominated by social revolutionaries, though the Siberians were more right wing than the Directory SRs. But the former had the support of the Czech Corps and consequently could impose their will on the Siberians as long as Czech support was forthcoming.

It was clear that with the Czech withdrawal from the front new arrangements would have to be made in the rear. Sir Alfred joked with Boldyrev about a *coup d'état* if the Directory and the Siberians failed to agree among themselves. As if to demonstrate this point Colonel Ward and his Middlesex Battalion arrived at Omsk. For the first time the Czechs found out that someone else would interfere in White affairs; so far they alone complicated the political situation by insisting on sanctioning any Russian minister before appointment. But with the British at Omsk to counterbalance their influence the Czechs were told by the Russians to mind their own business.[1] They were even forced to release arrested ministers of the Siberian government which obviously meant that the days of the Directory were numbered.

The circumstances of the Kolchak *coup d'état* are even now obscure. What seems obvious is that Omsk was ripe for a coup. The Czechs were withdrawing from the front, the commanding general was in Japan, the all-Russian Directory was a moribund body without mass support and the Siberians ready to assume political responsibilities. But the results of the coup were baffling: Admiral Kolchak

[1] Nettement to Regnault, 9 November 1918.

who assumed 'supreme power' was a British supported sailor with no political experience. All the same he dissolved the Directory, gained support of the Siberians and headed for a year and half the Provisional Government of Russia.

While the Omsk coup was on the way the long expected Allied Commander, General Janin landed at Vladivostok on 16 November 1918. Janin and Major Štefánik, now Minister of War of the Czechoslovak Republic, were anxious about the position of the Czechs. Štefánik conveyed his misgivings to the Quai d'Orsay from Tokio as soon as he found out that the Japanese would not help the Czechs any further.[1] Even before they reached Vladivostok Janin and Štefánik received messages indicating that the Czech collapse had started mainly due to the indiscipline of the Russians. On landing they were briefed in a similar vein by the Czech political leaders on the spot, Dr Girsa and Pavlů. Thus the first action of these Allied representatives was a quarrel with the local Russians as to who was responsible for the Czech collapse. General Ivanov offered his resignation in protest and Štefánik boycotted a Russian banquet given in his honour.[2] But the worst was still to come.

On 18 November 1918 while sorting out problems in Vladivostok Janin and Štefánik were told of the coup at Omsk. Admiral Kolchak became the supreme ruler thanks to Colonel Ward's Battalion and Ataman Volkov's and Ataman Krasilnikov's Cossacks. Janin was more shocked by the coup than Štefánik and genuinely believed that Kolchak was a British puppet and the coup an unsavoury British affair. However, the alleged British support was strictly local and definitely unauthorized. On 17 November 1918 the British War Cabinet finally recognized the Directory as a Russian government *de facto*. This decision was never made public, for in the meantime Colonel Nielsen's report on the coup arrived in London. The report did not throw any light on the rôle of the British in the coup but described it as an 'absolutely honest attempt at restoring order in Siberia'.[3] However, subsequent telegrams by Sir Charles were much less enthusiastic: he could not see the new highly irritable ruler putting anything right.[4]

Thus both the French and British governments faced with a *fait*

[1] Štefánik to Pichon, 3 November 1918.
[2] de Martel to Regnault, 19 November 1918.
[3] Nielsen to Curzon, 18 November 1918.
[4] Alston to Curzon, 28 October 1918.

accompli decided to acquiesce and the coup passed without official protests. On 19 November Janin ordered General Syrový not to interfere in the rear: 'the Czechs were in Russia to fight the bolsheviks and not to meddle in Russian internal affairs.' Janin's order ruled out any Czech attempt at overthrowing Kolchak, but the Czechs probably would not have tried, for General Gajda was a friend of Kolchak, and only he could have acted against the new régime. Nevertheless, the coup jolted at long last the Allies into a decision. On 26 November 1918 an Allied declaration made clear that General Janin was C-in-C of all Allied and Russian forces west of the Lake Baykal while General Knox was in charge of the rear, of training and supplies.[1]

But the decision came too late; it still assumed the situation under the Directory and made no reference to the Whites. But Kolchak was no Boldyrev and consequently such a decision could never be implemented in Siberia while he was Supreme Ruler. However impracticable, it was also the last decision on which Britain and France fully agreed. Henceforth suspicions and quarrels between the Allies and the Whites were supplemented by suspicions and quarrels between the French and the British.

III

General Janin's advantage in Siberia had been that he was Allied appointed and Czech recognized commanding officer of the Legion. Thus from the beginning he was able to talk to the Russian Whites from a position of strength. However, what seemed a strong position in October 1918 rapidly became a weak position in November and on his arrival in the war area in December 1918 his position was precarious to say the least. During November 1918 practically all Czech units ceased fighting and looked for a way home. Obviously Janin's first duty was to the Legion and he immediately inspected the front: he found that the Czechs were no longer a fighting force and could not be considered as such for some time.

Janin realized that the front would have to be reorganized; the Czechs practically withdrew and were only slowly replaced by the Russians. Since he was the nominal commander of all forces he tried to get an agreement with the new White leadership on the reorganization of the front. On 16 December 1918 Janin had his first tempestuous interview with the new leader, Admiral Kolchak, and could not agree on anything. Major Štefánik had to employ all his Slovak charm

[1] Ministère de la Guerre Statement 'Clemenceau', 26 October 1918.

to calm down the irascible supreme ruler of Russia. After the Omsk *coup d'état* and Boldyrev's departure the supreme command of the eastern front fell back on the youthful Czech General Syrový. Kolchak was unwilling to recognize any previous agreements and felt quite cold about the joint Allied declaration of 26 November 1918. However, Syrový's command and Czech collapse ultimately made a compromise possible. Thus Kolchak insisted that Janin should take over the supreme command from Syrový as Kolchak's plenipotentiary. Janin was deeply puzzled and had no choice but accept. On 20 December he left Omsk for Chelyabinsk to implement the new agreement.

From the beginning the implementation proved difficult. Janin took over Syrový's command and surveyed the military situation helped by experienced Chief of Staff, General Dieterichs. It was decided that Czech troops would have to be withdrawn and separated from Russian units. Since this was practically accomplished at the time of the decision it was no difficult matter. What was much more difficult was to take over the command of Russian troops. Janin felt pessimistic at the outset; he was convinced that the Russians would sabotage his efforts and simply disobey his orders. He left again for Omsk to strengthen his authority but became convinced that Kolchak would not help him, on the contrary would weaken him if possible. On 4 January 1919 during an interview he had with the Admiral he was told rather forcefully that the Czechs would have to be withdrawn and separated from the Russians, for they were demoralizing them. Kolchak then turned nasty and issued an ultimatum to Syrový to withdraw his Czechs or be disarmed.

This forceful speaking and ultimatum was obviously aimed at weakening the supreme Allied commander; but it did not improve the situation on the front. Janin needed no weakening anyway; his 1st Czech division was to all purposes non-existent, while the second was restless waiting for a suitable opportunity to leave the front. Its commanding officer, General Gajda, became commanding officer of the Siberian Army, a reward by Kolchak to his friend. This weakened still further Janin but kept the Czech division, however, reluctant, in the field. On 13 January Janin and Štefánik officially ordered Czech withdrawal from the front and on 15 January Syrový handed over the command of the Urals front to the Russians. Thus the Czechs ceased to be a military force and Janin supreme Allied commander.

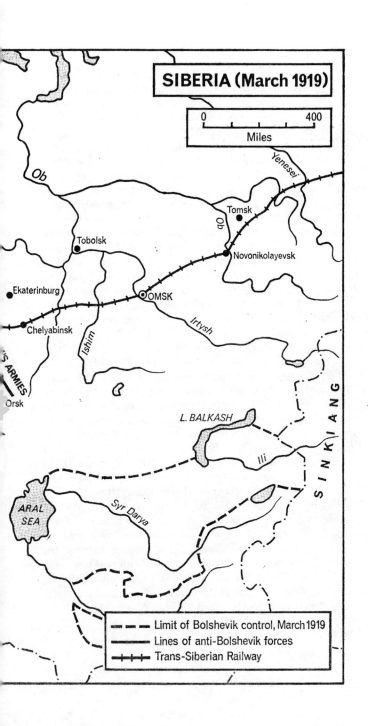

SIBERIA (March 1919)

```
0                              400
                 Miles
```

Yenesei

Ob

Tomsk

Ob

Tobolsk

Novonikolayevsk

Ekaterinburg

OMSK

Irtysh

Chelyabinsk

Ishim

'S ARMIES

Orsk

L. BALKASH

Ili

S I N K I A N G

ARAL SEA

Syr Darya

- - - - Limit of Bolshevik control, March 1919
———— Lines of anti-Bolshevik forces
+++ Trans-Siberian Railway

The Czech and Janin's withdrawal from the front had immediate effects on both Kolchak and the Czech division still fighting. Despite Gajda's retention the second Czech division began to show signs of mutiny. On 23 January Syrový rushed to inspect the division and was presented with a unanimous request for withdrawal. On 27 January orders went out for the evacuation of the 2nd division. Kolchak was left with no fighting men and a factious general: to all appearances he had achieved all he set out to do, but in doing so he weakened himself. Now he was ready for a new agreement with Janin, as he could not afford a complete rupture with the Allies, whose supplies he needed most urgently.

As the Czechs began to move out of the war area along the Trans-Siberian Railway which they were to guard, General Janin gave up all hope of ever directing military operations against the bolsheviks. Though he returned to Omsk to be near the Admiral he became incurably suspicious and extremely pessimistic. On 1 February 1919 he reported to Paris that the Russians were sabotaging absolutely everything he did, even Czech evacuation.[1] His report on 7 February illustrated his pessimism perhaps most clearly. With the Czech withdrawal and the fall of Orenburg, after a *coup de force* at Omsk and troubles at Krasnoyarsk, the Kolchak régime was looking for excuses and scapegoats and had turned openly against the Allies. Expressions of strong anti-Allied feelings could be heard at Omsk and the Allies were blamed for everything. But the fault was with the Whites. Politically the régime was a disaster: both the reactionaries and progressives suffered from inertia and were capable of enthusiasm and spirit only when fighting each other. The military situation was also depressing: Janin no longer attended the conferences at the Stavka (Supreme White Headquarters). According to him these staff meeting were purely ceremonial: elementary ignorance and muddle reigned everywhere. The Stavka officers were incapable of reorganizing the smallest units and did not know how to form a regiment. Only General Dieterichs had experience, but lacked the strength of character and consequently did not oppose the muddlers. Military incompetence and indiscipline extended from the top to the bottom. Even frontline units could not be controlled. Both officers and men acted like rabble: the city of Perm, the only success of the winter campaign, was to all purposes sacked by them. Admiral Kolchak did

---

[1] Janin to Clemenceau, 1 February 1919.

nothing to improve either the working of the Stavka or the discipline at the front. On the contrary he had complete confidence in his officers and on their advice issued nonsensical military orders from Omsk which would soon have disastrous effects on his own prestige. The régime as a whole was blind: it did not have even the most elementary intelligence service.[1]

From this report two things come out clearly. General Janin had completely given up the Whites and personally dissociated himself from the White command. He was also preparing the ground for subsequent defeats and disasters. On the spot he continued to exert a purely negative influence, since he was convinced that the Russians would sabotage anything else. On 18 February 1919 he blamed the Kolchak authorities for the mass desertions of Bashkir troops. With some justification he claimed that the authorities had been maltreating all the minor nationalities in Siberia and the desertions were the result of this treatment. At the same time he predicted a similar disaster on the southern front, if the Dutov HQ were not reorganized.[2]

Janin's reports had an obvious effect in Paris and it was now decided that since the French could not exercise direct influence and control over Admiral Kolchak and his régime, they could do so indirectly, by means of francophile Russians. This French decision was based on the British precedent: the French and Janin were convinced that Kolchak was a British nominee manipulated by the British and they wanted their own Russians. On 28 February 1919 Janin was informed of General Lavergne's arrival at Vladivostok. With him came a group of Russian officers, among them General Lokhvitsky, who previously commanded the mutinous Russian brigade in France: 'il est dans notre solde et est mis à la disposition de Kolchak'.[3] It is impossible to gauge Lokhvitsky's influence on Kolchak in favour of France, but in the end the General had his past experiences with mutinous Russian troops repeated in Siberia.

While the French were launching this devious attempt at indirect influence Janin was in charge of the French Mission and had to occupy himself with day-to-day activity. Thus he started to form and train units composed of the minor nationalities. Kolchak did not welcome this move and Janin soon experienced difficulties of his own: he lacked trained officers. Most of the French officers posted to Siberia were

[1] Janin to Clemenceau, 7 February 1919.
[2] Janin to Clemenceau, 18 February 1919.
[3] Clemenceau to Janin, 28 February 1919.

demobilized either *en route* or shortly after arrival.[1] The badly trained units were seen as a danger to Kolchak and Colonel Ward advised their dissolution. Kolchak did not press this demand, but then his armies collapsed and the national units either mutinied or went over to the bolsheviks and his fears were justified. However, Colonel Ward's influence with Kolchak aroused deep French suspicions.

March 1919 brought military victories to Kolchak. The jubilant Admiral listened to Colonel Ward's advice, as on the whole it concurred with his ideas and Janin was left out altogether. The French general began to see British intrigues in most unlikely places. Janin asked for increased French aid to the Whites to maintain French influence; the British gained their influence in Russia in this way despite their declarations, and contrary to this policy of non-intervention on the European continent.[2] Only as an additional reason Janin stated that the Whites needed three times as much aid as the British could afford to give them.[3]

But Janin's suspicions were shared by many other Frenchmen. The French political representative at Omsk was also restless. On 13 April 1919 he urged his government to send public congratulations to Admiral Kolchak on his victories on the eastern front. He pointed out that after the fall of Perm Sir Alfred Knox made his government to do likewise and it was much appreciated.[4] Other French voices were raised urging the French government to take advantage of the chaotic situation in Siberia and use it to its own advantage: 'do business with the Russians as the Americans were doing'.[5]

But the situation in Siberia, despite Kolchak's victories, never became easy enough for future plans. In April 1919 Janin had his hands full of the Czech problem. After their withdrawal from the front they were detailed to guard the Trans-Siberian. This seemed an easy enough asignment and to start with it was indeed. However, with the increased claims on the peasants by the Kolchak régime and decrease in the popularity of the Czech guardians, the Siberians began to form partisan detachments and attack the railway. Thus the Czechs were soon involved in fighting again and anti-partisan operations on behalf of the Kolchak régime were detested by the

[1] Janin to Clemenceau, 28 March 1919.
[2] Janin to Clemenceau, 23 and 29 April 1919.
[3] Janin to Clemenceau, 29 April 1919.
[4] de Martel to Regnault, 13 April 1919.
[5] Lasies to Clemenceau, 23 April 1919; 31 May 1919.

Czechs. Consequently the Czech soldiers were ready to mutiny again. They were war tired and wanted to go home.[1] Clearly the Czech government was also informed of this development and on 19 April the War Minister, Štefánik, on his return journey to Czechoslovakia, telegraphed Janin to withdraw the Legion from the guard duty and concentrate it round Irkutsk to be ready for the final evacuation.[2]

The position in which Janin found himself was intolerable. He was receiving orders from the Czech government to prepare the evacuation of the Legion and it was certainly a justified order. But he also received orders from his government which still counted on the Czechs to take part in the final military action against the bolsheviks. Thus for the time being at least Janin, obeying his government which pointed out to him the favourable situation on the front, chose to ignore Štefánik's order.[3] But from then on the Czechs and Allies were engaged in a kind of seesaw action: should the Legion be evacuated or not?

The Czechs at home, especially Dr Beneš, who was in Paris representing the new republic at the Peace Conference, were quite happy about the present position of the Legion in Siberia. While it did practically no fighting, it was a useful reminder to the victorious Allies that the Czechs were still fighting on their behalf and that they deserved benevolent treatment. The new republic had plenty of difficulties at the conference above all with its new borders. But, there was no clear Czech–Allied agreement on the Legion and while the Czechs wished it to remain passive the Allies had other plans. On 9 May 1919 Clemenceau asked Janin point blank whether Czech morale had been restored and if so, the Legion should be sent to the front.[4] Janin made another round of inspections, held consultations with Czech officers and came to the conclusion that the Legion was not in a fit state to be sent to the front again.[5] But even this report did not impress the Allies in Paris sufficiently.

Then suddenly the Czechs themselves manifested their hostility to any further fighting or stay in Siberia. On 13 June Janin reported large-scale mutinies among the Czechs. On the following day he analysed the causes of the mutinies: he singled out irresponsible

[1] Janin to Clemenceau, 5 June 1919.
[2] Štefánik to Janin, 19 April 1919.
[3] Clemenceau to Janin, 9 May 1919.
[4] Clemenceau to Janin, 9 May 1919.
[5] Janin to Clemenceau, 5 June 1919.

American propaganda which claimed that the Czechs would soon be replaced by American troops and thus enabled to go home.[1] Janin also telegraphed to Beneš: 'it is absolutely necessary to evacuate the Legion' and he wanted precise instructions as to how he should deal with the mutineers.[2]

Fortunately for Janin he did not have to deal with the mutineers. On his arrival at Irkutsk, the centre of the insurrection, all was quiet; the Czechs sorted out their troubles themselves. The mutineers were disarmed and placed under open arrest. But the victorious officers and political leaders urged Janin to start evacuation to avoid future mutinies. Janin speedily departed for Omsk and thence called for Czech evacuation in the immediate future.[3] This time the American and British governments were also warned by their representatives of the dangers to Siberia if the Czechs were not repatriated soon. Sir Charles Eliot was particularly insistent.

In Paris the Allied statesmen still refused to heed these warnings. They recognized that the situation at the front was serious and therefore thought that the Legion should make the last effort to save the hard pressed Whites. Since Janin told Paris that the Czechs would not fight directly, 'indirect plans' were discussed. On 23 June 1919 Sir Winston Churchill, new British War Minister, approached Dr Beneš with a plan of evacuation via Archangel or southern Russia: the latter alternative was preferable. The Legion would fight its way through the bolshevik front and join General Denikin; thence evacuation would be easy.[4] The plan was ingenious on the paper: the Czechs would get their evacuation, the Allies much needed troops and the Whites a morale booster, for this 'evacuation' implied that the bolshevik front would be broken. However, the plan never advanced beyond the planning stage. Churchill was able to persuade Beneš to sanction it and on 9 July 1919 Janin received orders for evacuation via Archangel or southern Russia. But in Siberia the plan made no sense. The Archangel alternative, if only for psychological reasons, was out of the question. The South Russian alternative presupposed a first class fighting force which would pierce the front and then march some 500 miles to the territories under General Denikin's control. While in April 1919 Kolchak's offensive was in full swing,

[1] Janin to Clemenceau, 13 June 1919.
[2] Janin to Benes, 14 June 1919.
[3] Janin to Clemenceau, 16 June 1919; Donop to Clemenceau, 16 June 1919.
[4] Churchill to Beneš, 23 June 1919.

Czech officers discussed this alternative on their own and they rejected it. With Kolchak's armies routed the alternative had no chance of being accepted and Janin's reply was swift: on 10 July he was informed by Syrový that the Czechs would not fight and passed the message on to Paris. On 12 July Clemenceau had Janin's reply, but all the same continued to impress Kolchak rather optimistically that the Czechs would in the end fight for him. They would be forced to do so, as the Peace Conference decided it.[1]

This was really wishful thinking, but all the same Allied leaders in Paris were determined to make the Czechs fight. Kolchak certainly was in great need and the Czech delegation in Paris dangled the Legion in front of the other delegations during negotiations. But in Siberia the situation was quite different: no one, not even Beneš, much less the local leaders could move the Czech soldiers to fight. They could not be sure to evacuate peacefully. The Siberian Czechs sent several delegations to Prague to request their evacuation, and the delegations finally arrived in July 1919. Now Prague was under pressure and evacuation would have to be carried out. Beneš went on ordering Janin to take the necessary steps, but Janin was busy rejecting French and Allied suggestions to evacuate the Czechs via Archangel or southern Russia.[2] In addition one of the local leaders in Siberia, Pavlů, suddenly changed his mind on the urgency of evacuation and postponed the final decision once more.

Janin's orders from Paris bid him to keep the Czech Corps in Siberia and he therefore seized on the Pavlů plan as on his last hope. The plan was nothing but a slightly modified version of the Churchill–Beneš proposals. Encouraged by Denikin's successes Pavlů dreamt of joining him in the joy ride to Moscow. From Siberia the victories in Russia appeared like a leisurely march and Pavlů did not want to miss it. Dr Kramář also came out in support of Pavlů's plan and thus it had the Czechoslovak Government's backing. If the soldiers could be persuaded to follow Pavlů, all would be well. To create a suitable atmosphere for the march to Moscow Pavlů sent Major Hajný to Omsk to negotiate with the Kolchak government incentives for the Czech soldiers. Pavlů himself started a newspaper campaign to convince his soldiers that they should march home via Russia. He wrote in the army journal about the Russian–Czech brotherhood and urged the soldiers to help the Russian Whites in their hour of need. He also

[1] Janin to Clemenceau, 12 July 1919; Clemenceau to Kolchak, 13 July 1919.
[2] Beneš to Janin, 18 July 1919; Janin to Clemenceau, 18 August 1919.

offered them danger money, for in the meantime Kolchak menaced by the bolsheviks in his capital Omsk was willing to hand the Czechs the Russian gold reserve provided they came and fetched it. But the scheme finally collapsed when Dr Kramář, no friend of Dr Beneš, was suddenly and unexpectedly dismissed as Prime Minister and Pavlů's plan repudiated by the Czech leaders in Prague.

In theory the last hope of making the Czech Corps fight rested with the Allied War Council. But the Council, since it was not sure that its order would be obeyed, never actually ordered the Corps to resume fighting, but its vacillations only delayed evacuation still further. On 28 July 1919 after so many orders and counter orders Janin told Beneš that he commenced to evacuate the sick and wounded.[1] When on 13 August Syrový requested Janin to issue an official evacuation order he was told that this could not be done, since the Allies and the Czechs could not abandon the Russian Whites; an official order to evacuate would be interpreted in this way.[2] After this partial evacuation Czech pressure on Janin to order a total one increased. On 26 August 1919 Janin had another telegram from Beneš urging him to start general evacuation and two days later he told Syrový that official orders would soon be ready.[3] He was obviously playing for time still torn between orders from the Czechs and the French. On 21 September 1919 Janin had to face a special Czech parliamentary delegation which arrived in Siberia on a fact-finding tour. The socialist leader of the delegation, Krejčí, told him to order immediate evacuation, but Janin still refused.

On 25 September 1919 probably after another contradictory order Janin tried to bargain with Beneš. He told him that only gradual evacuation was possible and only if the Supreme Allied Council agreed to it.[4] But even Beneš could no longer bargain. The problem of the 'forgotten Czech Legion in Siberia' became a burning domestic issue in Prague. Wives and relatives of the soldiers lobbied their deputies in parliament and street rioting broke out. The Czech government frightened by the riots issued firm orders to Beneš who passed them on to Janin. On 26 September 1919 Janin was told to evacuate the Legion even against Allied wishes. Beneš had apparently a grave report from Siberia: 'the Legion was ready to shoot its way out to

[1] Janin to Beneš, 28 July 1919.
[2] Syrový to Janin, 13 August 1919.
[3] Beneš to Janin, 26 August 1919.
[4] Janin to Beneš, 25 September 1919.

Vladivostok or negotiate its passage west with the bolsheviks.' This threat of mutiny finally decided the issue: on 29 September 1919 detailed orders of evacuation went out to all Czech units in Siberia.

IV

Throughout the intervention years in Siberia the Allies did not manage to come to a common agreement. Since the Czech Corps (Legion) started the 'intervention', Siberia first became the zone of interest of France. Britain and France then tried to engage other Allies in the intervention: but Japan and the United States were interested only in limited objectives not a general intervention. When they dropped out the burden for intervention fell back on France and Britain. The French based their intervention policy on the Czech Legion, and after Kolchak's rebuttal of Janin, they concentrated almost exclusively on this task. The British first arrived to aid the Czechs, but then diverted their efforts to helping Kolchak. By October 1919 both Allies were engaged in rear-guard actions: the French trying to extricate and evacuate the Legion; the British trying to save or somehow salvage the Kolchak régime.

Though the French task was easier it was no plain sailing. The final decision to evacuate was taken against some internal opposition. On 3 October 1919 Pavlů told General Syrový that it was premature to evacutate; the bolsheviks were on the point of collapse before General Denikin's forces and it was in Czech interest to go home via Russia. In Czechoslovakia Dr Kramář also tried to stop evacuation by publishing rumours about the return of the Legion via Denikin's southern Russia, but by then Kramář was a private politician not a Prime Minister hence his campaign lacked real strength. It did influence Dr Beneš who under pressure from the Allies hesitated once again. Throughout October 1919 he sent several enquiries to General Janin whether a limited or even large-scale action by the Czechs against the bolsheviks could be contemplated. On 31 October 1919 Janin replied rather categorically that the Czechs would not go to the front to fight and therefore had to be evacuated as soon as possible.[1] Needless to say all these hesitations slowed down the evacuation and when in October 1919 the bolsheviks suddenly broke through the front on the Tobol unimaginable confusion followed. General Janin realized the danger too late. He was the nominal commander of the

[1] Janin to Beneš, 31 October 1919.

Legion and therefore responsible for the evacuation, but in the end he lost completely control over the Legion and evacuation, and was glad to escape from the Baykal region with his train intact. But the evacuation almost ended in a tragedy: though the Legion did not collapse and surrender to the bolsheviks, it left Siberia with bolshevik consent and only after it helped the bolsheviks to bury its erstwhile friends, the Russian Whites. This tragedy was not exactly of Czech making, and certainly was enacted against the express orders of the impotent commander Janin, but both had a share in the responsibility for it. Even as late as 9 November 1919 Kolchak and the Whites were under the impression that the Legion would suddenly turn round against the bolsheviks and push them back from Omsk which was still the White capital. Pavlů even asked Kolchak to send a direct plea to President Masaryk to order the Legion to turn round, but Masaryk categorically refused and the evacuation continued. On 10 November 1919 the bolsheviks unexpectedly appeared in Omsk and took it with its immense stores of arms and ammunition intact. The floodgates of chaos were open and the Kolchak régime simply faded away.

As Omsk fell and everybody was retreating the inevitable collapse of the Trans-Siberian Railway ensued. The Czechs were then all entrained in readiness for evacuation and therefore had an immeasurable advantage over the panic-stricken Russians. Immediately disputes and recriminations arose between the Kolchak Russians and the Czechs and each tried to hit the other as hard as they could. On 12 November 1919 Pavlů, who until then was Kolchak's personal friend, publicly declared to the Czech soldiers of the 2nd Regiment that all the difficulties for the evacuation were caused by the Whites, whom he further qualified as butchers and their règime likened to assassins.[1] But it was not the only action the Czechs took against Kolchak and his followers.

The Czech General Gajda remained with Kolchak's Siberian Army even after the Legion withdrew from the civil war. He was successful with his army in the March offensive and so much so that in May 1919 Kolchak appointed him the commander-in-chief of all Russian forces. But in July Gajda quarrelled with Kolchak and was summarily dismissed and expelled from Omsk. He departed in a special armoured train accompanied by his Czech guards and remained since in his train at Vladivostok station. From Vladivostok Gajda began to plot the downfall of Kolchak. He easily persuaded the

[1] Lampson to Curzon, 14 November 1919.

Americans and even the French to back him in this attempt, but the British were resolutely against such adventure and the British Consul at Vladivostok, who listened too much to Gajda, was recalled to London.[1] Gajda decided to use for his attempt against Kolchak the Social Revolutionary Party and as early as September 1919 organized SR bureaux at Krasnoyarsk, Irkutsk and Vladivostok. The Bureaux were to launch coups against the Kolchak authorities whenever the situation permitted it. On 17 November 1919 Gajda led the first uprising at Vladivostok, but badly miscalculated. The Kolchak commander, General Rozanov, retained the confidence of the Japanese, and with their help put down the attempt next day.[2]

But the SR rebels were victorious at Krasnoyarsk and Irkutsk, and this had incalculable consequences for Kolchak and even for the Czechs. Krasnoyarsk was an important railway junction and disorders there meant delays in evacuation. On 16 November 1919 General Syrový refused to suppress the SR coup but instead ordered the Czechs to take over the Trans-Siberian west of the city. This meant that Admiral Kolchak and his army commanders could not move reinforcements into the uprising areas and in fact barred the very authorities from getting to and past Krasnoyarsk. While the Krasnoyarsk conspiracy was only encouraged by the Czechs, they took direct part in the Irkutsk one. For several months past Czech political leaders and soldiers promised aid to the Social Revolutionaries and they were given some arms by evacuating Czech soldiers. On 12 November 1919 the city *duma* and the *gubernya zemstvo* met and discussed future political development. These representatives then took over power in the city though the garrison still remained faithful to Kolchak who was *en route* somewhere west of Krasnoyarsk.

Though it was the Czech General Gajda who was responsible for most of Kolchak's trouble, not all the Czechs were in agreement with Gajda. The military leaders were more interested in the evacuation than any internecine Russian struggle, and opposed Kolchak only when the evacuation was threatened by his action. On 19 November 1919 the members of the Kolchak government arrived at Irkutsk and the Czechs had to decide whom they would recognize as masters at Irkutsk. The city was divided between the two Russian factions while the Czechs controlled the station and the railway track. In the end

[1] O'Reilly to Curzon, 26 October 1919.
[2] Lampson to Curzon, 17 and 18 November 1919.

the Czechs declared themselves neutral and let the Russians fight it out between themselves.[1]

In the meantime the fate of Kolchak was decided by the collapse of his armies. On 21 November 1919 the British representative in Siberia, Lampson, told Lord Curzon that the moribund Omsk was finished and that the Social Revolutionaries were coming up as the decisive political force in Siberia. As soon as Kolchak's armies dissolved all would come to an end.[2] Early in December 1919 Kolchak's armies split into innumerable small units and their leader-generals began to fight each other. General Voytsekhovsky shot dead General Grivin; then on Voytsekhovsky's order the Poles executed Colonel Ivakin at Novonikolayevsk. The quarrels of Generals Prince Galitsin, Matkovsky and Ostopov were delaying White retreat before the bolsheviks; on 7 December 1919 General Pepelyayev arrested General Zakharov and forced Kolchak to dismiss Zakharov as commander-in-chief of non-existing armies. General Kappel died on 11 December 1919 and his death only increased confusion. In the midst of all this chaos Kolchak lost his judgement and when the Czechs halted his trains and refused to let him through before their own troops were evacuated, he threatened the local Czech commander which was undignified and useless. But then he sent out insane telegrams to his subordinate commanders to oppose the Czechs with arms and even blow up bridges to prevent their evacuation.

Since the Czechs controlled not only the railway but also the telegraph Kolchak signed his own death warrant. On 10 December 1919 he was still able to get through a traffic jam at Mariinsk, but two days later he was stopped for a week at Krasnoyarsk. On 15 December 1919 only Czech trains were allotted fuel and all the other trains transporting Kolchak, his Russians, some Serbs, Poles and Rumanians came to a halt. When on 23 December 1919 the Czechs found out about Kolchak's orders to General Horvat and Ataman Semenov to stop them at all price, they simply told Kolchak's opponents to act. Kolchak was at Nizhne Udinsk while the pathetic remains of his armies were west of Krasnoyarsk cut from him by the rebels. Cheremkovo, on the way to Irkutsk was also in insurgent hands. Then on 24 December 1919 Irkutsk finally began to settle the issue with arms and within a week no Kolchak follower remained in the city.[3] Kolchak

---

[1] Lampson to Curzon, 24 November 1919.
[2] Lampson to Curzon, 21 November 1919.
[3] Lampson to Curzon, 27 December 1919.

himself was taken under Czech protection and on 7 January 1920 left Nizhne Udinsk for Irkutsk. He arrived there on 15 January and was handed over to the new authority, his Russian opponents.

Though the British tried their best to save Kolchak and his régime they failed. By December 1919 all authority collapsed: Janin was openly disobeyed by the Czechs, the Russians seemed without leadership and collectively the Allies were obeyed by no-one.[1] After the collapse of the Kolchak régime came the turn of the Social Revolutionaries and in the end only the advancing bolsheviks offered stability. In this atmosphere of each for himself the Czechs had to turn to the bolsheviks and demand their consent to complete their evacuation. They used the Irkutsk SRs as their emissaries and the gold reserve captured from Kolchak as bargaining points. On 11 January 1920 the SR delegation left Irkutsk to start negotiations, and with the Allies representatives safely in the Trans-Baykal region the Czechs could complete their bargain with the bolsheviks. The latter were not very enthusiastic. They thought that the remainder of the Czech Legion would be forced to surrender to them without any concession. After all the Serbs, Poles and Rumanians with whom the Red Army caught up with did so in the first days of January 1920. The Czech rear-guard had to fight hard, especially on 18 January 1920 at Nizhne Udinsk and then on 29 January at Tulun to keep the attacking Red units at a safe distance and continue with the evacuation. But after these successful skirmishes the bolsheviks became convinced that the Czechs would not surrender and on 7 February 1920 concluded an armistice with them.[2]

On the same day the Revolutionary Committee which replaced the SR administration at Irkutsk executed Admiral Kolchak, as the last remnant of his armies under General Voytsekhovsky reached Irkutsk and threatened to seize the city and liberate Kolchak. When they heard of the execution the exhausted Whites wanted to take their revenge on the city but were dissuaded by the Czechs not to do so. The Czechs continued their evacuation unhampered and as their last trains left the bolsheviks took over peacefully the abandoned territory. The Czechs who used the gold reserve to obtain an armistice from the bolsheviks were under Allied pressure not to abandon it to them. Clemenceau and Beneš sent several telegrams to their representatives on the spot urging them to save the gold reserve from the bolsheviks,

[1] Lampson to Curzon, 17 December 1919; Janin to Syrový, 14 January 1920.
[2] Janin to Lefevre, 7 February 1920; Krymzsa to Pilsudski, 4 March 1920.

but both Janin and Syrový were powerless to have their orders obeyed.[1] Rather than ship the gold to Vladivostok and thus break the armistice the Czech soldiers were prepared to mutiny. Thus the reserve remained at Irkutsk until 1 March 1920, when it was handed over to the bolsheviks when the last train left Irkutsk station *en route* to Vladivostok.

V

On 20 December 1919 a Foreign Office memorandum was circulated in the Cabinet. In it the British summarized all the troubles they had had with Siberia and its governments and formally announced the end of Kolchak's régime. In the conclusion it was stated that the British should pull out without further commitment; only the High Commissioner should remain, but only for the purpose of watching the Americans and the Japanese.[2] But even that proved hardly possible and the British representative Lampson had to retreat with the other members of Allied missions to China. On 12 March 1920 Curzon sent him a telegram to Pekin in which he announced that even the post of High Commissioner in Siberia had been abolished and the British mission dissolved.[3] British policy in Siberia failed, Kolchak's règime disappeared and the British drew a drastic but logical conclusion.

The French were in a different position from the British. In the Czech Legion they still had interests in Siberia, but these interests were remarkably unstable. The Legion ceased to obey the French commander-in-chief Janin in December 1919. Up to 15 January 1920 Janin tried to issue orders and interfere with the Czechs by means of telegrams from the various railway stations on the way to Chita. But after that he lost contact and the Czechs went their own independent way. Janin also finished in Pekin after he had failed to save both Kolchak and the gold reserve. He returned to France with his mission unfinished and was suitably reprimanded.[4] The Czech evacuation safe after the armistice dragged on throughout the summer of 1920. On 1 June 1920 the 10th Czech Regiment, the rear-guard, embarked on USN *Evelyn* at Vladivostok, but the last Czech convoy left the city on 2 September 1920.

---

[1] Beneš to Syrový, 1 February 1920; Millerand to Janin, 5 February 1920.
[2] Foreign Office Memorandum, 20 December 1919.
[3] Curzon to Lampson, 12 March 1920.
[4] Millerand–Janin interview, June 1920.

The Czechs were the chief executors of Allied policy in Siberia; they also failed. Though they started the upheaval, prematurely from the Russian Whites' point of view, they soon became confused and demoralized, so that in the end they not only ceased to execute Allied policy but positively upset it. They refused to fight the bolsheviks and support the Whites when bid by the Allies; to save themselves they abandoned Kolchak, the Whites and the gold reserve and ended their stay in Siberia without any apparent moral or material benefit to themselves. This was an utter fiasco and the only consolation was that elsewhere in Russia the Allied intervention ended in similar conditions.

CHAPTER SIX

SOUTHERN RUSSIA
AFTER THE ARMISTICE

I

In June 1918 the Allied intervention was launched for the publicly declared purpose of continuing the war against the Central Powers in Russia and of checking German influence in that country. After the armistice in the west in November 1918 the former factor became inoperative, but the latter, at least in the eyes of the Allies, became largely extended.

The process of re-formulation of Allied policies towards Russia is still obscure. The only certainty about it is that there was to be no common Allied policy. Instead each ally formulated its own attitudes and policies to suit particular national interests. However, there was agreement among the Allies on one or two points, whenever national interests coincided. Thus it was agreed that Germany was to evacuate all the annexed or otherwise occupied territory of pre-war Russia. It was also agreed that all German influence in Russia would have to be curtailed, if not eradicated, and since in Allied eyes the bolsheviks had been linked with the Germans they also would have to be rid of somehow. But this was the uppermost limit of Allied consensus.

The British attitude towards Russia was outlined before and after the armistice by the Prime Minister, Lloyd George, in several public statements: Great Britain wished to stand by her war ally, Russia, through thick and thin. She hoped that Russia would become again strong, secure and free. Though the Brest-Litovsk Peace Treaty irritated Britain, it did not change British objectives concerning Russia; she had no quarrel with the Russian people, not even with the bolsheviks, and wanted Russia to be great, powerful, but without German influence. The stress was on the last factor and the evacuation of Imperial Russia by Germany was a pre-condition to the armistice.[1]

[1] Extracts from War Aims Index of Statements by Allied, Enemy and Neutral Countries and Subject Nationalities, 1914–18; Lloyd George to Trade Unions, 5 January 1918; Balfour, House of Commons, 14 March 1918; Cecil, House of Commons, 16 May 1918; Lloyd George, House of Commons, 7 August 1918; Lord Northcliffe, *The Times*, 4 and 14 November 1918.

In fact British attitude towards the bolsheviks was more complicated than Lloyd George cared to admit publicly. The bolsheviks had always been thought of as German puppets and therefore viewed with extreme hostility; at the same time because of their successes fears were growing that the British would have to come to terms with the bolsheviks. However, after the armistice in the west victorious Britain could indulge in detesting the former ally represented now by the perfidious bolsheviks and Britain had additional, ideological reasons for detesting the new régime: wild social experiments were only increasing the misery and chaos of Russia. Though Lloyd George did not care to admit it Britain's attitude to Russia was hardening. Even before the signature of the armistice it was the bolsheviks who had taken the initiative to try to stop 'hostilities' in the east.[1] But this initiative was immediately rebuffed by both the British and the French. Balfour subsequently announced in the House of Commons in defence of the rejection of this peace feeler that 'the bolsheviks followed a deliberate policy of exterminating their political opponents ... we shall therefore not strengthen this government'. The bolsheviks could expect nothing but hostility from the British government.[2]

The French were guided by similar motives in consideration of their new policy towards Russia. But their announcements were couched in much stronger terms. They not only refused to 'strengthen the bolshevik government' but they definitely wanted to rid the Russian people of it. This government, according to the French, was responsible for the separate peace with incalculable consequences to France and also for the territorial losses of pre-war Russia. On leaving Russia Ambassador Joseph Noulens expressed forcefully French attitude: 'France and her Allies will not abandon the Russian people to the bolsheviks.' The statement had certainly the government's backing.[3]

But the ways and means for ridding Russia of German influence and the bolsheviks were never agreed upon by the Allies. It is true that both France and Britain reaffirmed their zonal arrangements on 13 November 1918. But the reaffirmation of the convention of 23 December 1917 did not solve anything; in fact it only complicated matters. After the declaration the Allies began to take separate decisions and undertake completely separate actions.

The British were militarily committed against the bolsheviks in

[1] Balfour, House of Commons, 12 and 18 November 1918.
[2] Chicherin to Balfour, 3 November 1918.
[3] Noulens, 18 December 1918 (*Le Temps*, 20 December 1918).

GERMAN OCCUPIED TERRITORY
IN NOVEMBER 1918

TROGRAD

Volga

Moscow

N

Oka

'itebsk

Tula

Mohilev

Orel

U S S I A

Dnieper

Gomel

Kursk

Bielgorod

Don

Kharkov

K R A I N E

Bug

Ekaterinoslav

Novo Tcherkask

Taganrog

Rostov

Nikolaev

lessa

Kherson

SEA OF
AZOV

Stavropol

C A U C A S I A

CRIMEA

Sevastopol

Novorossisk

L A C K   S E A

the north. They were determined to hang on to the Murmansk and Archangel bases until bolshevik collapse. However, in that area the British had not much choice: the expeditionary forces were literally frozen in by the Arctic Sea and could not be moved until May 1919. The same applied to Siberia, where there was a small British force and a naval battery as well as a training mission which was helping the Russian Whites to organize a new army. Immediately following the armistice the British were about to add to these 'frozen' commitments two new ones: they were to extend the occupied territories in the Caucasus and also help General Denikin and his Volunteer Army at Novorossisk.[1] Sir Winston Churchill called this "far-reaching". But coupled with the Balfour memorandum which refused to commit any British forces in Russia it really amounted to very little. The policy of strong words and sitting on the fence thus continued.

Balfour's memorandum made it clear that Britain was unwilling to get directly involved in Russia. The British were willing to go as far as to give the best possible chance to the pro-Allied Russians and then expected them to win.[2] The French were determined to act to the contrary. They had sorted out their Russian policy during November–December 1918 and the Foreign Minister, S. Pichon, was undoubtedly strongly influenced by the special Slavonic commission, which he had set up in December 1917, and which was dominated by East European non-Russian nationals.[3] Probably on its recommendation Pichon formulated his doctrine for the containment of the bolsheviks: a *cordon sanitaire* from Odessa to Riga. France then proceeded most energetically to implement this policy whose details became publicly known only much later.[4]

The idea of using French troops in Russia to underpin the success of the policy was coincidental. It was the unexpected military success in the Balkan area which suggested this move to Clemenceau. In November 1918 General Franchet d'Esperey and his forces, after the sudden collapse and surrender of Bulgaria and Rumania's re-entry in the war, were masters of Serbia and southern Hungary. Furthermore General Berthelot who had only just arrived in Rumania reported

[1] Sir Henry Wilson, Memorandum on our Present and Future Military Policy in Russia, 13 November 1918; War Cabinet Decision No. 502, 14 November 1918.

[2] Balfour Memorandum, 29 November 1918.

[3] La commission des affaires russes, arrêté du 7 décembre 1917; reference to Pichon's 'cordon sanitaire' in General Sir Henry Wilson's Appreciation of the Internal Situation in Russia, 2 January 1919.

[4] Foch to Clemenceau, 14 January 1919.

rather optimistically on the military situation in southern Russia. According to him the bolsheviks could easily be routed provided the French could aid effectively the Ukrainians and Russian Whites and establish a military zone beyond which General Denikin's armies could re-form and strike decisively against the bolsheviks.[1]

Clemenceau did consult Franchet d'Esperey on the direct French involvement in Russia and found out that the future *Maréchal de France* was opposed to it.[2] But Clemenceau chose to ignore the C-in-C's view; on 2 November 1918 General Berthelot was put in charge of the French intervention, though Franchet retained the overall command in the area. On 3 November the French naval forces were given orders to organize the immediate transportation of French troops to Odessa.[3] The French were to be joined by two Greek divisions which Premier Venizelos was persuaded to make available for this venture. On 15 November 1918 General Berthelot arrived at Bucharest to take charge of the intervention in Russia, while his forces were getting ready at Saloniki. He was to be the interpreter and chief executor of Pichon's idea of the 'cordon sanitaire'.

II

The French had made their decisions about intervention even before the armistice was signed. The Russian (only the pro-Allied ones) could not have been consulted but it was presumed that they would agree to it. Clemenceau, who had several Russian diplomatic representatives and many politicians in Paris, never bothered to discuss his plans with them. It would probably have been futile in any case and ultimately they all would have consented to the intervention. However, General Berthelot on the spot was in a different position. He was forced to 'prepare' the intervention politically whether he wanted it or not. It is not quite clear whether he sought authorization for his political enterprises after being appointed commanding officer in charge of the intervention; strictly speaking he did not have to. But all the same this political initiative complicated matters in the future.

On arrival in Bucharest Berthelot got immediately in touch with General Shcherbatchov, the former Russian C-in-C on the Rumanian front. Shcherbatchov was in contact with General Denikin's HQ and

[1] Clemenceau to Berthelot, 7 October 1918.
[2] Clemenceau to Franchet d'Esperey, 27 October 1918.
[3] ibid., 3 November 1918.

though he previously 'flirted' with Hetman Skorapodsky and the Ukrainians he was now considered Denikin's representative in Rumania. Berthelot quickly sought him out and told him about his appointment and plans. Shcherbatchov in turn telegraphed them to Denikin: according to confidential information imparted to me by General Berthelot the *Allies* were going to land twelve infantry divisions (mainly French and Greek) at Odessa where Allied HQ would be established. Allied forces would then push on to occupy Sevastopol, Kiev, Kharkov, the Donets and Krivoy Rog basins and would probably go as far as the Don, if it proved necessary. These Allied divisions were being sent to Russia to restore order, supervise German withdrawal and provide the Volunteer Army with a protective shield so that it could re-organise in peace and prepare to strike out at the bolsheviks when the right moment came. Shcherbatchov added that General Berthelot was in charge of both political and military operations.[1]

It is obvious that taking the local Russian commander into confidence was a tactical error. General Shcherbatchov misunderstood many things. First of all, he began to consider himself as the Russian representative with the Allied command. Then he took Berthelot's outline of intentions and plans as Allied 'demands and guarantees'. In turn his superior officer, General Denikin, felt that the Allies were consulting him before launching their intervention; he readily agreed to it provided the Allies stuck to the 'principles and conditions'. But when the intervention started and the principles were applied by French officers both Generals were most disappointed and later even dared to object to 'modifications in Allied plans approved by the Volunteers'. Berthelot's military consultations created a highly dangerous situation; his political initiative only confused it still further.

From the very beginning General Berthelot was not as free as he perhaps thought himself to be. The Allied ministers attached to the Rumanian government at Iassy had political instructions and authorization to prepare the ground for Allied intervention in southern Russia. Their spokesman with the Russians, Ukrainians and any other element in southern Russia was Consul Henno, formerly member of the Tabouis mission in Kiev and Captain of the Deuxième Bureau. The Captain evidently collaborated with General Berthelot, but politically was in a sense Berthelot's superior. He was the final interpreter of political orders from Paris and as such only

[1] Shcherbatchov to Denikin, 16 November 1918.

complicated Berthelot's mission. Henno's instructions were 'to check the bolsheviks (with menaces and without force), to insure that the German army does not hand over arms to them and to prepare the ways for the French landing in Odessa'. He interpreted this instruction to mean the convocation of an Allied–Russian consultative conference and thus only duplicated Berthelot's efforts.[1]

Though a tactical error it was a natural one and Henno was not alone in commiting it. The Allied ministers at Iassy, St Aulaire (France), Barclay (Britain), Vopička (United States) and de Visart (Italy) also saw in a consultative conference with the Russians the best way to prepare the French landing, and they sanctioned with their authority Henno's initiative. Henno ignored the Ukrainians and invited the pro-Allied Russians only, and did not make it clear to them what they were being consulted about. The Russian 'delegation' to the conference immediately misinterpreted its rôle. Its members even thought that they were asked to put a Russian sanction on the French landing, and approve Allied intervention as such. Since all these decisions had already been taken by the French the Russians were obviously wasting their time but since they were assembled on Allied bidding they thought that the best way to prepare for the Allied landing was to work out their own political programme.

As only the pro-Allied Russians were invited to the conference the approval of the direct Allied intervention in Russia was predetermined. But anything else, above all the Russian political programme, was sure to have a rough passage in this consultative assembly. The Russians took a long time before agreeing on two points only of the programme. They agreed that they would support the Allies in order to re-constitute Russia in its pre-1914 border (with the exception of Poland). They further agreed that this struggle would be waged under General Denikin's leadership: he was elected by the assembly Military Dictator. Since the Russians approved Allied intervention they in turn expected Allied approval of their programme, and this approval was assumed as automatic. Hence the conference dispersed with the false impression that the Allies had accepted the undertaking of re-constituting Russia in her pre-war border and that General Denikin was the supreme commander and leader by the grace of the Allies. Both conclusions had disastrous effect on Russo-Allied relations in the future.

Undoubtedly the French could have done without the conference.

[1] Iassy Conference, *Wrangel Military Papers*, Files 142–3.

They obtained a purely formal approval for the landing and plenty of complications as far as the Volunteer Army was concerned. The short term benefits of this conference went to General Denikin. It enhanced his authority and also gave him the impression that he would be the principal recipient of Allied military aid. This meant that he could subdue his internal opponents-rivals, the Don (Krasnov) and the Kuban cossacks and cherish the high hopes of becoming the leader of all the non-bolshevik Russians. As he had no inkling of any zonal arrangements between France and Britain he immediately began to exaggerate his own importance and unknowingly prepare the ground for Franco-British disagreements.[1]

In the French zone, namely in the Ukraine, the Crimea and the Donets area 'the decisions of the Iassy conference' created complications. Fortunately one great stumbling block in the form of Hetman Skoropadsky's régime disappeared before the conference dispersed. Skoropadsky's Ukraine, which had existed under German protection tried to change sides on 14 November 1918. Skoropadsky declared himself for the Allies and offered the non-bolshevik Russians a federal union. Since he was tainted by German collaboration and since Denikin and the Iassy delegates considered him 'a traitor to Russia' his advances were rejected by the Russians. The Allies hesitated, but before Skoropadsky could complicate their plans any further, he fell from power and became an unimportant refugee in Berlin. On 17 December 1918 Ukrainian nationalists seized power and declared the Ukraine an independent state.

This was an utterly unexpected turn of events for both the Russians and the French. They both hoped that the Ukraine would pass peacefully under their control and now suddenly a new factor made its appearance. On 13 December 1918 Clemenceau spelled out French embarrassment in the guidance to French military representatives on French aims in Russia. According to it the French intervention in the south was the logical outcome of the armistice: the French were there to control and supervise German withdrawal. Clemenceau then repeated his previous idea of a shield: the Volunteers would re-group and reorganize behind this French protective zone and then strike out against the bolsheviks. But the guidance assumed a peaceful takeover from the Germans and nowhere envisaged an offensive action by the French forces.[2] Consul Henno was therefore instructed to deal

[1] Journal of Meetings, File 143.
[2] Clemenceau to Janin, 13 December 1918.

with this Ukrainian complication. He was to solve all the political problems and prepare Odessa for the French landing. The 156th French Colonial Division was already *en route* from Saloniki.

Henno who had in the meantime moved from Iassy to Odessa had neither much time nor any force to solve the numerous problems. All he could do was to bluff and threaten. Without consulting the Iassy ministers whose spokesman he still considered himself, he issued an Allied declaration making the Ukrainian nationalist leaders personally responsible for law and order threatening them with French troops, still *en route*, if they allowed the Ukraine to lapse into chaos and anarchy.[1] Henno's empty threats were disregarded and the Ukrainians proceeded with military occupation of the Ukraine. But chaos was increasing as the result of nationalist moves. On 18 December 1918 some 500 French citizens stranded in the Donets area asked the French naval command at Sevastopol for protection against Red (meaning Ukrainian) violence. They specifically requested that German occupation authorities be allowed to remain as protectors until Allied troops' arrival.[2] An appeal to the Germans was obviously one way of dealing with the Ukrainian problem, but Henno rejected it and for a very good reason. On 18 December the French Minister at Iassy, St Aulaire, asked Pichon to intervene with the German government in order to stop the German High Command in the Ukraine from supporting the bolsheviks (the bolsheviks in this instance, of course, meant the Ukrainian nationalists).[3] Even if the Allies proved willing to retain German forces in the Ukraine the Germans themselves were not, and in any case would not have played the game according to Allied rules. Thus Henno had to wait for the arrival of the French division.

Nevertheless, Henno scored one concrete victory with his bluff. S. Petlyura, Ukrainian C-in-C, sent out a small detachment to take the city of Odessa for the nationalists. The detachment was strong enough to take the city but Henno's fulminations stopped Petlyura from issuing the final order. The Ukrainians deployed round the city which remained under the Hetman administration with small Polish and Volunteer units as forces of order. Odessa contained in the nut-shell all the problems of southern Russia and Henno was quite

[1] St Aulaire to Pichon, 7 December 1918.
[2] French Consul, Donets to French Naval Command, Sevastopol, 17 December 1918.
[3] St Aulaire to Pichon, 18 December 1918.

unable to cope with them. On 16 December 1918 he produced a memorandum for General Franchet d'Esperey which showed that he had learned nothing from the short experience he had had with the Russians and Ukrainians. The memorandum was a substantial document containing an historical introduction and analyses of German occupation and of the nationalist movement in the Ukraine. Henno deplored the swift collapse of German occupation and the seizure of power by the pro-German and pro-bolshevik nationalists, and recommended support of the Volunteers. In view of his experience with the Ukrainians he told Franchet d'Esperey that they should be ignored, but because of their military power the French zone should now be a narrow coastal strip, the 'zone de refuge'.[1]

On 18 December 1918 the naval units transporting French advanced forces arrived at Odessa. The Volunteer detachment in the city offered to clear it for the landing and with naval gun support was permitted to do so. On 19 December 1918 General Borius disembarked with some 1,800 men and marched through cheering Odessa with flying colours. The long-awaited French intervention in the south had just started; the landing of French forces was supposed to solve all the problems. Instead the landing was to create much greater problems involving not only the French and the Russians but also the British.

III

The French had originally taken on themselves to police southern Russia in the hope that soon there would be a common Allied policy towards Russia and French forces would be joined by other Allied forces. The hopes were to be fulfilled by the Peace Conference, for which the victorious Allies began to gather in Paris in December 1918. From the start it became obvious that a common Allied policy on anything, and in particular on Russia, would be a difficult task. Naturally each ally arrived in Paris with its own national policy, and only their reconciliation and harmonization would have brought about a common undertaking. But this proved impossible.

In the beginning there was a measure of agreement at the conference. The British basing their Russian policy on the zonal arrangement with France and on the cabinet decisions of 14 November 1918 (no direct troop commitments) suggested that all the Allies should make a concerted effort to 'give the non-bolsheviks the best chance

[1] Henno to Franchet d'Esperey, 16 December 1918.

to win.' But this proposal proved too vague. The French who wanted to be more concrete and had already had some unpleasant experience in Russia thought that all the difficulties were caused by the lack of coordination among the Allies. This analysis was probably right, but the remedy was difficult to arrive at. Coordination was only possible if the Allies agreed to reconcile their national interests in a common policy.

Even before the Peace Conference met the Allies failed to agree among themselves on who should represent Russia at the conference. In the end it was decided that no one should speak for her officially, but private individuals could be invited to address the conference on behalf of Russia and be listened to by the Allies.[1] When the Conference finally met, it had for its consideration one 'coordinated' draft proposal only. The Allied War Council, and in particular Marshal Foch, had prepared a military plan for Allied intervention in Russia. It envisaged a coordinated offensive against the bolsheviks by multi-national armies under Foch's supreme command. The nucleus of the intervention forces would be formed by the Rumanian, Polish and Baltic armies while the Czechs (their Siberian Legion) and the non-bolshevik Russians would play only a subordinate rôle. The Allies would equip these forces and with French officers firmly in command the plan would have probably had a good chance of success. However, the plan was narrowly military in its design and though some aspects of it were open to criticism it was on the whole plausible. Its chief weakness was political: the political aim of this military operation was the deliverance of Russia from bolshevism.[2]

On 12 January 1919 the Council of Five finally began to discuss the Russian problem. The political weakness of Foch's plan became immediately clear. The Russians objected to it claiming that it was crude interference in internal Russian affairs, and their objection was not insuperable. But the objection of the other states involved was decisive: they had no interest in re-constituting Russia by 'delivering her from bolshevism'. Clemenceau thought the plan was impracticable and both Lloyd George and President Wilson objected to it. On 22 January 1919 the Five Allied Powers rejected the plan and thus killed the only proposal for a common policy and action in Russia.

[1] Maklakov, Series B, I-5; also Paris Peace Conference Session, 16 January 1919.
[2] Foch to Clemenceau, 18 January 1919; Foch to Clemenceau, 17 February 1919.

Afterwards the Allies made impulsive efforts to solve the Russian problem, but since these efforts were not results of common agreement they also failed. One of these efforts initiated by Lloyd George highlighted the impulsiveness and Allied disagreements. During the preliminary discussions Lloyd George advocated negotiations with the bolsheviks as the most significant power factor in Russia since they could not be eliminated otherwise. President Wilson came round to Lloyd George's idea and drafted his own proposals on negotiations: all the parties engaged in the civil war in Russia were to meet at the Prinkipo Island off Istanbul and negotiate a peaceful settlement of their dispute. The conference would begin on 15 February and the only precondition of attendance was the cessation of hostilities.[1]

It is undoubted that if the idea of the conference worked it would have been an excellent way out of the Russian embroglio at least for Lloyd George and Britain. President Wilson who was hardly at all involved in Russia liked to play the rôle of a peacemaker and therefore was delighted with the conference. But the French gave only a grudging consent to the common Allied appeal for the conference convinced that the warring Russians would reject it. At first it seemed that even the Russian Whites would welcome it. The Crimean government misunderstood the conference thinking of it as an international tribunal by which the bolsheviks would be tried and outvoted.[2] But when it became clear that the purpose of the conference was not to judge but arrange a peaceful settlement the Crimeans rejected the idea. Both Admiral Kolchak and General Denikin also rejected it, because it arrived at the wrong moment. They were both preparing a large-scale offensive against the bolsheviks and none of them was as yet decisively beaten. Thus only the bolsheviks saw a direct benefit in accepting the invitation, but even they were prepared to attend on their own conditions. They demanded prior withdrawal of Allied troops from Russia and immediate halt of Allied military aid to the Whites.[3] These conditions would have probably wrecked the conference; however Clemenceau decided to take the onus for the failure from the bolsheviks. When he saw that no practical purpose could be served by such conference except bolshevik international recognition, halting of offensive preparations and incalculable blow to

[1] Herron Papers X – Prinkipo; Paris Conference Session, 14 February 1919.

[2] Maklakov, Series B, III-1.

[3] Chicherin to Wilson, 28 January 1919; Chicherin's note to Allies, 4 February 1919.

White morale he put pressure on the Whites who rejected this Allied proposal.[1]

The Prinkipo conference was the last 'commonly agreed' idea for the solution of the Russian problem. Henceforth the Allies reverted to the old unsatisfactory zonal arrangements, if anything more jealously enforced than previously because of disagreements. Uncoordinated actions, duplicated efforts and useless rivalry continued to bedevil the Russian situation and even endangered Franco–British relations, which by March 1919 reached a point of crisis.

IV

Even before the French landed in Odessa they sensed that Franco-Russian military cooperation would be difficult. Most of the Russian officers were also politicians and that made them unbearable military partners. They would judge French generals from a political point of view and the French could never understand this attitude. General Berthelot, whom the Russians had known before the bolshevik and indeed March revolutions, was very popular with them as long as he maintained his reputation of supporting the policy of 'one, indivisible Russia'. But on the whole it could be said that the Russians objected to and quarrelled with every French officer that ever set foot in southern Russia. It was perhaps not always entirely their fault, for apart from being politically ignorant or objectionable the French were given to lecturing and offensive condescension. They were the victors of the World War while their Russian counterparts exhibited such incompetence that they could not even deal with the bolshevik rabble without outside help. When Generals Erdeli and Dragomirov paid a visit to General Franchet d'Esperey he unashamedly treated them to a lecture on the moral decay of the Russian officer. Above all he showed indifference to 'one, indivisible Russia' and only busied himself with short-term problems such as the defence of his occupation zone. The seed of dissent was sprouting even before actual sowing.

General Borius arrived in Odessa with the vaguest political instructions ever issued: he was to give support to all patriotic Russians. The instruction did not even specify that the patriots had to be inhabitants of the French zone. Out of gratitude he appointed the youthful Siberian General, Grishin-Almazov, Military Governor of Odessa thus creating for the French the first problem; a whole series

[1] Janin to Clemenceau, 7 February 1919.

145

of the French-made problems was to follow.[1] Grishin-Almazov considered himself General Denikin's officer and therefore applied to him for approval which was granted. But General Denikin operated in the British zone and therefore strictly speaking had no authority over Odessa and French appointments therein. However, Grishin-Almazov was never enlightened on this point and a dangerous precedent was created. Henceforth Denikin began to consider his interference in the French zone as something natural, to the great annoyance of the French commanders, but again he was never told.

An open conflict between the French and General Denikin broke out shortly after General d'Anselme's arrival in Odessa. D'Anselme came with instructions to occupy the *zone de refuge* running from Odessa to Tiraspol, Kherson and Nikolayev, and to supply it, and especially the city of Odessa, with foodstuffs. The Volunteer Governor could not procure food supplies from General Denikin and it was therefore no wonder that d'Anselme soon sent his C-of-S, Colonel Freydenberg to negotiate with the Ukrainians who controlled grain supplies. The Colonel probably exceeded his power and offered the Ukrainians political recognition in return for food, but this point is still disputed. When these negotiations were leaked the Volunteers became extremely suspicious, and began to talk of French betrayal.

On 16 January 1919 General d'Anselme was suddenly told that there would be no further expansion of his French forces (. . . no more than one colonial infantry division . . .) but he would receive Greek and Rumanian reinforcements. When the Greeks arrived Freydenberg was able to send them to Kherson and Nikolayev thus fulfilling his original task, namely to occupy the French zone in southern Russia. But by then he had concluded several local agreements with the Ukrainians which went far beyond the original food negotiations. The French did not envisage the use of violence for the occupation of their zone, but the Ukrainians had sneaky habits and usually occupied territories evacuated by the Germans before the French or their Allies managed to arrive. It was obvious that this would have been the case with the Kherson and Nikolayev areas, and if this happened the French would have to dislodge the Ukrainians. Colonel Freydenberg therefore preferred to talk the Ukrainians out of this territory so that his Greeks could take it unopposed. But the Ukrainians demanded compensation; after all they were already

[1] This section is based on the reports of the Russian intelligence agency, *Wrangel Papers*, File 132–4.

supplying Odessa with food and now were giving up to the French large tracts of Ukrainian territory. Freydenberg therefore promised them that the territory and all it contained (stores etc.) would be held in trust by the Allies, and if and when evacuated, it would be handed over to the Ukrainians and no one else. When the details of this arrangement came out, the French had the Volunteers up in arms causing real trouble. But this was not the end of difficulties; the Ukrainians now demanded concessions in Odessa as well.

General Borius did not think twice when he appointed General Grishin-Almazov Governor of Odessa. After all the Volunteers did clear the city for the French landing and Consul Henno sanctioned the appointment. Grishin-Almazov was an efficient officer and reasonable administrator and there was therefore no reason to regret his appointment. He did have an irritating habit of referring to General Denikin before making major decisions, but it was thought that with time he would give up this habit and cooperate more fully with the French instead. But Grishin-Almazov undermined his own and Volunteer position in the French zone when his mobilization for the Volunteer Army failed hopelessly. Instead of resigning he blamed the French for obstruction and appealed to General Denikin to uphold his declining position. This was the last straw to the French, who under Ukrainian pressure to accommodate their wishes in return for food supplies decided to get rid of the Volunteer governor. But overnight the minor problem of replacing a governor blew into a political storm which ultimately involved the French not only with Denikin but also with the British.

Though southern Russia and the French zone was inhabited predominantly by Ukrainians Odessa was a microcosm of nationalities and races. It contained a strong Russian minority which recognized General Denikin as their leader and therefore stood behind his Governor. This powerful and vociferous group took up cudgels against the French on behalf of Grishin-Almazov. The Russians undoubtedly also recognized that Grishin-Almazov's successor would be a Ukrainian and thus this personnel argument became a political dispute. A Ukrainian Governor at Odessa meant that the French abandoned their policy of 'one, indivisible Russia' and sanctioned her dismemberment by separatist nationalities. The two Frenchmen responsible for this betrayal were General d'Anselme and Colonel Freydenberg and the Russians were ready to fight them tooth and nail whatever the consequences of this struggle may be.

At first they hoped that a compromise would be patched up. General Berthelot as superior officer of the two 'traitors' would put things right. He finally arrived at Odessa on 13 February 1919 and immediately received the local Russian leader, V. V. Shulgin. Shulgin was most impressed by Berthelot and wrote to Denikin that the former was not only a good man, but definitely wanted 'one indivisible Russia' and would help the Volunteers to re-constitute her. However, Shulgin could not understand that at the same time Berthelot spoke of the Ukrainians as 'our war-time allies' and not as hostile separatists to be ignored. It became obvious that Berthelot would probably also betray the Odessa Russians.

The Russians were quite wrong in imputing to Berthelot any political motives. General Berthelot, as much as General d'Anselme and Colonel Freydenberg were under War Ministry instructions 'to bring about the re-constitution of Russia' not her dismemberment. But they were equally under much stricter military instructions to maintain and defend the French occupation zone. In acting as they did they had purely French interests in mind and never envisaged the recognition of the Ukraine as an independent state, which in any case was not within the limits of their competence. French short term interests in southern Russia forced the French generals to seek limited military alliances with the Ukrainians which was all they were prepared to undertake. But they would have preferred to deal with the Volunteers, had these been powerful enough to help the French and had they been operating in the French zone.

General Denikin sent to Odessa another of his agents, General Sannikov, who was responsible for the whole of the French zone to the Volunteers. General Berthelot, who rather liked Grishin-Almazov, received Sannikov and told him that since the Volunteer mobilization proved such a failure they would have no further say in the military affairs of the zone and that the French themselves would mobilize and train a new force. Berthelot further said that French instructors would supervise training and advise their Russian fellow officers how to command. Sannikov could clearly see that this was the first step in ousting the Russian Volunteers from any influence in the French occupied territory. But he also clearly perceived the pretence under which this move could be combatted: French officers commanding Russian soldiers was a breach of a tacit Allied–Denikin agreement on the formation of White armies and above all it was a direct interference in internal Russian affairs. Sannikov therefore strongly rejected Berthelot's proposals and referred the matter to General Denikin himself, recommending that steps be taken in Paris to put a stop to these plans.

This was not a reasonable move and it brought no results except the deterioration of French–Volunteer relations. The Volunteers could not know that their demands for a decisive say in the French zone could not be granted because of the zonal arrangements. At the same time the French needed Russian troops to defend the zone against the bolsheviks, or their allies, and since the Volunteers could not oblige the French had to take steps to obtain the troops elsewhere. As for Volunteer demands to administer the French zone this also was unreasonable. For the French the Volunteers were in the zone not to administer but to fight the bolsheviks (*pour lutter, pas gouverner*) and in any case Volunteer administrative superiority would have implied that the French were in the zone in an auxiliary capacity and this was clearly unacceptable. But Berthelot irritated by Russian manoeuvres decided to act.

As Odessa depended almost entirely on Ukrainian food supplies General Berthelot was determined to secure their good will by handing them the civil administration in the city. He was further fortunate enough to find an acceptable Ukrainian: Captain Adro-Langeron, descendant of one of the French founders of the city, now spokesman for Ukrainian interests. This solution seemed too good to be true and indeed in the end proved unworkable. To the Volunteers Andro-Langeron was a Ukrainian separatist and they would fight to the end to prevent his appointment; to the Ukrainians he was the representative of the great landowners compromised unhealthily with the Russians. Since he also claimed to be of French descent both sides in the end turned against him.

At first General Sannikov thought that if General Berthelot met personally General Denikin all French–Volunteer difficulties could be smoothed over. But when it became clear that Denikin preferred to conduct his military operations to meeting Berthelot the French went through with their plans. On 3 March 1919 General d'Anselme received the leading Russians and told them of the proposed changes in Odessa. The Russian delegation led by Vernatsky rejected these proposals out of hand refusing to discuss them or to think of compromise solutions. On 8 March 1919 the Franco–'Ukrainian' agreement became publicly known and next day Captain Andro-Langeron and a delegation left Odessa for Denikin's HQ to acquaint the

Russians with the new arrangements in the city. On the same day General d'Anselme saw Shulgin, the other Russian leader, trying to persuade him to cooperate with the new administration, but failed to convince him.

It is not quite clear what happened to the Andro-Langeron delegation *en route* to General Denikin. However, it seems to have been the last gesture of good will by General Berthelot towards the Volunteers. Berthelot's health then gave way and he departed from Russia to France on 10 March. On 14 March Andro-Langeron was back in Odessa where the situation took a turn for the worse. At 9 a.m. on that day General d'Anselme informed General Grishin-Almazov that he had just declared martial law in the city and the zone and had taken over administration in both. D'Anselme then issued an order by which Captain Andro-Langeron was appointed Chairman of the Administrative Council at Odessa and General Schwarz, a Volunteer General, was made Head of the Military Section of the Council responsible for the defence of the zone. Grishin-Almazov was appointed CO of the Volunteer forces in the zone. This indeed was a shake-up quite contrary to Russian views and desires; they branded it as a *coup d'état* and determined to oppose it, even if it entailed the threat to the defence and security of the zone.

The French took these measures reluctantly, only after all other considerations had to be abandoned. The immediate reason for the 'coup' was the deterioration of the situation at the front. On 11 March 1919 Ataman Grigoriev, the roving Ukrainian cossack, who at that moment cooperated with the bolsheviks, took advantage of the friendliness of German troops towards him and with their connivance attacked Allied garrisons (mainly Greek) at Kherson and Nikolayev and compelled them to withdraw. This was obviously a great blow to French prestige in southern Russia, but meant no end to French troubles. Ataman Grigoriev's forces now began to advance on Odessa. On 18 March 1919 Allied forces engaged Grigoriev at the approaches to Odessa at Berezovka. During the engagement the Volunteer detachment (according to the French) refused to fight and the Greeks followed the bad example of the Zouaves and took to their heels abandoning all their heavy equipment, among it two French tanks, the first ones the bolsheviks captured. After this victory Grigoriev could have taken Odessa without much struggle and the bolsheviks certainly urged him to do so. However, Grigoriev was not a systematic warrior and therefore decided to wait until he could take the city without fighting at all.

150

The organizational decomposition in Odessa after the defeat was accelerated. When on 18 March General Denikin protested vehemently to Colonel Corbel, Head of the French Mission at his HQ, against the Odessa 'coup', he was told quite truthfully that the coup was necessary in order to save the situation there. But he refused to believe this explanation and immediately dispatched several telegrams to save the situation in his own way. Generals Grishin-Almazov and Sannikov were ordered to ignore the new administration and remain responsible to him. Two protest telegrams were sent to Paris and London representing the coup as flagrant interference in internal Russian affairs. All was prepared for a real French–Volunteer fight.

In Odessa the French were in desperate straits. General d'Anselme in addition to the setback at Berezovka had found out about a threatened mutiny in the French fleet at anchor off Odessa, and considered that further changes would be necessary. On 21 March 1919 General Franchet d'Esperey, French C-in-C in the Orient, arrived at Odessa to help with his superior authority General d'Anselme. They quickly enacted a whole series of measures: firstly Captain Andro-Langeron was dismissed and General Grishin-Almazov as Commander of the Volunteers was made responsible for the defence of the city. This was an obvious concession by the French who were really weary of the fight with the Volunteers. However, Grishin-Almazov completely misunderstood the concession. He went on thinking in political terms and demanded to know political concessions: were the Volunteers in charge of Odessa's administration and police? The puzzled French generals spoke of military matters and when Grishin-Almazov repeated the questions and refused to take up his appointment, Franchet d'Esperey dismissed him, accused him of sabotage and ordered him and General Sannikov out of the city at once. While Grishin-Almazov and Sannikov were on their way to report to General Denikin General Schwarz was put in charge of the Volunteer brigade which was rushed out to help in the defence of the city.

On 24 March 1919 General Schwarz tried to justify his assumption of command to General Denikin. He claimed that in the desperate situation he simply accepted General Franchet d'Esperey's order. On 26 March Franchet d'Esperey himself informed Denikin of all the changes he effected in Odessa and justified them by the gravity of the situation. General Schwarz was appointed by him when Generals

Grishin-Almazov and Sannikov refused to carry out his orders. General Timanovsky remained in command of the Volunteer brigade and cooperated with Schwarz. In any case the French command had the sanction of the Paris Russian Committee for all these changes. In the last moment Denikin, thoroughly alarmed, offered to meet Franchet d'Esperey to settle all differences, but the latter was not interested in meeting a local Russian commander, especially when Denikin at the same time refused to detail any force under his command to the relief of Odessa and in fact talked of withdrawing the small brigade from the city to the Crimea.

Disappointed by the Volunteers and under great pressure from Grigoriev forces the French Command heard of an open mutiny in the fleet. Its decisions were swift and desperate: despite previous denials the Odessa base had to be evacuated. On 3 April 1919 Consul Henno warned all foreigners in the city that evacuation was imminent. When on 4 April the news became known there was panic in the city. The French, tired of the Russians, looked purely after themselves and left behind most of the Russian refugees who wanted to evacuate with them. On 5 April 1919 Grigoriev's partisans arrived in the city and took it on behalf of the bolsheviks. This was then the result of grave mistakes by the French, but above all the result of the bitter quarrel between the French and the Volunteers. Furthermore the quarrel had serious repercussions on Franco–British relations.

V

It would be a simplification to say that the French-Volunteer quarrel was the only cause of Franco–British disagreements. After all in Paris Clemenceau and Lloyd George rarely saw eye to eye as far as Russia was concerned, and the Prinkipo idea which roused the French to such oppositon certainly embittered mutual relations. However, these disagreements in Paris were not decisive and a more fundamental quarrel lay at the root of this crisis. It was the zonal arrangement itself, once the only common point of interest, which was causing all the trouble.

The British differed very much from the French in their application of the zonal arrangement. They considered it valid in the strictest sense: for them intra-zonal factors became British factors. They arrived at their decisions on the zone in southern Russia more slowly than the French and above all were free from the complicating

Ukrainian question, though they had to cope with various cossack separatisms. Actual British commitments were the result of two reports by special military missions. The first one, under Colonel Blackwood, was put ashore on 23 November 1918 as soon as the British squadron could pass through the Turkish Straits and reach Volunteer controlled territory. On 6 December 1918 Colonel Blackwood sent off his first report from General Denikin's headquarters at Ekaterinodar. The report was based on information provided by Denikin's staff and contained many exaggerated estimates and inflated figures. Thus General Denikin envisaged that the Don army, which he considered as being under his command, would soon reach 250,000 men and the Ukrainian army would muster some 320,000. In addition he had some 50,000 of his Volunteers to care for and therefore asked the British to aid some 620,000 soldiers under his command. In London the figures were taken as exaggerated and another mission was sent to verify them. In any case the British could not look after the Ukrainian army which was in the French zone. However, one recommendation of Blackwood was accepted, namely that Denikin should be the chief recipient of British aid. He would then be responsible for channelling the aid to his subordinates, the cossacks and Caucasians under his command.[1]

Late in December 1918 General Poole arrived at Ekaterinodar to report in more detail on Denikin forces and thus help to finalise British decisions. Poole sent to London realistic figures of troops under Denikin and on these figures British aid was based. He did not mention hypothetical forces in the Ukraine, but endorsed Blackwood's idea on aid and urged London to recognize Denikin as Supreme C-in-C in southern Russia.[2] The British War Cabinet accepted these recommendations and on 14 January 1919 ordered first military supplies to be shipped to southern Russia. Within a month General Denikin received the first shipments of British aid and a powerful military mission led by General Briggs consisting of some 500 officers and men (1923 officers and men according to the bolsheviks). The mission's task was not only to control the use of British aid but also to advise General Denikin on military and political matters.[3]

[1] *Milner Papers*, Report on Visit of British Military Mission to the Volunteer Army under General Denikin in South Russia, 30 January 1919.
[2] Ibid., Major-General F. C. Poole Report, December 1918–January 1919.
[3] Shipping Ministry Memorandum, 5 February 1919.

Once decisions had been made and a mission and aid dispatched the British began to consider Denikin as if he were a 'British' general. He was completely dependent on Britain for supplies and a mission was with him to check him in case he tried to hamper British interests. This arrangement would undoubtedly been excellent had it not been for the decision to seek Allied recognition for Denikin as Supreme C-in-C in Southern Russia. The Allies willingly obliged and then the French suddenly (unreciprocally) sent their own mission to the Supreme Commander. It was not an important mission, led by a mere Lieutenant Colonel Corbel, with eleven officers (of which three were interpreters). They arrived in February 1919 and settled down in Ekaterinodar. But the British could not quite see the point of this mission in their zone, and finally decided that it was there on liaison duties. Colonel (*en mission*) Corbel did act as a liaison informing Generals Denikin and Briggs about the decisions and actions in the French zone.

However, soon even the French mission became a cause of dissention. General Denikin had his reports from the French zone on the Ukrainians and Colonel Corbel failed to explain French moves allegedly leading to the recognition of independent Ukraine. Volunteer suspicions communicated themselves to the British and General Briggs proceeded to alarm London. On 21 March 1919 Lord Curzon called in the French Ambassador, P. Cambon, and handed him a British note protesting against the activity of the French military representatives in southern Russia.[1] The British feared that the French without consulting them were really thinking of recognizing Ukrainian independence. However, the French firmly rejected British suspicions and accusations and explained their position in two notes delivered to Lord Derby at the Quai d'Orsay.[2] P. Cambon added in his personal letter to Pichon, which accompanied the British note that the Peace Conference should and could remedy the lack of cohesion and inefficiencies of Franco–British policies in Russia.[3] Suspicions, recriminations and quarrels began to threaten the substance of the Franco–British entente. Contrary to Cambon's recommendations the resolution of these conflicts would not come from the Peace Conference.

On 31 March 1919 Clemenceau sent his Under-Secretary of State for War to London to attend a cabinet meeting and put to it French

[1] Curzon to Cambon, 21 March 1919.
[2] Pichon to Derby, 22 and 23 March 1919.
[3] Cambon to Pichon, 22 March 1919.

proposals to resolve the present differences and arrive at a common policy. The French proposals were previously approved by the Council of Five and the cabinet meeting raised no fundamental objection to them. All the same it took no vote on them; further negotiations were necessary.[1] However, with the series of French concessions to the Volunteers in southern Russia the British became doubly suspicious. It was now thought that not only were the French dealing with the Ukrainians behind British backs, but they were ready to conclude a deal with the Volunteers without the slightest regard to British interests. Obviously a high-level meeting was necessary to resolve these fundamental differences and dispel suspicions.

On 4 April 1919 the first major effort was made to normalize Franco–British relations. On that day W. Selby of the Foreign Office and Major-General Radcliffe with Captain Woolcombe of the War Office met Monsieur Kammerer, Commandants Ganter and de Rougemont with Admiral Lanade and Capitaine Mottet at the Quai d'Orsay in order to resolve the difference between Generals Denikin and Berthelot. It was recognised that if these differences were successfully resolved the causes of Franco–British disputes would vanish, too. The meeting took place at the moment when French forces were evacuating Odessa. Chances for the re-establishment of mutual confidence were high; the French were in the mood for concessions and Kammerer opened the meeting with a categorical denial of any political deal with the Ukrainians; some French officers might have been indiscreet in their relations with the nationalists but it was most regrettable that the British believed such unworthy rumours. Seldy thanked Kammerer for his statement and enumerated British reasons why such an agreement was undesirable: Petlyura's Ukrainians differed very little from the bolsheviks and could therefore not be trusted. The British supported General Denikin and no one else in southern Russia. Kammerer agreed entirely with Selby and then spelled out French concessions: Russian units raised in the French zone would be commanded by Russian officers; no mixed units would be raised; General Denikin could appoint his political commissars with these units; in order to avoid another Kherson fiasco coordination of military moves would have to be established and troops and supplies would have to be permitted to cross or be taken over the zonal borders; there could be no political negotiations with other Russian factions without Denikin's representatives;

[1] Acting Secretary to War Cabinet to Admiralty, 1 April 1919.

155

Russian ships were to be allowed to fight for General Denikin. The meeting approved all these points and the Protocol of 4 April 1919 became the cornerstone of Franco–British cooperation in southern Russia.[1]

The success of this meeting was too great to last. At long last the Allies agreed to coordinate their actions in both zones and both firmly recognized General Denikin as the only and decisive Russian power factor in southern Russia. It took some time to approve all the decisions of the meeting embodied in the Protocol at the cabinet level. On 19 April the British War Office approved the Protocol and the French High Command accordingly sent instructions to the French C-in-C in the Orient, Franchet d'Esperey.[2] The political tidying up took even longer and on this level the process of watering down the Protocol began first. On 25 April 1919 Pichon asked Lord Derby to call on him and handed him a note which contained the agreed points on Franco–Denikin cooperation. Pichon asked Curzon to transmit the text of the Protocol to Ekaterinodar. But in the end Pichon repeated that the zonal agreement between France and Britain remained in force though it could be revised in the future.[3] This certainly was a peculiar reaffirmation of a principle which had caused so much trouble, especially since the Protocol only just signed spoke of future inter-zonal action. However, by this time France had no zone in southern Russia, if the Crimea, which was administered by a White government under General Denikin is excluded, and it was therefore futile to speak of it. On the other hand Pichon's allusion to the French zone indicated that France was probably thinking of reappraising her policy in southern Russia and perhaps even of creating a new zone.

The British also accepted the Protocol with high hopes; it cleared a way for a better Franco–British understanding. However, Pichon's hints on zones were carefully noted and Franco–British disagreements in Siberia (which was considered as part of the French zone) highlighted. Intervention policy moreover involved Britain in heavy financial commitments which began to hurt the economy. Britain was also getting ready for a reappraisal. On 11 June 1919 Selby who so successfully ironed out the April agreement wrote a memorandum which dealt with the whole of Russia. He pointed out the still pre-

---

[1] Procès-Verbal de la réunion tenue le 4 avril 1919 au Quai d'Orsay pour régler les rapports entre les Généraux Denikine et Berthelot.

[2] Foreign Office Memorandum, 19 April 1919.

[3] Pichon to Derby, 25 April 1919.

valent dissatisfaction with the zonal arrangements and stressed the disproportionate financial burden Britain had to bear. He recommended comprehensive Allied zonal and financial agreements.[1] This certainly was the most rational recommendation and had it been accepted it might have saved Allied intervention in Russia. However, no agreement was ever reached on it and the Allies continued their individual way of dealing with the Russian problem.

VI

In June 1919 after the success of the bolshevik offensive on the eastern front it became clear that Admiral Kolchak was badly beaten and even if he recovered from this defeat he would no longer be the decisive factor in the struggle against the bolsheviks. Meanwhile in southern Russia the Volunteer army and its cossack and Caucasian allies stood poised for an offensive whose objective was the bolshevik capital, Moscow. At this stage it was therefore natural that Clemenceau's attention shifted from Siberia to southern Russia, and while Britain began to complain about economic strain, the Tiger prepared for a bid for French influence in the British zone.

It is true that after the withdrawal from Odessa French prestige in southern Russia suffered a heavy blow but to Clemenceau's mind not an irreparable one. He knew full well that the Volunteers were informed about French good-will gestures in the April Protocol and that they needed aid from both Allies. He therefore warned the French Military Mission in Istanbul that a policy reappraisal was imminent. He undoubtedly did this in reply to the Mission's enquiry as to its purpose after the withdrawal from Odessa and signing of the April Protocol. Clemenceau explained first that the Protocol was a dead letter even before it was finally approved by the Allies because of French withdrawal. But the Mission would soon have a part to play, for the French were considering a new approach to the Volunteers. He then hinted that while economic and military aid was still a British monopoly the British could not supply everything. This was Clemenceau's tack: the French would soon try and fill the gap: they would furnish the Volunteers with the equipment which the British were unable to supply. But this was only an indication of Clemenceau's intention not a policy. In order to find out as much as possible about the Volunteers Clemenceau sent unobtrusive observers to their territory.

[1] Selby Memorandum, 11 June 1919.

157

One of these observers, who helped Clemenceau to make up his mind about southern Russia, was Captain Widhoff. He travelled extensively in southern Russia, met most of the leading Volunteer personalities and his final report and recommendations were greatly heeded by Clemenceau. Widhoff's report was a substantial document, and contained some interesting details on the Volunteers movement, especially on the period September–November 1918. According to Widhoff that was the time of the most acute crisis for the Denikin armies. As a consequence of bolshevik propaganda, Ataman Krasnov's policy and broken promises of 'Allied' representatives some 120,000 cossacks deserted and Denikin was left with hardly 40,000 men. However, thanks to British support and continuous military aid by the end of May 1919 Denikin had under his control some 100,000 men. But despite British advice and control Denikin's rear was badly organized and the General was committing grave political and military errors.

Widhoff then proceeded with the analysis of the Volunteer High Command. General Denikin was a faithful ally who had resisted German temptations even when Hetman Skoropadsky, Ataman Krasnov and General Mannerheim succumbed to them. He was a man who could be trusted by the western Allies. However, he was not a free agent and above all lacked a firm character being easily influenced by two monarchist and germanophile intriguers, Generals Lukomsky and Romanovsky. These two apparently 'ruled' in Denikin's stead while the General preferred to occupy himself with military affairs. Widhoff was impressed by Generals Mai-Mayevsky (energetic and good administrator), Kutepov, Ulagay and Sidorin. But he did not think much of Generals Shkuro and Pokrovsky who seemed to him to be simple, youthful (28 and 30 year old) cossacks whose only claim to prominence was that they commanded very rich troops (loaded with looted valuables) and they themselves were millionaire generals.

While the army was reasonably well organized and commanded the political set-up was unsatisfactory. To devote himself to military questions Denikin appointed a Special Council to deal with political problems. But General Dragomirov, whom he appointed as President of the Council, was an unsuitable choice: he was authoritative, xenophobic and suffered from delusions of grandeur. He hated the Paris Russians and chose the monarchist Sazonov to be his envoy there. His adjutant, Colonel Chaykovsky was a germanophile who

158

strongly influenced Dragomirov in his anti-French attitudes. The rest of the Special Council was impotent. The Cadet members, Astrov and Fedorov, could only write memoranda for the Allies, but could do nothing practical. The Council was in constant conflicts with the Don and Kuban Cossack Radas (Councils) and the cossacks who were the stronger elements, dared not suppress the former, for it enjoyed 'Allied' recognition and support.

The British mission was vigorous in controlling the use of aid, but otherwise had no consistent policy. It supported Caucasian republics against General Denikin, but on the other hand would not tolerate Cossack opposition against him. It acted confidently in its zone and was critical of French withdrawal from Odessa. The Mission's criticism permitted General Dragomirov to launch his anti-French campaign after the withdrawal. Colonel Corbel was a lonely and ostracized figure in Ekaterinodar.[1] It is obvious that the report re-emphasized all the failures and weaknesses of French policy in southern Russia. But it also stressed that the Volunteer movement in general and many generals in particular, were worth French support and this is probably what Clemenceau wanted to hear. He now waited for a suitable moment to launch his new Russian policy.

In July 1919 General Denikin not only issued his notorious order of the day bidding his armies to take Moscow, but also began to plan further extension of his armies and military bases. He needed more military aid and British help with organizing the bases. He chose the Crimea as the most suitable territory and asked officially the British for help. Denikin did not realize that the Crimea was in fact in the French zone and no approach to the French was therefore made. The British still thinking in terms of the April Protocol acceded to Denikin's demands and on 1 August 1919 Lord Curzon asked Lord Derby to deliver a formal British note informing the French of this *fait accompli*. Lord Derby called at the Quai d'Orsay with the note on 2 August.[2] It is not clear what exactly happened to this note and what impression it made on Pichon. However, Clemenceau saw it officially only on 27 August when the *fait accompli* was executed by the local British commander. Thus the British established a Russian base in the French zone without prior consultation with the French. To Clemenceau this was the final challenge and he was determined to

[1] Le rapport du Capitaine Widhoff, 28 June 1919; Clemenceau to Franchet d'Esperey, 26 July 1919.

[2] Derby to Pichon, 2 August 1919; Curzon to Derby, 1 August 1919.

restore French influence in southern Russia by launching a new French policy which he had been considering for some time.

This new policy was drafted in August 1919 and was contained in the 'Note sur la Mission Française auprès du Général Denikine'. The note stated that the new policy was necessitated by the successes the Volunteer army which was then approaching Odessa and Kiev, and also by the British measures for the establishment of the new Russian base in the Crimea. It stated further that this new situation required a new, more powerful French mission to General Denikin: (comme les Anglais nous devons envoyer un General) like the British a General should be sent there. The Mission's aim should be three-fold: (i) Political: the re-establishment of French prestige with General Denikin and his government with whom at the moment relations were extremely unsatisfactory (facheusement tendues). (ii) Military: offer military adivce to the Volunteers, if asked for, and control French aid and (iii) Economic: defend French economic interests in Russia.[1]

These new French moves were launched at the moment when Franco–Volunteer relations had reached their lowest point, but also at the moment when the British began to show signs of restlessness. Though it was in May 1919 that General Dragomirov released the Volunteer 'Yellow Book' dealing with French 'betrayals' at Kherson, Nikolayev and Odessa, the French obtained a copy of this 'insulting pamphlet' at this time and protested most vigorously to the Volunteers and the British.[2] Furthermore the Denikin–Ukrainian conflict caused a flood of recriminations between the Volunteers and French, when the latter tried to conciliate between the two, and urged combined operations rather than mutual clashes.[3] They were rebuffed rather tactlessly by General Denikin, who, however, could again plead ignorance as excuse: previously he 'annexed' the Crimea and called the British into what was in fact the French zone. Now he was telling the French to mind their own business not realizing that the Ukraine was French business, indeed, because it was a part of the same French zone. Denikin's ignorance must have had a great mitigating effect on Clemenceau, for he never gave vent to his irritation on seeing France treated so badly by the Volunteers.

The British realized as early as June 1919 that Russia and British

---

[1] La note sur la Mission Française auprès du Général Denikine, août 1919.

[2] Pichon to Maklakov, 18 August 1919.

[3] Pichon to Clemenceau, 12 September 1919.

aid were becoming serious liabilities. But General Denikin's successes temporarily silenced misgivings and irritation. But Allied aid arrangements were so irrational that the British decided to challenge them once again. On 21 August 1919 Lord Curzon circulated a memorandum in which he spoke of disproportionate aid by Britain to non-bolshevik Russia. This unbalanced situation could not continue much longer; soon Britain would have to overhaul its aid policy to Russia.[1] While this memorandum expressed British dissatisfaction in general, other memoranda showed particular dissatisfaction with General Denikin. At the height of Denikin's successes the British remained sceptical. They justifiably pointed out Admiral Kolchak's fate and instead of enthusiasm began to tighten up control over British aid. On 2 September 1919 General Holman, Head of the British Military Mission and Denikin's supporter, openly criticized the Russians saying that they had been most wasteful with British supplies and equipment.[2] But when the Volunteers became involved in conflicts not only with the Ukrainians but also with the Rumanians and the Caucasian nationalities Britain's real interests were disturbed and signs of British impatience with Denikin began to multiply. By November 1919 Volunteer retreat from central Russia was in full swing and the British realized that once more they backed the wrong horse. From then on the British government anxiously waited for a suitable moment to pull out of Russia altogether. But in the meantime recriminations continued. To British reproaches the Volunteers replied with counter-accusations: the British forced on them certain strategic mistakes (the Tsaritsyn drive) and politically had several times undermined Volunteer morale. Denikin could not forget Lloyd George's Prinkipo proposals; but British secret approaches to the bolsheviks were also known to the Volunteers. When in November 1919 Lloyd George made a public allusion to the possibility of negotiations with the bolsheviks British prestige and influence in southern Russia reached its lowest ebb.

It was at this moment that Clemenceau chose to send his new, high-powered mission to General Denikin. Late in October 1919 the Quai d'Orsay made tactful enquiries at the foreign affairs section of Denikin's headquarters whether it would be propitious for Denikin to receive General Mangin, a war commander of high reputation, and his mission. On 1 November 1919 Head of the Section, Neratov,

---

[1] Curzon to Balfour, 21 August 1919.
[2] Holman to Churchill, 2 September 1919.

intimated that the mission would be welcome.[1] Within a week General Mangin was in southern Russia and Clemenceau had his first report. Mangin found out that both General Denikin and Romanovsky were francophiles and worthy of support. The Volunteers were badly in need of economic and military aid. Only the British and the Italians were helping a little, but if France wanted to replace British influence she only had to send military aid and the Volunteers would come to love her again.[2]

Perhaps Clemenceau was unaware of Volunteer–British tension, but the ease with which British influence could be supplanted certainly surprised him. Mangin who was equally surprised did not realize that the Volunteers had no choice but to fall back on the French, since the British became very cold, indeed, towards them. But obviously Clemenceau was not after an easy victory over the British, in Russia, though he probably wanted to oust them from there. He had two main reasons for wanting to act decisively in Russia in place of the British: 1. He was convinced that it was France's last chance to recoup some of her economic losses in Russia and 2. That he could achieve this recuperation by organizing the non-bolsheviks in Russia and Eastern Europe against the bolsheviks more efficiently. It is surprising that such an experienced politician as Clemenceau, could misjudge so completely the Volunteer movement. At the moment when the British considered it quite moribund Clemenceau hoped that by means of it he could accomplish the satisfaction of French economic interests. Undoubtedly Clemenceau's overall strategy for Eastern Europe was responsible for this misjudgement.

It is well known that Clemenceau did not favour the Foch plan for intervention in Russia when it was presented to the Allied Peace Conference early in 1919. However, with the failure of Admiral Kolchak, General Yudenich and General Denikin he began to see the merits of the plan. It was clear to him that separately the Russian non-bolsheviks could achieve nothing. But combined with the border nationalities, and especially with the Poles, who in June 1919 became the sole responsibility of France, they could achieve much. It is therefore in the light of this plan that Clemenceau's actions must be judged. Thus to knock out British influence with the Volunteers Clemenceau offered the latter a credit of 30 million francs. Though ultimately the Volunteers received very little aid from this credit it

[1] Neratov to Pichon, 1 November 1919.
[2] Mangin to Clemenceau, 7 November 1919.

opened the door to French influence and forced the Volunteers to follow French advice.

Though Marshal Foch envisaged in his military plan of intervention a combined front of Finns, Estonians, Latvians, Lithuanians, Poles, Ukrainians and Rumanians with the Volunteers thrown in in the south, Clemenceau's priority was a combined Polish–Volunteer offensive. He now instructed General Mangin to try and bring about a Russo–Polish *détente* which would ultimately be turned into an *entente cordiale*. Separate Volunteer–Polish actions could achieve nothing; a coordinated offensive would bring about bolshevik downfall.[1] But such a *détente* was greatly problematic, for the partners mistrusted each other very much. To start with the Volunteers were remarkably well misinformed about the Poles. It is true that they had their friends and agents sometimes in the highest spheres of Polish leadership but reliable intelligence was scarce. Thus on 1 October 1919 the Volunteer Warsaw agent reported that on the whole the Polish press was not hostile towards Russia (meaning the Volunteers) and since after all the Polish army was successfully fighting the bolsheviks the Volunteers should not be hostile to Poland.[2] But the same agent reported only a month later that the Polish War Council, with the exception of General Haller, voted to declare war on the Volunteers in September 1919 and was only dissuaded from actually doing so by the threats of the French and British Ambassadors who wanted to leave the country and cut off economic and military aid.[3] While this report was obviously an exaggeration of a debate within the Polish Military leadership it was widely accepted as true by the Volunteer leadership. No alliance was possible with such people; however, the true Polish position was even less favourable to an alliance with the Volunteers.

If the Volunteers distrusted the Poles the latter openly hated them. For the Poles the Volunteers were successors of the hateful tsarist Russia, and even the bolsheviks seemed less objectionable to General Denikin's movement. On 19 November 1919 the Volunteer agent in Warsaw summarized unwittingly the true Polish position towards Russia: the Poles wanted the bolsheviks to beat Denikin and Denikin to beat the bolsheviks.[4] Though this was correct, no one, least the

[1] General Staff Memorandum, 4 December 1919.
[2] Ibid., 1 October 1919.
[3] Ibid., 17 November 1919.
[4] Ibid., 19 November 1919.

French, believed that this attitude was inflexible, and General Mangin continued optimistically his efforts. On 4 December 1919 he urged Clemenceau to force the Poles to commence immediately an offensive against the bolsheviks in order to relieve pressure on the retreating Volunteers. As soon as the latter re-formed, a combined operation could be planned. Mangin went on to Taganrog and procured the British Mission's sanction for the combined plans. At the same time he met again General Karnicki whose mission had been with General Denikin since August 1919 and tried to infuse new life into it. Karnicki was by then convinced that the Poles could expect nothing from the Volunteers and was anxious to go back to Poland. Now Mangin optimistically suggested that the two sides should meet and negotiate in his house, on neutral ground and in his convivial presence come to some kind of agreement.[1] But nothing came of the meeting and though the French continued to reconcile the irreconcilables their efforts were doomed.

General Mangin's mission was ultimately a failure. He not only failed to bring the Volunteers and Poles together but also misinformed Clemenceau about Volunteer capacity. Mangin probably felt that he was competing with the British mission for influence with the Volunteers and this sence of competition made him send Clemenceau very curious reports. Thus according to Mangin General Denikin was a most impressive character. He and General Romanovsky were the staunchest francophiles in the Volunteer camp. While to the British they were rapidly fading weaklings, to Mangin they were political and war leaders worthy of French support.[2] He urged French support for them so strongly that even Clemenceau became suspicious. He planned for the Volunteers a minor rôle in his grand design for Eastern Europe and Mangin urged him to assign them the principal one. But Clemenceau decided to ignore Mangin's advice and the Volunteers, without solid support from both Allies, slowly wasted away.

By November 1919 the British became convinced that General Denikin and his volunteers could not win the civil war and began to draw logical conclusions from this finding. First of all, aid would be gradually stopped and the Volunteers would be encouraged to come to terms with the bolsheviks. While France was still thinking of giving the Volunteers limited aid and encouraging them to fight on, Britain definitely set out to close this embarrassing chapter of British

[1] Mangin to Clemenceau, 4 December 1919.
[2] Mangin to Clemenceau, 12 November 1919.

policy in Russia. On 14 November 1919 Lord Curzon appointed Professor Mackinder, MP as High Commissioner to the Volunteers.[1] Mackinder's appointment was in fact that of the liquidator; he made a long journey via Warsaw and Bucharest to southern Russia, was knighted *en voyage*, and returned to the United Kingdom within a month. He successfully told General Denikin that he would henceforth play a small part of the overall Allied intervention plan based on the border nationalities, that he would have to liberalize his internal régime in order to obtain Allied aid and support and that, since he could not win the war, he would have to conclude peace with the bolsheviks. Denikin was indeed in a difficult position and was willing to heed British advice in everything except the last. But for the British the last point was the only logical and meaningful one; they had no faith in either the grand design or in the internal reforms, for by January 1920, when Denikin declared himself for all these concessions, there was hardly anything left to reform. Mackinder therefore withdrew leaving Denikin to his unenviable fate.[2]

But the Volunteers' fate was sealed as early as December 1919 and not in southern Russia but in London. Early in December 1919 Clemenceau went to London to meet Lloyd George to iron out a number of political points between them; one of them was Russia. On 13 December 1919 France and Britain agreed on a common policy for Russia and Eastern Europe; since the policy of supporting the non-bolshevik Russians failed, they would no longer receive Allied support; instead, in order to prevent bolshevism from spreading out of Russia and in order to isolate Germany from Russia Allied support would go to the border states.[3] This agreement which in fact meant the abandonment of the non-bolsheviks was in a sense a return to Pichon's 'cordon sanitaire'. It was a design for static and defensive policy, but since this aspect of it was unsaid, it promised some interesting interpretations of the agreement and obvious differences in the future. From the beginning it was clear that Britain was prepared to abandon the Volunteers more than France, and while Clemenceau remained in power nothing really happened to demonstrate the Franco–British difference in emphasis. But on 18 January 1920 Clemenceau resigned when he failed in the election for Presidency, and his successor, Millerand, soon showed the British that he

[1] Curzon to Mackinder, 6 December 1919.
[2] Mackinder to Curzon, 21 January 1920.
[3] Anglo–French Meeting, London, Session 13 December 1919.

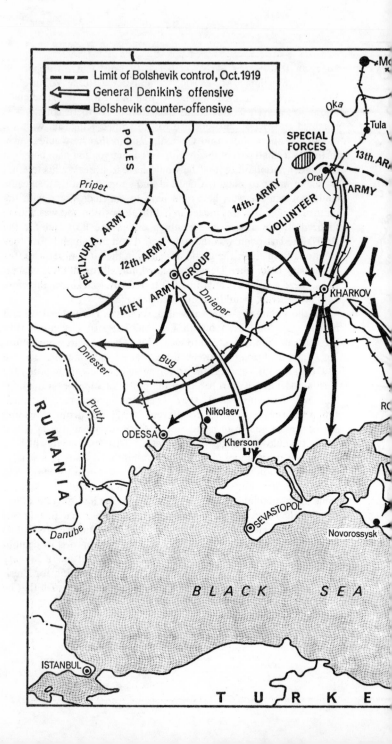

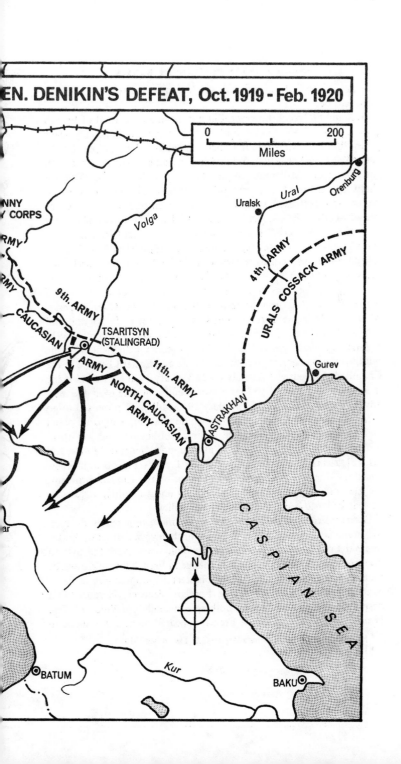

EN. DENIKIN'S DEFEAT, Oct. 1919 - Feb. 1920

0   200

Miles

NNY
CORPS

RMY

Volga

Uralsk   Ural   Orenburg

RMY

9th. ARMY   4th. ARMY

CAUCASIAN   URALS COSSACK ARMY

TSARITSYN
(STALINGRAD)

ARMY   11th. ARMY   Gurev

NORTH CAUCASIAN
ARMY

ASTRAKHAN

C A S P I A N   S E A

N

BATUM   Kur   BAKU

was much less disillusioned with the Volunteers than even Clemenceau had been.

Millerand's ascent, however, did not mean any reversal of French policy. He still believed that bolshevism had to be contained by means of the border states, but the containment could be helped by the remaining non-bolsheviks. While Clemenceau had almost written off the Volunteers, Millerand, despite the reverses they were suffering at that very moment, had a small rôle for them to play. The reasons for Millerand's increased support for the Volunteers were not to be found wholly in Russia itself. This ex-socialist had for internal reasons to support the non-bolsheviks more vigorously than Clemenceau; in the Chamber he was relying on right-wing support and at the time when France was having her own social and economic troubles he had to prove, right and left that he was a resolute opponent of bolshevism. But possibly the most important factor in Millerand's change of emphasis was the new Secretaire General at the Quai d'Orsay, Maurice Paleologue, former French Ambassador in Petrograd, and now Millerand's chief adviser in foreign affairs. On 23 December 1919 Clemenceau made his last anti-bolshevik policy statement when he outlined the new common plan for Russia and Eastern Europe in the Chamber of Deputies.[1] Already on 21 January 1920 Millerand made it clear in the Chamber that Clemenceau's outline was the new government's policy. On 5 February 1920 Millerand proposed to go even further than Clemenceau: he would not only support Poland and Rumania in their struggle against bolshevism and aid them directly, if attacked, but he would also support General Denikin and his Volunteers despite their reverses. In January 1920 Britain knew about the divergence of views with France on the Russian problem; the December agreement was in jeopardy and something had to be done in order to bring about a common policy.

But the Franco–British difference was more apparent than real. Millerand's strong statements were probably meant entirely for internal French consumption and the Volunteers were the first to discover that there was hardly any change in French attitude towards them.[2] On 6 February 1920 the Volunteer Plenipotentiary in Paris, Sazonov, telegraphed the acting Foreign Minister, Neratov, that despite Millerand's statements nothing concretely pro-Volunteer had been done. It is true that the French appeared more sympathetic to

[1] La session de la Chambre des Deputes, 23 December 1919.
[2] Ibid., 5 February 1920.

Volunteer views, but Russian finances in France were still frozen and the Volunteers could not use them to buy arms. However, there was one danger in France Sazonov feared most, namely that Millerand would follow Lloyd George's example and revise his Russian policy according to the British pattern. This meant a *de facto* recognition of the bolsheviks.[1] Sazonov was obviously right when he stated that Millerand despite his public proclamations would not be able to do much more for the Volunteers that Clemenceau was able to do. But he was obviously wrong when he thought that Millerand would follow the British and recognize the bolsheviks. Millerand could not afford the recognition politically without being open to criticism of pro-bolshevik sympathies and that would have been fatal to his career as Premier. Sazonov also exaggerated the British position, for Britain was not yet at the point of recognizing *de facto* the bolsheviks.

During February 1920, while the French and British discussed what should be done with the Volunteers, the British were still directly involved in south Russian affairs. It is true that with Mackinder's departure from Russia his mission as High Commissioner came to an abrupt end, but not only the British Military Mission was left behind, but also the special political representative, General Keyes, stayed on. British aid continued to arrive and to outer appearance Britain was still busy helping the Volunteers and not preparing their abandonment or downfall. In fact General Keyes was very busy helping General Denikin to come to an agreement with the Georgians and various other Caucasians, as well as with the Green Guards, who had had such a disastrous effect on his Moscow offensive.[2] In addition the British were supervising Denikin's implementation of his agreement with Mackinder to reform his internal system. The General rushed through a number of reforms, even against the opposition of his chief allies, the Don and Kuban cossacks. Thus he formed a new government based more widely on political parties but since he retained the premiership even this concession was thought as purely formal. All the same it prevented Britain from stopping completely aid which was still trickling in.[3] Denikin also showed willingness to recognize *de facto* the various succession states, such as Poland, the Baltic Republics and the Georgians and Armenians.[4] But here again

[1] Sazonov to Neratov, 6 February 1920.

[2] Percy to Churchill, 8 March 1920; Keyes to Curzon, 11 March 1920.

[3] Mackinder–Denikin Protocol, 10 January 1920.

[4] Denikin to Lukomsky, 14 January 1920; Curzon to Wardrop, 22 December 1919; Wardrop to Curzon, 6 January 1920.

the British proved unsuccessful: due to misunderstandings and sabotage no formal recognition by Denikin was announced. For all these concession Mackinder promised General Denikin that the British would evacuate all the 'compromised' officers and their families, if the situation in the Volunteer occupied territory became untenable. By March 1920 the situation was grave indeed, but Denikin relying on British undertakings refused to consider it so and then suddenly an internal intrigue removed him from the leadership.

To the last moment General Denikin had the British worried about his plans and intention. He had them guessing as to where he would evacuate from Novorossisk when this became necessary. The British wanted him and his Volunteers to go to the Crimea and not to Batum where he would have preferred to go. They feared that the bolsheviks would be drawn by him to attack Georgia and Armenia and thus had to spend many anxious days before Denikin declared that he would comply with British wishes. He was helped in making up his mind by an alleged monarchist plot he suddenly discovered. He saw General Keyes, explained to him the nature of the conspiracy and announced that he was dismissing Generals Dragomirov, Lukomsky and Wrangel, who apparently were the principal privies of the plot.[1] General Keyes was not enthusiastic about the dismissals, for he recognized that General Wrangel was the only capable field commander the Volunteers had, but acquiesced in the end. However, the dismissals did not prove sufficient to restore Denikin's position. While under pressure from the bolsheviks officers in the field began to sabotage Denikin's orders and operations. Something very drastic had to be done, if he was to reassert his leadership.[2] Denikin then tried the last remedy left to him and dismissed front-line officers in such numbers that no sabotage was necessary for his operations to go wrong. Seeing that all he had tried failed he decided to resign.

On 1 April 1920, a few days after his arrival in the Crimea from Novorossisk, Denikin called back his monarchist opponent, Dragomirov, and instructed him to convoke an officers council which would elect his successor.[3] After the election General Denikin would appoint the new leader by a public order and then leave Russia to go into exile. Since the Crimea was flooded with anti-Denikin officers it was clear that the General was serious about his resignation. He was

[1] Keyes to Curzon, 4 March 1920.
[2] C-in-C Mediterranean to Admiralty, 7 March 1920.
[3] Curzon to de Robeck, 1 April 1920; de Robeck to Curzon, 2 April 1920.

not even surprised when his bitterest opponent, General Baron Wrangel, was elected to succeed him. Sadly disappointed he immediately left the Crimea without any political or diplomatic gesture. He was a simple soldier to the last, who always disliked politics and always felt uneasy about diplomacy. His disappointment reached despair when his friend and fellow exile, General Romanovsky, was assassinated by a man in a Russian officer uniform as soon as they arrived at Istanbul. This was the gratitude that his Volunteer army for which he sacrificed his entire life, had shown him. Once again he left Istanbul a lonely figure without a country and a refugee under indifferent British guard.

His successor, General Wrangel arrived in the Crimea from his exile on 4 April 1920. He was an excellent field commander and as such had his conflicts with General Denikin. However, politically he was a dark horse. Somehow, probably because of his mastery, everyone, the liberals and the monarchists, the pro-German and the pro-Allied officers, had confidence in him and he proved reasonably successful when he finally took over power. However, it would have been difficult to be less successful than Denikin. Wrangel arrived at the Council with the copy of a British note telling the Volunteers of the termination of British aid to them. This was an irreparable blow and in practice meant the end of the Volunteer movement. But the note also contained other suggestions which offered a way out of the present impasse. The British wanted the new leader to come to terms with the bolsheviks and proferred their good offices with the latter.[1] Immediately Wrangel proved to be a much shrewder politician and more skilful diplomat than his predecessor. Though he was not at all optimistic about the Volunteers he decided to try his utmost against the bolsheviks with Allied aid. His first decision was to reply to the British note in the most conciliatory way throwing the onus of contacts with the bolsheviks on the British government. He was rightly convinced that Britain would no longer support him and his movement. But he could not afford an open rupture with her and her peace offer could come useful in the future.[2] With Britain out of the way Wrangel had to find a replacement and immediately turned to France. For the first time the Volunteers began to play one ally against the other and benefit from it. In many ways this was a natural move, but so far the Volunteers shied away from it for sentimental or possibly

[1] Curzon to Wrangel, 4 April 1920.
[2] Wrangel to Curzon, 4 April 1920.

still other reasons. Wrangel, however, cared more about victory than dignity and the task of exploiting Franco–British differences was an easy one.

VII

In December 1919 France and Britain came to an agreement about concentrating their efforts in Eastern Europe in the border states. This obviously meant that the Russian anti-bolsheviks would get less aid, but otherwise their fate was left undefined. It was also agreed that Poland would become the chief beneficiary of the policy change, but the reason for increased aid was again left out. Perhaps the Allies did not really think out the reasons, but it seems more probable that they thought them out incompletely. Within a month two interpretations of the agreement became apparent, one French and the other British.

The French had an excellent excuse for 'misinterpreting' the agreement, for Clemenceau who had negotiated it, disappeared from power. But his successor Millerand took over Clemenceau's plans and policies almost without a change and therefore could not use this excuse. On 14 January 1920 General Weygand on Foch's behalf. presented another intervention plan to Clemenceau; on 20 January Millerand was Premier and Foreign Minister, and the plan was accepted as the basis of French policy in Russia and Eastern Europe. It was not a strikingly new plan; if anything it was an improved variation of the old Foch Plan rejected by both France and the Allies in 1919. But conditions in Russia and Eastern Europe had changed so much that this variation had in it certain plausibility. The most important aspect of it was that it was an offensive plan, not a defensive one as the British had understood it. In fact it envisaged the annihilation of the bolsheviks by means of a Polish thrust into Russia. The Poles were to be protected on their flanks by the Baltic and Rumanian armies. After initial successes Ukrainian and non-bolshevik Russian forces would be thrown in to continue the drive towards the Dnieper. After consolidation and re-grouping a combined Polish and Volunteer operation against bolshevik central Russia would 're-establish order in Russia' (. . . en vue du rétablissement de l'ordre en Russie'' ..). But the plan had only a chance of success if the Allies stuck to their December agreement, maintained a firm attitude towards the bolsheviks, retained the unity of aims in Russia and continued common support of the Poles.[1]

The existence and the discussion of this plan in France indicates that the French completely misunderstood the British attitude to Russia, and Eastern Europe. But above all the British were not consulted about the plan, or at least they were not given details of it. Somehow the French thought that they were given a free hand in Eastern Europe by the British and went full speed ahead with the implementation of the plan; consequently differences soon became apparent. On 27 January 1920 Lloyd George received the Polish Foreign Minister, Patek, and tried to discourage him from taking hostile actions against the bolsheviks. Lloyd George went as far as to impress on Patek that Britain would prefer to see the Poles coming to terms with the bolsheviks.[2] The Poles had probably quite different intimations from the French and disappointed Patek told Millerand about contrary British pressure. On 5 February 1920 Millerand sent Lloyd George a cautious note in which he argued against a hasty peace between Poland and the Soviets. He did not absolutely reject the idea of peace negotiations but he strongly disapproved British pressure.[3] On 16 February 1920, after the Americans also expressed their misgivings, Millerand felt forced to explain himself to the Allies. In a note to Lloyd George he stated that France did not want to excite the Poles against the bolsheviks, and in fact urged them to adopt non-aggressive attitude towards them. But if Poland was attacked by the bolsheviks, France would give the Poles 'all the necessary assistance' (. . . toute son assistance . . .).[4] Millerand made it quite clear why France had an intervention policy against the bolsheviks; it was a preventive policy, for he firmly believed that the bolsheviks would soon attack in Eastern Europe, especially in Poland. The note also showed that France and Britain parted completely from a common policy. Millerand finally spelled out that France would actively support the Poles, the Rumanians, the Balts and the Volunteers, while Britain was thinking in terms of a passive political alliance and then peace with the bolsheviks. Once again without consultations each ally went its way.

The British now decided that they would pursue actively their policy of peace negotiations with the bolsheviks. It is true that

[1] Foch (Weygand) to Clemenceau (Millerand), 14 January 1920.
[2] Curzon to Rumbold, 27 January 1920.
[3] Millerand to Curzon, 5 February 1920.
[4] Millerand to Curzon and Lansing, 16 February 1920.

G   173

both France and Britain were secretly negotiating with the bolsheviks at Copenhagen, but these negotiations conducted by the special Soviet envoy, Litvinov, the British Minister and French Consul General, were limited to the exchange of prisoners.[1] When the French began to implement their 'offensive' plan the British began to implement the opposite. Taking as an excuse General Wrangel's consent to peace negotiations the British took the plunge. A cabinet decision on peace negotiations was not popular even at the Foreign Office; however, after some delay Lord Curzon sent a radiogram to Chicherin to enquire under what conditions the Soviets would be willing to terminate the civil war. He proposed an immediate cessation of hostilities in southern Russia and an amnesty for all enemy combatants.[2] This was obviously an exploratory sounding, but Chicherin's reply was swift indeed. On 14 April 1920, one day after Curzon's radiogram Chicherin said that the Soviets were interested in the proposals, but demanded direct negotiations between Litvinov and Curzon in London and release of Russian prisoners of war in Austria as a gesture of good will.[3] There followed a pause of three days, while the British were puzzling out Chicherin's cryptic demands. Chicherin radioed again on 17 April renewing his offer to negotiate and requesting an answer from London.[4] On 19 April the Foreign Office explained to Chicherin the delay; the Secretary of State was abroad and the reply had to wait for his return.[5] The bolsheviks were undoubtedly very anxious to pursue these peace proposals, for Chicherin radioed by return that the delays were no fault of the Soviet government.[6] On 24 April he finally received Curzon's reply in which Chicherin's suggestion for direct negotiations was rejected. The release of Russian PoWs in Austria had nothing to do with the problem under negotiation and the bolsheviks were bidden to confine themselves to southern Russia.[7] On 29th, after some hesitation, Chicherin asked Curzon if the Wrangel forces would surrender completely.[8] On 3 May Curzon assured Chicherin that they would indeed

[1] Sablin to Sazonov, 11 December 1919; Duchesne–Litvinov Agreement, 20 April 1920.
[2] Curzon to Chicherin, 13 April 1920.
[3] Chicherin to Curzon, 14 April 1920.
[4] Chicherin to Curzon, 17 April 1920.
[5] Curzon to Chicherin, 19 April 1920.
[6] Chicherin to Curzon, 20 April 1920.
[7] Curzon to Chicherin, 24 April 1920.
[8] Chicherin to Curzon, 29 April 1920.

surrender and urged him to make a direct approach to Wrangel and commence negotiations.[1]

But by now the bolsheviks began to hedge. On 5 May 1920 Chicherin agreed to the direct approach to Wrangel, but nothing much seems to have happened.[2] On 17 May Curzon had to urge Chicherin again to contact Wrangel.[3] Four days later Chicherin replied evasively that the bolsheviks were still considering the terms of the promised amnesty.[4] It is obvious that the bolsheviks originally agreed to negotiations with Wrangel in order to get him out of the way and then come to an agreement with the Poles. But when the Poles suddenly invaded the Ukraine and Wrangel remained passive, obviously out of weakness, they were not interested in further negotiations. It would be more convenient for them to deal with him after the Poles had been dealt with, and negotiations with Britain were broken off. However, negotiations would have been broken off for another reason, which the British failed even to consider, but of which they immediately took a good advantage.

Shortly before Chicherin's signals faded Lord Curzon found out that General Wrangel, whom he had tried to save, was planning to launch an offensive against the bolsheviks. At first no one could believe it; thus it took the British some considerable time to deliver their protest. But Wrangel's preparations went on and this apparent defiance was finally seized upon by the British as a pretext for a complete break with the moribund Volunteers. On 1 June 1920, too late to stop it, Curzon instructed the High Commissioner in Istanbul, Admiral Sir John de Robeck, to deliver an ultimatum to General Wrangel: if he launches the offensive, he can expect no more support from Britain.[5] Wrangel, who was kept informed about the progress of Anglo–Soviet negotiations, realized that his offensive would embarrass Britain, and all the same he wanted to avoid an open break. But in June 1920 he was convinced that Britain wanted to write him off completely.[6] He tried to explain his offensive as an attempt to feed his Crimean population; in any case the British ultimatum came too late to stop the offensive.[7] On 11 June 1920 the last act of

[1] Curzon to Chicherin, 3 May 1920.
[2] Chicherin to Curzon, 5 May 1920.
[3] Curzon to Chicherin, 17 May 1920.
[4] Chicherin to Curzon, 21 May 1920.
[5] Curzon to de Robeck, 1 June 1920.
[6] Seymour to Wrangel, 19 April 1920.
[7] Wrangel to de Robeck, 5 June 1920.

Anglo–Volunteer relations was played. Previously Volunteer forces successfully broke out of the Crimea into the Ukraine thus ignoring the ultimatum. Curzon therefore instructed de Robeck to withdraw the British Military Mission and break off all relations with the Volunteers.[1]

VIII

British withdrawal from southern Russia was in a sense a French victory. After all this was what Clemenceau was planning in June 1919, though perhaps he did not envisage such a total victory. But both the French and the Volunteers did anticipate British withdrawal; this anticipation became a certainty in April 1920 when General Wrangel was elected Volunteer leader. Wrangel had really no choice but to turn to the French and the French were quite willing to support him subject to certain conditions. He had to prove to them that he was a liberal and that his pro-German reputation was false. Wrangel thought that the latter was more urgent and acted immediately. The Crimean peninsula under General Denikin's Governor, General Schilling, became the refuge of all the pro-German elements, and above all officers, of the Volunteer movement. These officers were largely responsible for Wrangel's election as leader and they therefore expected something in return. But Wrangel was realistic enough to see that a pro-German policy was simply impracticable and thus, instead of rewarding the pro-German elements, he purged them. Quite resolutely Wrangel dismissed a number of pro-German officers and in their stead appointed officers with pro-French reputation.[2]

The purge in the army was extended to the Volunteer diplomatic corps, especially to the old representatives in Paris. The new people, who emerged from the purge, such as Struve and Basily, were not only more efficient but also *personae gratae* with the French in general, and with Millerand and Paléologue, in particular. As early as April 1920 the French decided to give Wrangel a chance and refused to support British negotiations with the bolsheviks which would inevitably involve them in recognizing the bolsheviks.[3] Instead they

[1] Curzon to de Robeck, 11 June 1920.

[2] *Staatsarchiv*, Vienna, Belgrade Embassy to Ministry of Foreign Affairs, 21 March 1920; esp. 18 October 1920.

[3] Maklakov to Struve, 1 May 1920.

began to plan the restitution of the Volunteer army, the transfer of Russian troops from various European territories to the Crimea and above all bring about closer Polish–Volunteer cooperation.[1] Millerand was still convinced that the Volunteers could become a valuable link in his military plans, and in time even in his political plan, in the 'cordon sanitaire'. On 7 May 1920 Paléologue told discreetly Krivoschein, an important Volunteer conservative, that France was willing to help actively Wrangel in his defence of the Crimea.[2]

General Mangin who had moved from the Kuban to the Crimea with the Volunteers was still in charge of the French Military Mission and he did his utmost to bring about Volunteer–Polish *rapprochement*. This *rapprochement* was indeed topical, for during May 1920 the Poles scored so many military successes in the Ukraine that it was quite possible that they would emerge at the approaches to the Crimea. According to the Weygand Plan this would have introduced the second stage of military operations against the bolsheviks. Mangin therefore wanted mutual political recognition and then military integration for the drive to Moscow. The former was no problem and Wrangel was ready to recognise Poland any time; but the Poles were much more reluctant to do likewise. The latter, quite unthinkable under General Denikin, looked like a probability, for Wrangel had no illusions about his grandeur, and was willing to subordinate himself and his armies to the Polish High Command. A start was made when the Bredov Corps was put under Pilsudski and fought successfully with the Poles in the Ukraine.[3] But there was the other stumbling block, the Ukraine, whose independence the Poles, and the Bredov Corps were indirectly upholding. In all these negotiations Wrangel proved an extremely skilful diplomat. He simply refused to be drawn into any political discussions on the Ukraine and showed great willingness to coordinate military plans with the Poles. He left the question of overall command to the French: they would have to clinch off any particular agreement themselves.[4] Still Mangin could see through these manoeuvres, and began to press Wrangel on concrete points of the agreement, especially on his attitude to the Ukrainians. The matter became urgent in view of the

[1] Krivoschein to Paléologue, 7 May 1920; Paléologue to Krivoschein, 8 May 1920; Memorandum on the Bredov Corps, 19 May 1920.
[2] Paléologue to Krivoschein, 7 May 1920.
[3] Trubetskoy to Struve, 28 May 1920.
[4] Trubetskoy to Mangin, 17 May 1920.

impending Volunteer offensive, which would probably bring them in contact with the Poles and the Ukrainians. Though the offensive was prepared in utmost secrecy, the French were kept informed.[1]

But Wrangel would not be forced into an awkward position; he would not make policy pronouncements until he reached a stage when this would be appropriate, and not before. Thus the French had to get accustomed to the unpleasant fact that Wrangel while recognizing his weakness would not be a puppet. The British, apart from other considerations, probably arrived to the same conclusion and acted in the opposite sense. General Wrangel had a British promise that, if necessary, British naval units in the Black Sea would come to his assistance. He counted on British naval support for his offensive. But when the British decided to withdraw their Mission it also meant the ships. While the naval commanders on the spot were most disinclined to leave, they were ordered to do so from London and obliged. On 6 June 1920 when the British decisions became known in Paris General Weygand requested immediate direct French aid to General Wrangel.[2] But while support in principle was promised immediately, actual aid was slow to arrive.

In June 1920 the French were preoccupied by the Polish situation. For them Poland was their first priority and they were willing to support Wrangel as much as it would relieve the Poles. But they had to be discreet so as not to upset the British too much. On 8 June 1920 Millerand received Struve and told him again that the British should not be antagonized. He promised French aid and requested cooperation with the Poles. However, both agreed that while the British would be kept happy by diplomatic manoeuvres, cooperation with the Poles could not wait. The Bredov Corps would definitely be transferred to the Crimea, but the Volunteers would have to start their offensive immediately.[3] On 21 June Millerand met Lloyd George at Boulogne and tried to impress on him the importance of General Wrangel for both the Polish situation and for negotiations with the bolsheviks. He obviously failed to carry with him the British ally, for next day Millerand alone stressed his support for the Wrangel government by declaring that it was 'a good and popular government.'[4]

[1] Maklakov to Neratov, 6 June 1920.
[2] Weygand to Millerand, 9 June 1920.
[3] Maklakov (Struve) to Neratov (Trubetskoy') 8 June 1920.
[4] Struve to Wrangel, 22 June 1920.

Britain and France now utterly disagreed on the handling of the situation in Russia and Eastern Europe. While the former wanted peace negotiations with the bolsheviks, the latter wanted to stop the Polish retreat and then by a combined operation defeat the bolsheviks before talking to them. Millerand needed Wrangel for this plan and the further the Poles retreated the more he was prepared to support him. On his return from Spa where again Poland was discussed he told the Wrangel representative in Paris that he would recognize South Russia as a government *de facto* and send a High Commissioner to the Crimea.[1] This promise was made against the explicit wishes of the British who wanted to start immediately negotiations with the bolsheviks on both Poland and southern Russia. But Millerand was determined to block any such negotiations. He told Struve that British proposals for peace negotiations would endanger military positions of both the Poles and the Volunteers and he would be no privy to such proposals.[2] However, now even the bolsheviks, encouraged by their victories in Poland turned a deaf ear to British proposals and France felt free to declare open support of Wrangel. On the eve of Millerand's declaration the Volunteers delivered a special note at the Quai d'Orsay emphasizing their importance for the Polish situation. They claimed that their offensive had kept sixty-three infantry and thirty-two cavalry divisions in southern Russia. With this force in the west the bolsheviks could have finished the Poles.[3] But the note was unnecessary; Millerand was ready to make a public announcement: all the same before he made it he once again consulted the British. On 27 July 1920 Millerand met Lloyd George again and because of the gravity of the situation in Poland wrested from him a more flexible attitude towards Wrangel and more rigorous attitude towards the bolsheviks. When on 4 August Marshal Foch urgently requested emergency supplies for the Volunteers Millerand approved the request and on 11 August 1920 recognized the Wrangel government as the *de facto* government of southern Russia. The recognition was obviously a triumph of Volunteer diplomacy and their hopes were raised again. But they needed both Allies and with Britain out of the picture Wrangel found himself in Denikin's position: he was now a 'French General' as Denikin before him was a 'British General'. The Volunteers were completely dependent

[1] Basily to Struve, 11 June 1920; Millerand to Basily (undated, 10? July).
[2] Neratov to Struve, 20 July 1920; Basily to Neratov, 22 July 1920.
[3] Basily to Paléologue, 23 July 1920.

on French good will and even their interests were negotiated and furthered by the French Prime Minister.[1]

Apart from the diplomatic triumph the most important short term benefit of the recognition was the French promise of immediate military aid. To begin with it looked as if the French really meant business. They put real pressure on the Rumanians to release the Russian war stores which had been in Rumanian custody since the Brest–Litovsk Peace in 1918.[2] The Rumanians gave way and promised to send these stores to General Wrangel in the Crimea in time for his Kuban offensive. But as previously difficulties cropped up and the arms and equipment arrived too late and in insufficient quantity. But in Paris Marshal Foch took an optimistic view of the supply situation in the Crimea. He told Millerand that measures had been taken to assure the 'satisfactory solution of the supply problem'.[3] On 19 August 1920 Foch asked General Miller, Wrangel's military attaché in Paris, to keep him informed daily of the Wrangel army requirements.[4] The French High Command even went as far as to plan combined Polish–Volunteer operations, but without encouragement from Millerand. After the failure of Wrangel's offensive in the Kuban area Millerand became very cautious towards the Volunteers.[5]

The Kuban failure had shaken Millerand considerably. The British had constantly warned him that this would inevitably happen. But Millerand disregarded these warnings as long as there was the slightest hope. His recognition of Wrangel and military measures were taken against fierce British opposition. By August 1920 Franco–British disagreements on this subject reached such a pitch that the French ceased to consult the British and mutual relations reached another point of crisis. The British dissociated themselves completely from French policy and protested to the unbelieving bolsheviks that they had nothing to do with General Wrangel and his movement.[6] In the meantime the situation in Poland improved and the

---

[1] Basily to Neratov, 3 August 1920; Foch to Millerand, 4 August 1920; Wrangel's call for recognition and acceptance of French conditions in Trubetskoy to Struve, 31 July 1920.

[2] Foch to Millerand, 20 August 1920.

[3] Basily to Paléologue, 3 August 1920; Foch to Millerand, 24 August 1920.

[4] Foch to Miller, 19 August 1920.

[5] Struve to Maklakov, 1 September 1920; Foch to Millerand, 11 September 1920.

[6] Curzon to Grant-Watson 'for Litvinov', 6 August 1920.

bolsheviks were in full retreat. It was obvious that they would turn next on the Volunteers; the question was could they save themselves as the Poles did before them? Millerand was still determined to help them, but this time his aid would have to be more discreet, for he would not engage himself fully on Volunteers' behalf, as a distinct possibility of their defeat loomed large. The French High Commissioner arrived at Sevastopol and pledged again French support. But at the same time Paléologue had a long talk with Prince Basily, the Russian chargé d'affaires, in Paris. He strongly urged the Volunteers to drop any plans of offensives. They should consolidate and increase their forces, dig in, construct suitable defences and wait.[1] The French were obviously at a loss as to what to do with the Volunteers. The British now warned them for the last time: they received a secret report which claimed that the Wrangel army was on the verge of collapse.[2] But the French were too deeply involved to pull out. At the same time short of a direct French involvement only a miracle could save the Volunteers.

As long as Millerand remained Prime Minister France would not treat with the bolsheviks and would continue to aid the Volunteers morally and materially. But even moral support would be limited. In turn Millerand did not hesitate to put pressure on the Poles to help the Volunteers. He instructed the French Ambassador in Warsaw, Panafieu, to request the Poles to delay the signature of the peace treaty with the bolsheviks as long as practicable to detain as many bolshevik troops on the Polish front as possible. This particular move was however misinterpreted by the Volunteers; they came to believe that the French would not permit the Poles to sign a peace with the bolsheviks at all. They therefore went on with the planning of combined Polish–Volunteer operations even when it was clear to everyone that there would be a peace treaty between Poland and the Soviets. Somehow General Wrangel expected the French to make greater gestures towards him and could not understand Millerand's caution. In September 1920 the most urgent Franco–Volunteer supply negotiations began to drag. It is probable that by then the French came to the conclusion that the Volunteers were a dying force and that it would be wasteful to send them further military supplies. General Wrangel, however, thought that the difficulties were only technical and since he needed the supplies most urgently

[1] Paléologue to Basily, ? September 1920.
[2] Foreign Office Memorandum, 16 September 1920.

he offered to come to Paris in person to speed them up. Though Marshal Foch urged Millerand to receive the General, Millerand replied with a firm 'fin de non-recevoir'.[1]

In any case the Volunteers, even in their desperate situation, were no easy ally. Throughout August and September 1920 intensive talks were going on between the French and the Volunteers on military aid. Extensive Volunteer requirements were compiled and the problem of credits tackled in many ways. The French, however, fearing further economic losses were most reluctant to send any supplies to the Crimea without cash payment. In the end discussions centred on a million franc *insured* loan, but were brought to nought by a curious leak. On 30 August 1920 the *Daily Herald* suddenly published an apocryphal text of the 'Franco–Volunteer Economic Treaty' which gave exorbitant advantages to France. The text as well as the existence of such a treaty were most emphatically denied by the Quai d'Orsay.[2] There were no further negotiations with the Volunteers after this 'leak' and Millerand felt further justified in his caution.

In October 1920 when it was quite clear that the Volunteers would collapse under the first attack from the bolsheviks the French had a chance to abandon the sinking ship of the Volunteer movement. Millerand resigned as Prime Minister on his election to Presidency and the new Premier, Leygues, could have changed his policy towards Russia: but he refused to do so. On 22 October 1920 he received the indefatigable Struve and promised him his personal support in aid of negotiations then again under way.[3] He refused to recall the French Mission though by now it was in danger of being captured by the bolsheviks. But de Martel's stay in the Crimea lasted exactly three weeks. The bolshevik offensive was imminent and its consequences were incalculable. On 23 October 1920 de Martel together with Admiral de Bon and General Brousseau promised General Wrangel full French assistance in the coming battle, but Wrangel could see that this was really moral encouragement.[4] When on 4 November the bolsheviks drove through the outer defences of the Crimea he ordered preliminary evacuation. On 10 November he

[1] Millerand to Foch, September 1920.

[2] Basily to Neratov, 25 September 1920; 27 September 1920; Maklakov to Neratov, 15 October 1920.

[3] Basily to Struve, 25 and 27 September 1920; Maklakov to Tarishchev, 22 October 1920.

[4] Martel–Wrangel Interview, 23 October 1920.

told Admiral Dumesnil that all was lost; the Frenchman promised that he would help with the evacuation of the Volunteer forces and their dependents in every possible way.[1] France remained determined to help the Volunteers and stand by them to the last.

On 17 November 1920 all the Volunteers and their families embarked on the Franco–Volunteer ships and set sail for Istanbul. The evacuation was perfectly organized and for the last time Franco–Volunteer cooperation proved most successful. But with the disappearance of the organized struggle in Russia a new phase in Allied–bolshevik relations was ushered in.

[1] Dumesnil to Wrangel, 11 November 1920.

CHAPTER SEVEN

POLAND, THE ALLIES
AND THE BOLSHEVIKS

I

Many Soviet historians call the 1920 campaign against Poland 'the last march of the Allies against Soviet Russia'. But even they must be conscious of the simplifications they are committing by labelling the war operations against the Poles in this manner. Firstly, they can hardly substantiate this claim with documentary evidence. Secondly, they deal with a complicated enemy, Marshal Pilsudski, and even more complicated Allied foreign policies, which make their claims look often contradictory and sometimes unrealistic.

Thus to unravel the complexities of the Polish episode and demonstrate the implausibility of Soviet arguments it will be necessary to follow the development of Allied–Polish relations from their very beginnings in 1918. Pilsudski will obviously be the key to all the problems, and in this context it is important to remember that Polish struggle for independence was directed from two centres, Paris and Warsaw. During the war the latter was under German control; Pilsudski who dominated it was therefore in a sense on the other side in the war.

Allied–Polish relations began in the accepted sense after the collapse of Germany on 9 November 1918. It is true that France and Great Britain had dealt with Poland before the armistice, but these dealings concerned mainly friendly, pro-Allied Poles centred on Paris. Thus on 5 January 1918 Lloyd George promised the pro-Allied Poles independent Poland and on 1 June 1918 France and Britain pledged themselves publicly to establish a unified and independent Poland.[1] But these promises were certainly not directed at the Regency Council or even at the Polish government after the armistice had been signed. In fact the Allies cold-shouldered the Warsaw Poles and gave them to understand that they were not the real representatives of Poland.

Naturally the Poles on the spot had an incalculable advantage over the Poles in Paris, or even in America, but since they fought for a

[1] Extracts from War Aims Index of Statements by Allied, Enemy and Neutral Countries and Subject Nationalities, Lloyd George, 5 January 1918.

common gaol Dmowski and his Paris associates did not want to push their claim to precedence over the collaborating Poles too far so as not to harm Poland itself. Pilsudski's arrival in Warsaw from a German prison helped to bridge the differences between the two centres. On 10 November 1918 the German appointed Regency Council named Pilsudski Head of State and dissolved itself. The appointment was made primarily for internal reasons, for Pilsudski was then the only person capable of preventing a civil war from breaking out in Poland. But to a certain extent the appointment was dictated by the necessity of having the least compromised Pole as Head of State capable of a compromise with the 'foreign' Poles and skilful enough to deal successfully with the victorious Allies. Pilsudski was supposed to have these qualities and while at home his prestige and leadership could not be doubted, in foreign affairs he was in a difficult position. The Allies could, if they wished so, use their Poles against him and thus delay the consolidation of post-war Poland. However, both Dmowski and Pilsudski realistically recognized their mutual need of each other and soon struck a bargain.

The Allies were extremely suspicious of Pilsudski. It would be wrong to say that they did not know him and the forces he represented, but the more they knew of him the greater their suspicions became. Pilsudski and his C-of-S, Colonel Sosnkowski became notorious when in 1916 they refused to swear allegiance to the German Governor of Poland, General von Beseler, while in command of the German sponsored Polish Legions. Afterwards they both went to prison in Germany, but contact with them was not lost altogether. Their deputy in Poland, Colonel (later Marshal) Rydz-Śmigly made several attempts to get in touch with western Allies. He was then in charge of the Polska Organizacija Wojskowa, an underground organization, destined to become the nucleus of the future Polish army. In August 1918 Rydz-Śmigly went to Moscow to meet Colonel Lavergne, the French Military Attaché, and discussed with him military problems. However, he had not come to Moscow to negotiate nor sign an agreement pledging his forces to fight on the Allied side and thus his organization and its clandestine leaders, Pilsudski and Sosnkowski, remained on the list of suspect organizations.

Rydz-Śmigly's refusal to engage his organization in an open struggle against the Germans was dictated by the necessity of preserving at least one military force intact and capable of action on German collapse. Even the reluctant French must have seen his reasons, for they knew of several precedents which ended rather badly for the Poles. In February 1918 Colonel Haller, who commanded the Austro–Polish Legion, had broken through the front with his troops and surrendered to the Russians.[1] Haller thought that he and his men would join the other Polish Corps in the Ukraine, but in May 1918 the Germans caught up with the Corps, defeated and dissolved it.[2] Though Colonel Haller and some of his soldiers were evacuated to France, they ceased to be both military and political factors in Poland and justifiably Rydz-Smigly wanted to avoid similar suicide for his organization. But the French disliked this caution and to help the underground Poles to decide to come out and fight, they heaped honours and influence on unsuccessful Haller. He was promoted General and in November 1918 appointed GCO of the four Polish divisions formed in and equipped by France.

But politically Rydz-Šmigly's refusal was justified. An open combat with the Germans would have destroyed the last Polish military instrument and create conditions for chaos in Poland. The other objection, namely that the Warsaw Poles were too pro-German to fight them, was probably exaggerated. On the whole the Poles divided their hatreds about equally between the Russians and the Germans. But undoubtedly there was an element of truth in this accusation and the Allies could not but notice that when the armistice became effective and Pilsudski was back in Warsaw, he allowed von Beseler to depart practically unhindered. Between 10 and 19 November 1918 German troops in Poland were peacefully disarmed and Pilsudski made it clear that he would not permit any violent incidents. These actions made the most unfavourable impression on the Paris Poles, but also puzzled the Allies. They came to believe Dmowski that Pilsudski was pro-German, but this belief did not remove Pilsudski from power. Dmowski at first thought that perhaps he could get rid of Pilsudski in this way and remembering his socialist past accused him of being infected with bolshevism, which was patently false. But the accusations failed to rouse the Allies to action and the Poles were left to fight it out among themselves.

However unfavourably the Paris Poles and the Allies might have thought of Pilsudski, in Poland he was an absolute master of the country. He not only rid Poland of the collaborating Regency Council

[1] Panouse to Clemenceau (General Barter to Lord Milner), 18 February 1918; Wardrop to Milner, 4 March 1918.

[2] Summary of Intelligence, 13th series, No. 10, 12 March 1918.

but also prevented his fellow-socialists from staking their claim for the control of the new state thus probably precipitating a civil war. Thus at home all the Polish political parties with minute exceptions were prepared to work under Pilsudski, and only under him. But Pilsudski was lucid enough to see that this was not sufficient: Poland needed international recognition and he could not obtain it, or better obtain it sufficiently quickly, solely by keeping Poland internally stable and under his control. He needed above all Allied recognition and support and there was no other way to obtain it but by striking a bargain with Dmowski and the Poles in Allied countries. Needless to say that he had tried to do without it; on 26 November 1918 Pilsudski as C-in-C of the Polish forces sent a situation report on Poland to Marshal Foch, the Supreme Allied C-in-C.[1] But this gesture of submission to the Allies and effort at dealing with them directly failed. Dmowski was strong enough to outmanoeuvre Pilsudski abroad, but Poland's position at the Peace Conference would have been even more unfavourable, had they not reached an agreement. As it was, an 'American' Pole, Paderewski, stepped in and with the powerful backing of President Wilson proposed a compromise. Since both parties were willing Paderewski set out to effect it personally. On 26 December 1918 he left Paris with the Allied (Franco–British) Mission for Warsaw passing through Pozań, Dmowski's political bastion. His aim was the 'fusion of domestic and foreign Polish forces in a new Poland'.

As previously with Pilsudski, Dmowski would not give up without a struggle. Though Paderewski's was a peace mission Dmowski's supporters were determined to exploit it to strengthen their own hand in negotiations with Pilsudski. On arrival at Poznań Paderewski and the Allied Mission witnessed demonstrations and riots in favour of Dmowski. Though the Pilsudski authorities easily suppressed them they were clearly warned. Paderewski reached Warsaw only to find out about a *coup d'état* against Pilsudski. Prince E. Sapieha and Colonel M. Januszajtis led a rebellion against the Head of State on 4 January 1919, but the coup collapsed next day. At the time it was said that Pilsudski provoked it prematurely in order to show Paderewski that he really was master of Poland. Thus Dmowski's failures prepared the way for a compromise, for both sides now realized that they could not do without each other but would derive great advantages from acting in concert.

[1] Pilsudski to Foch, 26 November 1918.

On 13 January 1919 Pilsudski recognized Dmowski as the head of the combined Polish delegation to the Peace Conference in Paris. Then on 16 January Paderewski was appointed by Pilsudski Prime Minister of Poland. This was a great victory for Pilsudski for without surrendering any power he pacified two of his most serious opponents-rivals. With Dmowski and Paderewski as his representatives he finally obtained international recognition of Poland which he so desired. But the compromise had also a calming effect on home politics. On 26 January 1919 a general election took place and Dmowski's National Democratic Party emerged as the strongest single party in the new Sejm. Its member, W. Trampczynski, was elected Speaker, but no other political changes took place. Paderewski remained Prime Minister and Pilsudski, who on 20 February 1920 lay down his powers as Head of State and Commander-in-Chief, was reinvested with them by the Sejm.

In the long run the Pilsudski-Dmowski compromise paved the way for the division of interests. Pilsudski had a free hand at home and in the unsettled 'Polish' east, while Dmowski reigned supreme abroad and in the 'Polish' west. But the compromise would not have been effective if the partners did not stick to it in their respective spheres. Soon Pilsudski, who had some interesting ideas about the rearrangements in the east, came into conflict with the Allies. Dmowski, who did not care much about the east, loyally defended him and was in turn upheld by Pilsudski when he demanded German concessions to Poland in the west. However, of the two Dmowski realized more clearly that no Polish eastern policy was possible without Allied support. Pilsudski made several efforts to prove this false and it took him over two years to learn the lesson.

II

Many Polish historians when dealing with the problem of Allied–Polish relations have come to the conclusion that Poland fitted into post-war Allied planning only in so far as it served as a buffer between Russia and Germany, or possibly as the cornerstone of the 'cordon sanitaire' against bolshevism. In Allied plans Polish national aspirations hardly counted and at best were coincidental. Thus they rightly point out that the Franco–British Agreement on Russia of December 1917 assigned Poland to France without the slightest regard to the Poles and their wishes. They further thought that because of this arrangement Britain was persistently anti-Polish. But even Allied plans for intervention in Russia were made out without any reference to Polish interests. Marshal Foch's plan envisaged Poland as a base for the re-constitution of Russia which to the Poles who had gained independence on Russia's ruin, seemed incredible and ridiculous. Hence they were most reluctant to be drawn into this Allied intervention. But all these objections are really misinterpretations of Allied policies. The Allies genuinely wanted independent Poland and publicly committed themselves to this aim. During the war and even after, the Allies could not consult the Poles about their views on intervention in Russia or the rearrangement of Eastern Europe, for there was no common Allied policy, each ally formulating and pursuing its own national policy. France's inclusion of Poland in her sphere of influence rested more on her claim to influence in Poland on account of the Haller army rather than on the Franco–British Convention. After all France had formed and equipped that army and was naturally determined to control it even after it was transferred back to Poland.

These misinterpretations perhaps come out best of the British 'Memorandum on Our Present and Future Military Policy in Russia'. The treatment of Poland within this Russian context is natural and has no national or political implications. What later became known as the Foch Intervention Plan appears in this memorandum as one of three possibilities to be discussed, adopted or rejected. The British were inclined to reject the Foch variant, for it placed a great burden on the border states which in British views could not be relied upon either politically or militarily. Poland's interests or aspirations are never mentioned, for they were unknown to the British. In fact very little was known about the Poles: Pilsudski figures nowhere as C-in-C and only the 'Russian' General Dowbor is singled out and his reforms and reorganization of the Polish army are discussed. The British estimated that Poland had only some 70,000 reliable troops of which General Haller's French equipped army formed about a half; it therefore could not be counted upon to be either a base or a decisive instrument of the Allied intervention in Russia.[1] Thus the British had written off Poland as early as November 1918. Subsequently they objected to the French proposals and Foch's plan was rejected by the Council of Five in January 1919. With the failure of a common Allied policy Poland was dropped by both Allies as a

[1] General Sir H. Wilson, Memorandum on Our Present and Future Military Policy in Russia, 13 November 1918.

power factor for the intervention against the bolsheviks until December 1919.

The chief reason for discarding Poland as an intervention factor by the Allies was its military weakness. But this weakness was relative, for in the chaotic conditions of Eastern Europe conventional military calculations were inapplicable. In fact the small and badly equipped Polish army was the only serious force in that area and the Poles were very conscious of it, though it took the Allies almost two years to discover it. Now left alone and without intervention commitments Pilsudski began to think of using his army for his own purposes; the British labelled these purposes 'national aggrandizement' while the Poles considered them as 'just historical retribution'. But as soon as Pilsudski made public his eastern interests and began to take steps to implement them, he disturbed the peace of the area still further, and this automatically provoked Allied opposition to his plans. In February 1919 the Poles clashed with the bolsheviks in Byelorussia for the first time; in April 1919 it was Lithuania's turn. The armed conflict with the Ukrainians which broke out in 1918, reached its climax and violent solution at this time. By all these actions Pilsudski was proving to the Allies that they miscalculated his strength; but by the total disregard of Allied views and wishes Pilsudski was also acquiring the reputation of being a Polish warrior bent on imposing his will on Eastern Europe. This illusion of grandeur and the complications it created in Eastern Europe were the root of Allied resentment and lack of sympathy towards the Poles. Thus throughout 1919 Pilsudski acted on his own, certainly without British encouragement and definitely against French intentions.

France had her own policy and well-thought out plans and for the French Pilsudski should have considered himself honoured to be part of them. Since France invested so heavily in Polish independence in the form of the Haller army she felt justified in expecting the Poles to cooperate with the French in carrying out the idea of the 'cordon sanitaire'. But Pilsudski refused to be what he thought was a tool of the French, and by his actions upset the other components of the cordon sanitaire. France wanted a solid alliance of the border states, the Baltic states with Poland, Rumania, the non-bolshevik southern Russian and the Caucasian states. Instead Pilsudski's actions antagonized the Lithuanians, and even the Latvians, definitely the Ukrainians and even the Rumanians not to mention the Russian Whites. There could be no cordon sanitaire while the participants were fighting each other. But Pilsudski managed to quarrel also with the Czechs over the Cienszyn (Těšín) territory and the French were ready to teach him a lesson.

After all, France still possessed a trump card in the Haller army and Pilsudski was well aware of its importance. On 14 February 1919 the French representative at the Peace Conference, Ambassador Noulens, proposed that an Allied commission be sent to Poland to supervise the 'correct use' of Polish troops hinting thus rather obviously at the future employment of the Haller army which was awaiting repatriation.[1] The French struck in the most sensitive spot, the army, and would undoubtedly have carried the day if they really pressed their attack home. Pilsudski needed this army and its equipment very badly; without it he would be forced to pause with his actions. But he was also determined to avoid French control which was the first step for the French to tame him and make him fall in with their plans. In Paris it was argued that before releasing the Haller army a special French mission should precede it to help the Poles to reorganize their army in Poland. On 11 March 1919 Colonel Henrys was chosen to lead the mission, but after long and skilful manoeuvring the Poles managed to counter the French bid for control of the Polish army and General (*en mission*) Henrys left for Poland in purely advisory capacity.[2] After this failure the French simply gave up the Poles and the 'cordon sanitaire' for the time being. In April 1919 Haller went home with his troops and full equipment and other smaller Polish detachments from Russia were also repatriated to Poland. Thus Pilsudski was doubly victorious: he fended off a French attempt at controlling him and at the same time gained the forces he needed to implement his own policies in Eastern Europe.

III

On 3 March 1919 the Polish delegation in Paris presented its demands to the Peace Conference and had most of them squarely rejected. Dmowski had failed to convince the Allies that it was just that the new Polish state should inherit the old kingdom's historical frontiers. If Polish demands were granted Poland would have become another Austria–Hungary, a multi-national republic. But the Allies and per-

[1] Peace Conference Session, 14 February 1919.

[2] Peace Conference Session, 11 March 1919; General Sir H. Wilson, Appreciation of the International Situation in Russia, Section Poland, 2 January 1919.

haps even Dmowski, thought that this was impracticable; Pilsudski not only thought the contrary but was now prepared to try his plans out. He was a Lithuanian Pole, with intimate knowledge of the area: he observed the chaos after the collapse of Russia and after the withdrawal of Germany from this area and became convinced that Poland could and should step in and replace the two powers. According to his idea Eastern Europe could be pacified most effectively by means of a Polish-dominated confederation. The confederation rested on two foundations: the unifying factors were (i) The common cultural element based on the historical presence of Poland and (ii) The fear of bolshevism (or for that any new Russian régime). All the peoples concerned had tasted in the past the higher culture of Poland and he therefore expected the Lithuanians, Latvians, Estonians, Ukrainians, Tartars and Byelorussians to gravitate towards his confederation in their own cultural interests. He thought that the second factor would operate even more strongly in his favour than the first, for by 1919 all these nations had tasted the 'barbaric' occupation by the bolsheviks and would necessarily be drawn into this grouping for protection. Poland would be the natural leader as it was the most historical nation of them all and also militarily most powerful. From the East European point of view there was plenty of logic in Pilsudski's plan, but to the Allies it was an illusion and a dream and they resolutely opposed it.

The plan had many weak points. First of all, these new arrangements in the East were far from being unanimously endorsed by the Poles; in fact many opposed and ridiculed them. Then it seemed questionable that all the nationalities would gravitate so naturally towards the confederation; many of them perhaps thought of the Poles as the alternative to the Russian oppressor. Only few of them were conscious of a common culture but many were aware of historical differences. But these considerations apart, the important fact was that Pilsudski himself was convinced of the practicability of his project and as the head of a powerful state his conviction certainly carried weight: only experience could prove to him whether he was right or wrong and he was ready to try. On 8 April 1919 Pilsudski wrote to his friend, L. Wasilewski, on the way he would carry out his Eastern plans: he would soon be ready for the solution of the Lithuanian and Byelorussian problem 'with a revolver in my hand.'[1] The confederation would be forged with iron and order

[1] Pilsudski to Wasilewski, 8 April 1919.

would be created with military might. On 12 April 1919 Pilsudski announced his intentions publicly in Paris. Paderewski, another 'Eastern' Pole, laid before the Commission for Polish Affairs his plea (Pilsudski Plan) for the creation of the United States of Eastern Europe. Simultaneously Pilsudski launched a series of military offensives; by 19 April he controlled Vilno and Lida. On arrival of the Haller army the Ukrainian problem was solved. On 14 May Pilsudski launched an offensive against the Ukrainians in eastern Galicia and drove them beyond the river Zbrucz. He then tried to negotiate with them, but negotiations soon collapsed, for the Ukrainians were still capable of a counter-attack. General Bredov's forces advanced against the Poles, but were too weak to keep up pressure. On 15 July Pilsudski counter-attacked and overran the whole of Galicia. He then switched his operations to Byelorussia and on 8 August took Minsk, the capital. The advance then continued towards Borisov and Bobruisk. This was Pilsudski's exemplification of the solution 'with a revolver in my hand'. As soon as he defeated decisively the Ukrainians in Galicia, he offered them an armistice and new peace negotiations. He was to employ this two-pronged tactics elsewhere, but it really worked with Petlyura's Ukraine only. The armistice was followed by an agreement in August 1919; Hetman Petlyura was in grave difficulties being attacked by the bolsheviks, Volunteers and the Poles at the same time. For varied reasons both sides then began to talk of closer cooperation, but it had to wait until April 1920, and even then it was not real. The Poles had always treated the Ukrainians as defeated opponents; the master-suppliant attitude could never produce real cooperation. Nevertheless, the agreement with the Ukrainians was the first success of Pilsudski's eastern policy.

By September 1919 Pilsudski reached the limit of his military capability; up to then Polish victories were relatively easy. Despite shortages in military equipment, food and other supplies the Polish army marched on defeating the raw or unorganized forces of their opponents. But even policing this extensive, newly acquired territory stretched the Polish capacity to its limits. For further expansion and decisive defeats of the bolsheviks, Pilsudski needed more equipment and ammunition, and could only get them from the western Allies. Thus his independent action had to come to a halt and Allied wishes had to be re-considered. Pilsudski also miscalculated and now had to pay the price: he was forced to modify his tactics.

Poland's great weakness was always the question of supplies. To start with Pilsudski hoped that he would be able to use the equipment left behind by the withdrawing Germans. But somehow they refused to hand over arms and ammunition to the Poles, and even Foch's intervention did not improve the situation. Then in January 1919 Pilsudski tried to lay his hands on Hungarian arms and equipment. He sent negotiators to Budapest and though he found Colonel Vyx, French High Commissioner, willing, nothing came of this move.[1] As time went on and supplies became short, frantic efforts were made to buy equipment elsewhere and reached a climax in July 1919. The Poles had tried to buy arms in Danzig, Berlin, Paris, Washington, Belgrade and the Hague and failed everywhere.[2] The realization of dependence on the Allies then forced Pilsudski to a *volte face*. His final objective, the confederated Eastern Europe, still remained, but was much less stressed, while the danger of bolshevism was seized upon and exploited.

On 14 September 1919 Paderewski made a peculiar gesture in Paris. He offered Lloyd George a Polish army of 500,000 men to march on Moscow for £600,000 sterling. The Allies who suspected that sooner or later the Poles would run out of ammunition and would turn back to them, were all the same suitably surprised by this offer. But Paderewski addressed himself to the wrong ally who had no direct responsibility for Poland. Lloyd George could not quite see what he would do with Polish-occupied Moscow and therefore rejected the proposal.[3] Pilsudski's *volte face* was clumsy, it annoyed the Allies and did not bring in the desired results. If anything it confirmed Allied suspicions of the Poles; they were most impulsive and incalculable. The British War Minister, Winston Churchill, expressed these suspicions in a speculative memorandum shortly after Paderewski's offer: would Pilsudski march again or would he conclude a separate peace with the bolsheviks?[4] But both Pilsudski and Paderewski went on talking about their march against the bolsheviks, nonetheless, making it clear that without abundant Allied aid there would be no march. Their persistent pressure on the Allies finally succeeded in December 1919, but the change in Allied attitude towards the Poles was probably much less due to the pressures than to the failures of

[1] Captain Zwislowski to Pilsudski, 10 January 1919.

[2] Depesza z Gdanska, w sprawie zakupu i transportu municji; z Berlina; z Paryza; z Waszyngtonu; z Belgradu; z Hagi, 28 July 1919.

[3] Peace Conference Session, 14 September 1919.

[4] Churchill Memorandum, 22 September 1919.

British and French policies in Russia. In December 1919 they had no choice really; Pilsudski was the only remaining opponent of bolshevism with a reasonable chance of success.

IV

The French High Command had not really given up its plans for an intervention in Russia via Poland even after the rejection by the other Allies. Marshal Foch kept turning back to them from time to time only to have them rejected once again. In June 1919 the Poles conscious of the sympathies they enjoyed in the Supreme Allied Military Council tried to exploit them. Paderewski made another of his surprising and superfluous gestures: he offered to place the Polish army under Foch's supreme command. It is not clear why on 12 June 1919 the Allies accepted this offer; the agreement was made public on 14 June.[1] It is difficult to gauge the significance of this move, but it was probably based on unrealistic hopes: the Poles hoped for arms and Foch for control of the Polish army for his Russian plans. Nothing of the sort followed, but Poland remained the pivot of Allied planning.

Shortly after the agreement concerted French and British military pressure was put on Pilsudski. The Allied command wanted him to come to amicable arrangements with the non-bolshevik Russians, and above all with General Denikin and the Volunteers. In July 1919, at the height of the arms crisis, Pilsudski had to give in and announced that he would send a mission led by General Karnicki, who had a pro-Russian reputation, to negotiate with Denikin. On 8 August Karnicki was given detailed instructions and also questions to be put to General Denikin: what was his attitude to Poland, her borders, the Ukraine. The mission was also charged with finding out Denikin's military strength and his relations with Admiral Kolchak, General Yudenich, Germany, Japan and the Allies.[2] On the satisfactory replies of Denikin and subject to a favourable report on his strength Pilsudski was prepared to come to Denikin's aid by moving against the bolsheviks on the western front. In this affair Pilsudski had fundamental doubts and suspicions of General Denikin and his Russians and would probably not have moved even had he been given satisfaction by the Volunteers.

---

[1] Peace Conference Session, 12 June 1919; Memorandum for the Quai d'Orsay, 14 June 1919.

[2] Colonel Haller to General Karnicki, 8 August 1919.

General Karnicki's mission remained in southern Russia until 1920 mainly on account of Allied pressure. The Allies continued to hope against hope that a Polish–Volunteer entente was possible, but Karnicki knew in November 1919 that there was no substance in these hopes. On 15 November 1919 he made it quite clear to Pilsudski that Denikin's Russians were of no interest to Poland. According to the report they were all Great Russian chauvinists, who at present postponed tactically any political pronouncements, but in their hearts were for 'one, indivisible, pre-war Russia'. General Denikin was interested in short-term military agreements with the Poles and would not commit himself on the future frontiers.[1] Thus the Poles had no incentive to become the left wing of Denikin's advance on Moscow, and in fact began to watch Denikin's progress with growing apprehension, as the British Ambassador in Warsaw, Sir Horace Rumbold, pointed out in his dispatches.[2]

Seemingly the Poles were giving way to Allied pressure and Marshal Foch was quick to try and force Pilsudski to join another half-baked Allied enterprise. In the North General Yudenich's North Western Army was ready to start its march on Petrograd and Foch wanted the Poles to march on its right wing. On 30 August 1919 Foch submitted a memorandum to Clemenceau in which he advocated a combined Russo–Baltic–Polish drive on Petrograd. It took Clemenceau a fortnight to reject the memorandum without comments: he had more pressing tasks to attend to than consider unrealistic plans.[3] Foch's latest idea never reached the Poles, but they would have been equally unwilling as in the case of Denikin. When General Yudenich finally launched his offensive the Poles proved as apprehensive as before; White successes in fact always alarmed them.[4]

In the end Pilsudski made his position quite clear: he would not be anybody's wing. On 7 November 1919 he told Sir Horace what he thought of the Russians: to him Denikin, Kolchak or the bolsheviks were the same Russians, enemies of Poland. Whoever ultimately won in Russia, he would be forced to call in foreigners to organize the country for him. Pilsudski himself was not interested in Russia, but concerned himself exclusively with the defence of Polish eastern frontiers, and for this he needed urgently military supplies. If he did

---

[1] Karnicki to Pilsudski, 15 November 1919.
[2] Rumbold to Curzon, 19 October 1919.
[3] Foch to Clemenceau, 30 August 1919; bordereau du Quai d'Orsay.
[4] Rumbold to Curzon, 27 October 1919.

not get them from the Allies he would be forced to turn to Germany.[1] Thus Pilsudski made it abundantly clear why he gave in to Allied pressure and negotiated with General Denikin and the Whites. At this late stage he also hinted at his latest attempt at getting supplies from the Allies, Germany, but it was quite unnecessary, for the Allies were in the process of reappraising their policies in Russia. On 8 December 1919 Sir Horace urged Lord Curzon to stop wasting arms and ammunition on the Whites and instead send them to the Poles who needed them and would put them to a better use.[2] On 12 December 1919 Lloyd George and Clemenceau reached an agreement by which military aid would be switched from the Russian Whites to the Poles and Poland would become the Allied stronghold against bolshevism. Pilsudski was recognized as the most important leader in Eastern Europe and would get aid practically on his own terms.

V

After the Allied decision to aid Poland had been taken it took some time to work out practical details and start the flow. In the meantime the reports from Poland were far from encouraging. Thus Colonel Tallents, British High Commissioner in Latvia, reported from Wilno that Polish morale there was low. Everyone seemed drunk, the officers and the soldiers. Sir Horace quoted Pilsudski that economic and military position was critical.[3] General Henrys, head of the French mission, was immensely worried by the arrival of bolshevik reinforcements on the Polish front, after their victorious offensive against the Volunteers. Most energetic measures would have to be taken to save Poland.[4]

Despite the common Franco–British decision to support the Poles Poland remained the primary responsibility of the French. They were responsible for the bulk of military aid and also for operational planning. On 14 January 1920 Marshal Foch produced another variant of his plan for Eastern Europe. It was in fact worked out by General Weygand and presented to Clemenceau. It again envisaged the Polish army in the centre of a wide front against the bolsheviks, supported on the right by the Rumanians and on the left by the

[1] Rumbold to Curzon, 7 November 1919; interview with Pilsudski.
[2] Rumbold to Curzon, 8 December 1919; Savory Memorandum.
[3] Tallents to Curzon, 7 December 1919; Rumbold to Curzon, 17 January 1920.
[4] Foch to Clemenceau, 14 January 1920, quoting General Henrys.

Balts. Ukrainian and Byelorussian forces were to be used by the Poles after initial successes on their drive to the Dnieper; henceforth a combined Polish–Volunteer operation 'would re-establish order in Russia.' This was the rehashed old intervention plan and Clemenceau rejected it, because by now he was thinking more in defensive than offensive terms. But a few days later he resigned and Millerand became Prime Minister of France.

The Poles heard rumours of Allied policy reappraisals and Pilsudski decided to send his Foreign Minister, Patek, round the Allied capitals to find out more about the changes. While in Paris Patek was told of the old-new Foch plan, but he did not find out whether Clemenceau managed to modify it or whether Millerand accepted it as a basis for his policies. He left for London where to his great surprise Lloyd George promised British support, but urged the Poles to come to terms with the bolsheviks.[1] This was a great disappointment for the Poles, for they expected the new policy to be more aggressive towards bolshevism. However, Pilsudski found out that he would get arms and that the Allies, despite agreements, had no new ideas nor common policy for Russia or Eastern Europe. This ambiguity and the arms would enable him to act on his own.[2]

First of all he had to discredit the idea of peace negotiations with the bolsheviks. Pilsudski established contacts with the bolsheviks as early as 3 November 1919 during the crisis on their southern front. But these were exploratory contacts which were soon broken off. In turn the bolsheviks made their peace proposals on 22 December 1919 and made them public on 28 January 1920. Pilsudski used Patek's absence abroad to ignore the bolshevik offer, but when the latter returned the Poles delayed their reply still further and in the meantime began to raise doubts about Soviet sincerity.[3] But Pilsudski would not negotiate in any case at this stage, he needed a military victory to start negotiations, so he continued to delay.

The Poles were killing two birds with one stone: they would not negotiate with the Soviets because the conditions were not right and at the same time were impressing on the Allies that the bolsheviks could not be trusted and were difficult to deal with. But the British, dissatisfied with the delays, began to put pressure on Pilsudski and this if allowed could upset Polish plans. Pilsudski therefore skilfully

[1] Curzon to Rumbold, 27 January 1920.
[2] Rumbold to Curzon, 23 January and 10 February 1920.
[3] Rumbold to Curzon, 30 and 31 January 1920.

exploited Franco–British differences to gain time and ward off British pressure. Throughout January 1920 the British refused to see Pilsudski's difficulties with the bolsheviks and instead urged him to start negotiations. The French were finally informed and Millerand wrote to Lloyd George asking him not to push Poland too much towards a peace with the Soviets; a delay in negotiations could be of benefit to both Poland and Western Allies.[1] But when Lloyd George replied rather pessimistically that Poland was not really worth disputing about and should be abandoned like the Russian Whites, Millerand felt obliged to come out strongly in favour of the Poles. But he was careful to point out that France was not discouraging the Poles from negotiating with the bolsheviks, and would only get involved directly, if the bolsheviks attacked Poland.[2] It was obvious that the French and the British did not see eye to eye and this could only be to Pilsudski's advantage. The French, in order to counterbalance British discouragement, even announced Marshal Foch's visit to Poland to assess the military situation in person.[3] Though the visit was ultimately not realized Pilsudski had the Allies quarrelling over him leaving him free to prepare his own plans.

In January 1920 Pilsudski told openly Sir Horace Rumbold about his ultimate plans in Eastern Europe. They were in fact his old confederation and though Sir Horace reported them to London, they were not taken seriously either by him or Curzon.[4] However, many significant pointers indicated that Pilsudski's plans should have been taken more seriously; in 1920 conditions in Eastern Europe were markedly more favourable for their realization. Ukrainian nationalists were completely defeated and controlled only a small area in Western Ukraine. General Hetman Petlyura resided in Warsaw, his arrival there was passed over without any commentary.[5] Pilsudski's federal proposals to the Lithuanians were also considered unimportant, but obviously much depended on the success of the Ukrainian–Polish *rapprochement*.[6] When the Poles began to talk about buffer states in Byelorussia and Volhynia both Allies considered the scheme as fantastic, though the French would have liked it, had it been

[1] Millerand to Curzon (Lloyd George), 5 February 1920.
[2] Millerand to Curzon (Lloyd George), 16 February 1920.
[3] Rumbold to Curzon, 16 February 1920.
[4] Rumbold to Curzon, 23 and 26 January 1920.
[5] Rumbold to Curzon, 14 December 1919.
[6] Rumbold to Curzon, 26 January 1920.

POLAND IN 1920

0   100
Miles

BALTIC SEA

LIVONIA

COURLAND

Riga

Dünaburg   Drissa   Polotsk

SAMOGITIA   Dzisna

Smole

Niemen

Kovno

WHIT

KÖNIGSBERG   VILNA   Boriso

Goldlap   LITHUANIA   MINSK   Mogi

Sowalki   Grodno   RUSSI

DANZIG

Lomza   Bialystok   Wolkowysk   Slutsk   Beresina

Ostroleka

Vistula   PODLESIA   Pripet

Modlin   Brest   Slutsk

Warsaw   Litovsk   Pinsk   Mozyr

Wieprz

Deblin

Chelm   Kovel

Lublin   Lutsk

Zamosc   V O L H Y N I A   KIE

Katowice   San   Zhitomir

Cracow   Lwow   UKRAI

Teschen

EASTERN   Tarnopol

Drohobycz   Husiatyn   Bar

GALICIA   Stanislavov   PODOLIA   Bug

Dniester

Pruth

N

---   Polish frontiers in 1920

◄——   Bolshevik offensive, June-July, 1920

⎯▷   Polish counter-offensive, Aug.-Sept., 1920

▨▷   Polish southern offensive, Sept., 1920

possible, as it fitted well into their 'cordon sanitaire'.[1] Pilsudski's public declarations and manoeuvres only confused the Allies and they were now incapable of even guessing what he was after. But Pilsudski knew well that even if his confederative plans failed, he would still benefit, for he was getting in this way short-term local allies against the bolsheviks, and Allied aid and support as well.

Throughout the winter lull Pilsudski had been strengthening his army. He still had difficulties with supplies, as Generals Henrys and Knox (recently back from Siberia), could not agree on priorities and it was always hard to extract direct aid from the Allies.[2] But indirectly the French were helping him; they put discreet pressure on the Austrians to sell the Poles war surpluses and the Austrians discreetly complied.[3] Direct French supplies also began to arrive so that the Poles could face resolutely bolshevik danger should it arise. Pilsudski now decided that he would make it rise.

While still officially pursuing peace negotiations with the bolsheviks the Poles began to spread alarming rumours abroad. Bad economic conditions in Poland were well known abroad and they made it likely that a new bolshevik attack would finish off the Poles.[4] The rumours and the realization of this possibility moved even the hostile Czechs to worry about the Poles and consider aiding them. On 29 February 1920 Dr Beneš, Czech Foreign Minister, told the British Minister in Prague, Sir George Clerk, that he had reliable information about an impending bolshevik attack on the Poles within the next four weeks. The Czechs would be happy if Polish–Soviet peace negotiations were pursued to a successful conclusion, but if the bolsheviks attacked, they would follow the Allies and aid the Poles.[5] Without any doubt Dr Beneš told the French about his information and made clear his position, but this undoubtedly was exactly what Pilsudski wanted. He probably planted the information on the Czechs and used them to alarm the Allies and gain a free hand for himself in the defence of Poland.

On 15 February 1920 the Poles made public conditions under which they were prepared to discuss peace with the bolsheviks. The

[1] Rumbold to Curzon, 10 February 1920 (General de Wiart's interview with Pilsudski).

[2] Quai d'Orsay Memorandum, February 1920.

[3] Cambon to Derby, 4 May 1920.

[4] Rumbold to Curzon, 9, 22 November 1919 and 2 February 1920; Gibson to Lansing, 13 February 1920 and 17 January 1920.

[5] Clerk to Curzon, 29 February 1920.

conditions far exceeded Allied notions of justified Polish demands, but the bolsheviks did not find them extreme enough to break off negotiations. In fact they wanted to force Pilsudski to negotiate really.[1] All along the western front they increased local attacks and bolshevik renewed activity was noticed by the foreign military missions.[2] But Pilsudski would not strike back. He wanted to show the Allies that he was reasonable and at the same time put the bolsheviks into an awkward position.[3] There were limits to these 'provocations' but for the time being the Poles contented themselves with beating off bolshevik attacks and holding the front line intact.[4] On 27 March 1920 Pilsudski sent his negotiators to Borysov after he had rejected Chicherin's proposals to hold negotiations in other, preferable foreign cities.[5] He knew well of bolshevik concentrations in this sector and was determined to embarrass them to the utmost, for it was clear that the Polish delegation would observe the concentrations and hamper their movements by its presence. When the bolsheviks approached the Allies in an attempt to get out of Pilsudski's trap, they only convinced them that they were planning something sinister against the Poles and that the latter were justified in mistrusting the bolsheviks.

But by the end of March 1920 bolshevik activity on the front calmed down. They could see that the Poles would not be forced into negotiations by a few local attacks and therefore stopped them. However, Pilsudski now prepared for his counter-attack.[6] It was launched first on the diplomatic front. By March 1920 he had concluded several local alliances and they were to be used in the coming military offensive. In December 1919 Pilsudski reached a discreet agreement with the Latvians whose results were the bolshevik defeat at Dvinsk and the taking of the city. On 15–20 January 1920 the Poles attended the Baltic States Conference in Helsinki hoping to exploit the Latvian success and cement a Baltic alliance against the bolsheviks, but when they failed Pilsudski turned to the Russian Whites. B. Savinkov arrived in Warsaw and concluded an agreement with Pilsudski by which

[1] Rumbold to Curzon, 15 February 1920; Gibson to Lansing, 19 February 1920.

[2] British Mission to War Office, 1 March 1920; Rumbold to Curzon, 13 and 29 March 1920.

[3] Rumbold to Curzon, 15 March 1920.

[4] British Mission to War Office, 23 and 25 March 1920.

[5] Rumbold to Curzon, 29 March 1920.

[6] British Mission to War Office, 31 March 1920.

General Balakhovich's Corps as well as General Romanovich's Tartar Cavalry came under Pilsudski's operational orders.[1] But the most important agreement was concluded with the Ukrainians.

When Hetman Petlyura reached Warsaw to deal with Pilsudski he was in a hopeless position both politically and militarily. Politically he was still unrecognized by any one except the Poles, and militarily he was completely defeated and did not even have an army. But Pilsudski treated him with consideration and proposed to conclude an alliance with him against the bolsheviks. When in February 1920 rumours of it reached the Allies they reacted rather forcefully. On 9 February 1920 Curzon warned the Poles that they could expect no British support for any aggressive move even against the bolsheviks. On 24 February 1920 the Supreme Allied Council repeated this warning.[2] It was clear that the Allies would not sanction a preventive war against the bolsheviks which was the real meaning of the Polish–Ukrainian alliance. The Allies would only support the Poles if they were actually attacked or war was imposed on them by bolshevik actions.

This Allied warning made it clear to Pilsudski that in any offensive action he would have to rely on himself. All the same he tried hard to make the Allies believe that the bolsheviks were forcing him into action. On 14 April 1920 Patek, his Foreign Minister issued an urgent warning to the Allies about the increasing tempo of bolshevik military activity.[3] Five days later Patek bitterly complained about Dantzig's blockade by the Germans: Allied aid could not reach Poland, 'the bulwark against bolshevism.'[4] The Poles were obviously preparing a surprise and it was only on 20 April 1920, four days before the Polish offensive, that the British heard rumours about it.[5] Two days later the British Mission basing itself on rumours claimed that an offensive was imminent.[6] It can be reasonably assumed that the French were kept in comparable darkness, though perhaps for different reasons: Pilsudski did not want to put them into a difficult position vis-à-vis their British ally.

On 24 April 1920 Pilsudski and Petlyura signed a treaty of alliance and a military convention by which Poland promised the Ukraine

[1] Pilsudski–Savinkov Agreement, 8 August 1920.
[2] Rumbold to Curzon, 10 February 1920.
[3] Rumbold to Curzon, 14 April 1920.
[4] Rumbold to Curzon, 19 April 1920.
[5] Rumbold to Curzon, 20 April 1920.
[6] British Mission to War Office, 22 April 1920.

independence in return for military aid against the bolsheviks.[1] On signing the treaty 'retaliatory' actions against the bolsheviks started. Pilsudski personally took command in the field and four Polish armies together with their local allies struck deeply into the Ukraine.[2] On 26 April Pilsudski issued his manifesto to the Ukrainian people promising them freedom and independence. On 29 April a circular note to all the Polish embassies made clear the aim of the offensive operation against the bolsheviks: Russian imperialism was to be rooted out and non-Russian territories were to be detached from her. Pilsudski risked everything in this one stroke; he followed his armies in the Ukraine where at Vinnitsa he brotherly embraced Petlyura. On 7 May 1920 the Poles occupied Kiev.[3]

Everybody was surprised but satisfied. The Allies failed even to protest: the unpredictable Poles had done it again. But it was recognized that Pilsudski was largely forced into action by the bolshevik provocation. In addition he needed a victory over the bolsheviks in order to negotiate with them successfully. The British who had hampered Pilsudski's aggressive manoeuvres right to the moment of the offensive, acquiesced surprisingly quickly to the situation, and in the Foreign Office everyone wished Pilsudski the best of luck.[4] But how long would the luck last? The Allies still maintained that Pilsudski's confederation was a dream and even his Ukrainian alliance a short term palliative. The chief reason for the offensive was undoubtedly Pilsudski's desire to strengthen his hands for subsequent negotiations. On 30 August 1920 Sir Horace analysed Polish motives in similar terms. He also observed that Marshal Pilsudski also needed a victory for the coming election of the President of Poland.[5] But the latter was obviously incorrect; Pilsudski waged the war against the bolsheviks to carry out his confederation idea thus creating a new order and peace in Eastern Europe.

While he was successful all was well and British pessimism seemed unjustified. But soon after the fall of Kiev difficulties began to crop up. The Ukrainians began to question the vague promises made by the Poles. The Polish army proved most reluctant to relinquish its authority in occupied Ukrainian territory and as early as 30 April 1920

[1] Rumbold to Curzon and British Mission to War Office, 24 April 1920.
[2] Rumbold to Curzon, 26 and 30 April 1920.
[3] Rumbold to Curzon, 30 April and 9 May 1920.
[4] Minutes of a Foreign Office Meeting on Poland, 27 April 1920.
[5] Rumbold to Curzon, 30 April 1920.

the Allies received reports on these tensions. They decided to send to the Ukraine their own observers to find out exactly about the situation and also to conciliate if necessary. Thus they witnessed the great turn-out of Ukrainian peasants to welcome Pilsudski on 24 May 1920. But they also saw that these peasants failed to join their own armies, which were to take over from the Poles as soon as order had been restored. However, the peasants had no reason for joining the forces of the new régime: the régime did not even announce a land reform. The Allies began to worry.[1]

On 5 May 1920 the bolsheviks protested against 'Polish imperialism', but their protests fell on deaf ears. However, the Allies realized that they were capable of more than protests. On 10 May Trotsky, War Commissar, declared that relentless class struggle would be waged against the imperialists, but the Polish nation would be treated well.[2] This statement made bolshevik aims crystal clear: they intended to strike back and invade Poland. This was what the Allies always feared and it was the reason for their opposition to Pilsudski's plans. The bolsheviks delivered their first 'surprise' attack at Potock on 15 May 1920. The British were immediately alarmed and though Sir Horace spoke reassuringly about Polish measures to protect Kiev anxieties were rising in the west about the turn of events in the east.[3] Within ten days of the 'surprise' attack the bolsheviks launched a general offensive and Allied misgivings began to be justified. With the Ukrainians unwilling to fight for themselves the Poles were easily outflanked and forced to retreat. On 8 June they were back at Borisov and on 10 June Kiev was evacuated.[4] However, even swifter defeats and retreats followed and Polish jubilations turned quickly into dark depression.

With the military reverses in the Ukraine Poland was in the grip of a political crisis. The Polish cabinet resigned on 10 June 1920 and Poland remained without a government for a fortnight. Panic invaded the capital and fear of pogroms and the spread of bolshevik doctrines could be detected everywhere.[5] The Poles wavered between two extreme: they wanted to start immediate peace negotiations with the bolsheviks, which could not be contemplated since there was no

[1] Rumbold to Curzon, 3 and 24 May 1920.
[2] Trotsky to Dzerżiński (Lenin), 2 May 1920; Lenin to Trotsky, 5 May 1920; Trotsky to Central Committee, 10 May 1920.
[3] Rumbold to Curzon, 15 May 1920.
[4] Rumbold to Curzon, 10 and 12 June 1920.
[5] Rumbold to Curzon, 12 and 20 June 1920.

Polish cabinet, or they hoped that the Allies would go to war on their behalf. Thus on 19 June 1920 Marshal Pilsudski advised General Carton de Wiart, Head of the British Military Mission, that Britain should declare war 'not on Russia but on the bolsheviks'.[1] This dispatch indicates that even Pilsudski was surprised by the turn of his gamble and now hoped that the Allies would get him out of the precarious situation. Nevertheless amidst these fluctuating emotions the Marshal was taking concrete steps to organize Polish resistence to bolshevik advance. On 20 June 1920 new classes were called up and to prevent bolshevik subversion in the rear a League for Combating Bolshevism was formed. This militia then protected most efficiently the rear of the armies, especially after the bolsheviks appealed to the Poles to start a 'national insurrection' on 17 June 1920.[2] On 1 July 1920 the Council of National Defence was formed at last uniting all the political parties in the supreme effort to beat off bolshevik invasion. On 6 July 1920 Grabski, who managed to form a cabinet, appealed to the Allied Supreme Council, then in conference at Spa, to come to Poland's aid and initiate peace negotiations with the bolsheviks. On 10 July Grabski went to Spa in person and was forced to listen to rather humiliating British recriminations. But in the end the British promised to try and open talks with the bolsheviks. Lord Curzon radioed to Chicherin his proposals on 11 July 1920.[3]

The French were unable to help the Poles diplomatically, for they had no contacts with the bolsheviks but rather with the opposition in southern Russia. But when the events in the Ukraine began to take a bad turn they tried hard to increase the flow of supplies.[4] In this they were gravely hampered by the German blockade of Dantzig and difficulties in Czechoslovakia where Czech railwaymen refused passage to French munition trains destined for Poland.[5] On 10 July Marshal Foch requested General Henrys to send him a detailed report on Poland and Polish army to be delivered in person by a staff officer. Recommendations as to the most urgent need were also requested.[6] At the same time the Supreme Allied Council decided to

---

[1] Rumbold to Curzon, 14 June 1920.
[2] Rumbold to Curzon, 20 June 1920.
[3] Curzon to Chicherin, 11 July 1920.
[4] Foch to Millerand, 8 and 18 May 1920.
[5] Beneš (Paris) to Foreign Ministry (Prague), May 1920.
[6] Foch to Henrys, 10 July 1920.

send to Poland a high-powered, fact-finding mission led by Lord d'Abernon and General Weygand to boost up Polish morale.

Despite these remedial measures chaos and confusion was increasing in Warsaw: another cabinet was formed on 21 July 1920. W. Witos, the new Prime Minister, immediately proposed to the bolsheviks an armistice and peace negotiations. But Witos' appeal as well as that of the British Foreign Secretary, were left unanswered. As soon as the Polish appeal reached the Soviets the C-in-C, S. Kamenev, asked for the suspension of operations against Poland. But since Lord Curzon's proposals also dealt with the southern front and envisaged a composite armistice with Pilsudski and Wrangel, Trotsky refused Kamenev's request. He would only consent to an armistice in the west; the southern front had to be left out of negotiations altogether.[1] In the end Lenin personally decided the issue, proclaimed British initiative a swindle and ordered military operations to continue. On 17 July Chicherin rejected Curzon's proposals and asked for direct Russo–Polish negotiations.[2] The Red Army crossed the ethnic line and invaded Poland proper. The Soviets now acted as Pilsudski had acted before: they continued their advance, but at the same time left the way open for peace negotiations on their terms. It was clear that the farther they got into Poland the better their position in subsequent peace negotiations would be. On 23 July Tukhachevsky, CO of the bolshevik armies in the north, issued an order by which Warsaw was to be captured.

VI

The order for the capture of Warsaw was never carried out, for in the meantime Polish forces rallied and successfully counter-attacked. Somehow they retained combat efficiency even after so many weeks of retreat and demoralization. With Allied moral support and Pilsudski's strategic genius they defeated the triumphant bolsheviks at the gates of the city.

The restitution of Polish morale began with the arrival of the Allied mission on 25 July 1920. Many historians, above all the Soviet ones, allege that the Allied mission was responsible for more than raising morale. It is undoubted that General Weygand did offer the Poles

[1] Trotsky to Lenin (Kamenev), 12 July; Trotsky to Chicherin (Lenin), 13 July 1920.

[2] *Lenin Memorandum*, 13 July 1920; Chicherin to Curzon, 17 July 1920.

military advice, but this did no more than raise Polish morale, as the French General addressed himself constitutionally to the Chief of the Polish General Staff, General Rozwadowski, and not to the C-in-C. It so happened that Pilsudski conducted operations without really taking Rozwadowski into confidence. If Weygand's advice had an effect on the General Staff it seems problematic but in view of its impotence it was unimportant. To all accounts Weygand's rôle in the preparation of the offensive was negligible. Thus on 30 July Weygand told Rozwadowski that a line of defence should be fixed and held at all cost. He also recommended the creation of strategic reserves and control over the execution of orders.[1] This advice was so defensive that it seems probable that like Rozwadowski Weygand was not told of Pilsudski's projected offensive.

On 1 August 1920 Weygand went as far as to warn Rozwadowski against premature counter-attacks. He sketched out concretely what he considered the best line of defence; it was to run from Omulew, to Ostrolnika and then along the river Bug. He again urged the Poles to create new reserves.[2] Rozwadowski patiently listened to Weygand, but could not affect Pilsudski's plans. The latter changed his plans without telling Rozwadowski and we cannot say whether Weygand was given any details of the changes. Thus on 2 August 1920 when he heard about a limited Polish probing attack which he had opposed previously he urged Rozwadowski again to halt the operation, transfer troops to the north and consolidate the front there.[3] He was most distressed by the abandonment of the Bug line and proposed a northern thrust to throw the enemy back across the river. But cautious as he always was he advised the most meticulous preparation and concentration of reserves to ensure success of the counter-attack.[4] From all these communications between Weygand and Rozwadowski it is clear that Weygand did try to influence the Poles but was politely ignored. Perhaps this was quite right, for the French general could not help but think in terms of western armies and world war operations and this type of thinking was out of place in Poland. Pilsudski was now ready to show Weygand what really had to be done.

On 8 August 1920 while Pilsudski issued his handwritten orders for the offensive Weygand was busy telling Rozwadowski that he should

---

[1] Weygand to Rozwadowski, 30 July 1920.
[2] Weygand to Rozwadowski, 1 August 1920.
[3] Weygand to Rozwadowski, 2 August 1920.
[4] Weygand to Rozwadowski, 3 and 5 August 1920.

throw all the available forces into the defence battle round Warsaw.[1] As he spoke of moving troops by all the means he was undoubtedly thinking of Paris and its defence in 1914 and 1918. Three days later Weygand was finally told of the offensive that Pilsudski was to launch 'soon' and his only comment was a recommendation to transfer further reinforcements to the north and concentrate them in the area Modlin–Serotsk.[2] On 12/13 August Pilsudski left Warsaw for the front and issued his final orders orally. The Polish General Staff was probably told roughly of the plan, but it did not know of any modifications that Pilsudski might have introduced after inspecting the front personally. However, Weygand felt compelled to send Rozwadowski a warning that the planned action by tanks and aeroplanes was projected too far back from the front and would therefore prove ineffective.[3] It is not known what was Pilsudski's reaction to this last minute warning, if it ever reached him. On 16 August 1920 the Polish 4th Army counter-attacked at Wieprz from the Deblin-Kock sector and was immediately successful. The striking group reached the Narew on 22 August thus cutting off the line of retreat for Tukhachevsky's 4th Army. On 28 August the bolsheviks were again defeated at Grodno-Wolkowysk, completely collapsed and fled in confusion. Pilsudski's victory was decisive and in September 1920 his armies occupied Slutsk and Minsk again.

The Polish leader who only recently was threatened with mortal danger from the bolsheviks could now resume peace negotiations, for this seems to have been ultimately the only practicable thing. Though victorious he had to abandon his greater plans and bury, at least for the time, his confederation. His delegates were already in Russia and after some delay finally met their Soviet counterparts at Baranowiczi. But the bolsheviks tried to delay talks until Warsaw fell. They had wrested some concessions from the British about Polish frontiers and while still under the impression of an imminent Polish defeat were trying to force the Poles to accept them. Lenin instructed his delegation to take advantage of the British weakness, but when finally the two sides got down to negotiating at Minsk on 17 August, no one knew of the situation at the front and progress was very slow.[4]

[1] Weygand to Rozwadowski, 8 August 1920.
[2] Weygand to Rozwadowski, 11 August 1920.
[3] Weygand to Rozwadowski, 14 August 1920.
[4] Lenin to Sklyansky, August 1920, five telegrams; Lenin to Danishevsky, 11 August 1920.

The bolsheviks presented maximum demands and had them rejected by Dabski, the leader of the Polish delegation. Both sides anxiously waited for the news from the front. But it was slow to filter through to Minsk and the talks were therefore adjourned. Then on 2 September 1920 both sides knew with certainty of bolshevik defeat and immediately arrived at their first agreement: the talks were transferred to Riga. Although there were still some difficulties ahead the military defeat of the bolsheviks had a decisive influence on negotiations. On 12 October 1920 a preliminary treaty was signed and on 18 October 1920 the Soviet–Polish war was over. The final Peace Treaty was concluded at Riga on 18 March 1921.

VII

After the war the Soviets soon advanced the claim that the Polish–Soviet episode was the result of an Allied conspiracy with Pilsudski. Though it would have been in his interest Pilsudski, while alive, remained modest and silent about the real Allied attitude towards him. On the contrary he allowed the legend of the Allies aiding the Poles to save themselves from bolshevism to grow and prosper. But at least one ally knew well that it was Pilsudski and the Poles themselves who defeated the bolsheviks practically with no assistance from the Allies. The French were in fact so impressed by Polish performance in the war that within six months they consented to conclude a treaty of alliance with them.

CONCLUSION

It was very difficult for the Allies to decide on the intervention in Russia. This was so above all because of the lack of a single historical precedent. Even in 1917 it seemed inconceivable that one great power, or several allied great powers, could infringe the sovereignty of another great power by intervening directly in internal affairs. Thus it took the Allies a long time to decide whether any form of intervention was possible and when the decision was finally made the Allies had missed a number of suitable opportunities and in the end intervened on behalf of the old 'pro-Allied establishment' identifying themselves with by then disintegrating factions of Russian society.

Apart from these legal, political and philosophic difficulties technical shortcoming affected Allied decisions. The planning of the intervention was extremely unsatisfactory. A completely unprecedented situation arose in Russia requiring 'revolutionary' decisions; the established institutions of the Allies could not cope with this situation efficiently. It would be possible to say that apart from conventional international reactions to events in Russia, which by then had already run their course, there was no real planning at all. The Allies had no planning boards to deal with the political, military, supply, psychological and economic contingencies of the Russian situation. While on the national level certain institutions (foreign ministries) could react and muddle through, on the international level there was absolutely nothing at all. The Peace Conference (the world directorate) proved quite incapable of decisions; on this level the Allies did not even succeed in formulating a common and comprehensive policy for intervention.

The French who probably wanted the intervention most of all were committed in terms of military power to the Western front and were therefore the weakest *vis-à-vis* the intervention in Russia. Moreover, their military concepts were narrowly Western front and consequently any 'operation' launched in Russia would have to serve to relieve the Western (home) front and nothing else. The British, while capable of wider concepts in so far as Russia was concerned, were equally unable to commit their own troops and therefore suffered from the same weakness as the French. The two allies could plan, advise and urge, sometimes even make promises, but fundamentally they were incapable of decisive intervention.

However, even carefully planned and prepared operations failed. The chief causes of these failures were exceptionally bad intelligence on the spot and international rivalry affecting vitally the local situation. Thus the Murmansk–Archangel operations in 1918-19 proved a failure largely because of faulty intelligence; the bolsheviks were much harder to fight than anticipated, and public opinion in the three Allied countries (France, Britain and the United States) involved in the fighting, was so averse to further operations, that hasty retreat had to be effected. The Siberian intervention which was really based on the Japanese and American involvement was first of all disturbed by the unexpected revolt of the Czechoslovak Legion, which upset the timetable, and then stalemated by the American–Japanese rivalry.

After the armistice in November 1918 additional reasons were found for Allied intervention in Russia. The defeat of Germany in the west meant to the Allies the elimination of German influence in the east, especially in the bolshevik-controlled Russia, which on the whole was considered as a puppet régime created by the Germans. The elimination of German influence was conceived to mean the evacuation by the Germans of all occupied territories in the east, and the destruction of the puppet (bolshevik) régime. But this Allied presupposition could never be implemented, for not even France and Britain, the principal allies concerned, could see eye to eye. At first the French tried to destroy the bolsheviks by a direct intervention. But their insufficient forces soon suffered setbacks and after a disastrous evacuation the French came round to the British view that the best way to destroy the bolsheviks was to support the local, anti-bolshevik forces. But this was about the limit of Franco–British understanding and instead of coordinated aid and support the two allies soon quarrelled and only aggravated the internecine struggle in the non-bolshevik movements.

In Siberia the French controlled the Czechoslovak Legion and tried unsuccessfully to use it to hold on to and expand the White Siberian State. But because of insufficient aid and internal demoralizations of both the White Siberian movement and the Legion, Siberia collapsed and was overrun by the bolsheviks. In the south both the British and the French theoretically supported the White movement led by Generals Denikin and Wrangel. But here again internal White weakness and Franco–British rivalry paralysed Allied interventionary actions. Because of the utter lack of coordination and inter-allied quarrels Allied intervention instead of strengthening and stabilizing the White movement only weakened it morally and materially.

When one by one the Russian White movements failed to defeat the bolsheviks the Allies turned to Poland, a succession state of the old Russian Empire, trying to induce the Poles to lead the struggle against the bolsheviks. If with Allied aid the Poles had managed to unite the Ukrainians, Georgians, Armenians, the Balts, Finns and the remnants of the Russian Whites they might have defeated the bolsheviks. But while Britain and France could not agree on the extent of aid to the Poles, the latter had their own ideas on the struggle for power in Eastern Europe. Once again because of fundamental disunity and lack of coordination the intervention via Poland failed, the Poles were themselves in danger at one stage and though they ultimately scored a decisive victory which enabled them to conclude an advantageous peace with the bolsheviks, they failed to achieve their own and Allied aim, the destruction of bolshevism. They in fact did not even decisively cripple the bolshevik régime, but by means of their victory postponed the power settlement in Eastern Europe for another generation.

The overall failure of the Allied intervention was caused by Allied inability to harmonize national interests in the struggle against the bolsheviks. Both France and Britain pursued their own interests in Russia separately, actively combating any other interests and above all ignoring completely Russian national interests. This inevitably led to internecine struggle among the Allies and ultimately antagonized even the submissive Whites. When the latter observed that their interests hardly counted, despite their vital stakes they opposed Allied policies, especially, on the lower echelons of the White movements.

Another Allied inability was to proclaim clearly their aims in Russia. Thus Britain advocated different policies in different parts of Russia; now favouring national separatism now opposing it. In the end even the Whites suspected the British and thought that they wanted to dismember Russia permanently and occupy parts of it, especially certain Asiatic territories. France could not decide either whether the Russian element or the separatist ones would help her most in her pursuance of national interests and French support fluctuated accordingly. Had only once these contradictory policies coincided and had the Allies concentrated their support on at least one movement the struggle against the bolsheviks might have ended differently. Thanks to Japanese support a non-bolshevik republic in the Far East survived longest (1922) when all the other movements had been eliminated one by one. Thus Allied intervention policy proved a fiasco from which ultimately no one benefited either politically or economically. German influence and 'German puppets' (bolsheviks) were not only not eradicated, but in many ways forced really together. Economically both France and Britain lost their investments in Russia and commercial relations were resumed only slowly after long delays. Needless to say Russia did not derive any benefit from the intervention which in fact stimulated and kept going the civil war. On the other hand the intervention, while never vitally threatening the bolsheviks, helped them to divert the attention of the Russian people from domestic political and economic problems and disasters and put the blame for them on interventionist forces.

In the international sphere the intervention caused a 'revolutionary' reaction to it. The bolsheviks became convinced that to defeat it they had to prepare and organise a world revolution. In the world revolution they saw the only defence against the 'international imperialist conspiracy' which aimed at the destruction of the 'young revolutionary régime'. Though the Allied decision to intervene in Russia involved no long-term consideration on the part of the Allies, the intervention had long-term repercussions in international relations. Even nowadays it is used as an argument against an East–West *détente*; it definitely influenced Stalin in 1939 when he spurned Western approaches and chose to ally himself with Germany. But above all the intervention in Russia proved utterly futile, as it damaged everybody and profited no one.

BIBLIOGRAPHY

Austrian Sources (Unpublished)

HAUS-, HOF-, UND STAATSARCHIV
St Petersburg: Politische Kasten 4
Slawische Angelegenheiten 1899–1918
Kramarz Prozess 1916
Russland 1914–20
Interna – Panslawismus

KRIEGSARCHIV
Generalstab: Evidenzburo 1914–20
Militärkanzlei 1914–20

VERWALTUNGSARCHIV
Böhmen 22 1880–1918

British Sources (Unpublished)

FOREIGN OFFICE
Russia: War Aims 1914–18
Confidential Prints: Russia, Poland 1914–20
Baltic Provinces and North Russia, 1914–20
Documents on British Foreign Policy 1914–18
Allied Relations with Russia, 1917–18
Diary of Russian Affairs from the Revolution to Peace with Germany
Summary of Correspondence Concerning Allied Intervention in East Russia
  Northern Department 1919–20
Correspondence respecting the Affairs of Russia 1919

LORD MILNER PAPERS, OXFORD
Carton A: Russia 1917
Carton d-2: Kaledin, Buchanan, Knox
     G-1: General Shore
     B: Foreign Office Memoranda
Fascicle 32: General Wilson
     E-2: Czechs, Japanese
     E-1: Extreme Orient
     D-3: Ataman Semenov

215

French Sources (Unpublished)

QUAI D'ORSAY ARCHIVES (Inventaire de la nouvelle Série reliée 1897–1918)

Russie

Dossier général volume 4 October 1906–July 1914
Sibérie-Caucase volume 1 October 1896–July 1910
Agitation rev.-anarchiste volume 1 October 1880–1904
    Volume 2 October 1905–July 1918
Presse volume 1 October 1896–July 1913
Alliance franco–russe volume 11 October 1913–July 1918
Relations avec l'Autriche volume 1 1897–1914
Chemin de fer volume 3 1904–18

Allemagne

Relation avec la Russie volume 1 1897–1904
    Volume 2 1905–14

Austriche–Hongrie

Tchèques volume 1 1897–1918
Slovaques volume 1 1897–1918
Dalmatie–Bosnie–Herz. volume 1 1897–99
    Volume 2 1900–3
    Volume 3 1904–6
    Volume 4 1907–8

Angleterre

Relations avec l'A. et la Russie volume 1 1896–1920
Relations avec l'Autriche et les pays balkaniques volume 1 1897–1918
Correspondance politique – Russie 1896–1920

MINISTERE DE LA GUERRE ARCHIVES

Russie

Carton No. 12 Rapports des Attachés Militaires 1914–20
Carton No. 67 Renseigeignement général
Carton No. 68 Liaison 1906–14
Carton No. 72 Organization 1906–14
Carton No. 73 Correspondance et télégrammes 1915–18
Carton No. 78 Missions 1914–24
Carton No 79 Mission de colonel Langlois
Carton No. 80 Rapports 1915–24
Carton Nos. 81–86 Missions-dossiers personnels
Carton No. 87 Sibérie
Carton Nos. 88–90 Sibérie 1918–23

Columbia University, New York
Milyukov Diaries
Denikin Diaries and notes
Shatilov Memoirs
Khagondakov Memoirs
Abrikosov Memoirs
Sannikov Memoirs
Ya. G. Kefeli, S. Generalom Shvartsem
Tomilov Memoirs

Pilsudski Institute, New York
Adjutantura generalna naczelnego dowodztwa 1918–21

Hoover Institution, Stanford, California
Documents and Papers belonging to the personal archives of General
   P. N. Wrangel
Military Archives, General Wrangel
Maklakov Papers, Series a, b, c.

German Sources (Unpublished)

AUSWÄRTIGES AMT (Captured German Documents)
Ukraine 1917–20
Siberien 1916–20
Akten betreffend Tchecho-Slowakei 1819–1920

Documents

Browder R. P. and Kerensky A. F. *The Russian Provisional Government
   1917, Documents*, 3 vols, Stanford, 1961.
Bunyan J. and Fisher H. H., *The Bolshevik Revolution, 1917–1918*, Stan-
   ford, 1934.
Bunyan J., *Intervention, Civil War and Communism in Russia*, December
   1918. Documents and Materials, Baltimore, 1936.
Cumming C. K. and Pettit W. W., *Russian–American Relations, March
   1917–March 1920, Documents and Papers*, New York, 1920.
Degras J., *Soviet Documents on Foreign Policy*, vol. 1, OUP, 1951.
Denezhnyye dokumenty Generala Aleksyeeva, *Arkhiv russkoy revolutsii*,
   vol. 5, pp. 345–57, Berlin, 1922.
Dokumenty vneshney politiki SSSR, vol. 1, Moscow, 1959, vol. 2, Moscow,
   1958.
Dokumenty o geroicheskoy oborone Tsaritsyna v 1918 godu, Moscow, 1942.
Dokumenty o protilidové a protinárodní politice T. G. Masaryka, Prague,
   1953.
Dokumenty o protisovětských piklech československé reakce, Prague, 1954.
Dokumenty po istorii grazhdanskoy voyny v SSSR, vol. 1, Moscow, 1941.

Dokumenty o geroicheskoy oborone Petrograda v 1919 godu, Moscow, 1941.

Golder, F. A., *Documents of Russian History, 1914–1917*, New York, 1927.

History of the Great War Based on Official Documents: The Campaign in Mesopotamia, 1914–1918, vol. 4, London, 1927.

Iz istorii grazhdanskoy voyny v SSSR, 3 vols, Moscow, 1960–1.

Les armées françaises dans la Grande Guerre, 58 vols., tome VIII et IX, Paris 1928–34.

Lenin V. I. *Ob inostrannoy voyennoy interventsii i grazhdanskoy voyne v SSSR*, (1918–1920gg.), Moscow, 1956.

——, *Voyennaya perepiska* (1917–20), Moscow, 1957.

Listovka grazhdanskoy voyny v SSSR, 1918–22 gg., Moscow, 1942.

Mirnye peregovory v Brest–Litovske: polny tekst stenogramm, vol. 1, Moscow, 1920.

Moulis E. and Bergonier E., *La guerre entre les alliés et la Russie, 1918–1920*, Paris, 1937.

Petliura, Simon V. Un appel du president Petlioura à la democratie française, (letter to Jean Pelissier, October 22, 1919). (Hoover Library).

Piontkovskii, S. A. (ed.). *Grazhdanskaia voina v Rossii, 1918-1921 gg: krestomatia*. Moscow: Izd. Kom. universiteta im. Ia. M. Sverdlova, 1925.

Pobeda Velikoi Oktiabr'skoi Sotsialisticheskoi Revoliutsii v Turkestane. Tashkent: Gosizdat, USSR, 1947.

Protokoly tsentral 'nogo komiteta RSDRP(b), August 1917–Fevral' 1918. Moscow: Institut Marksizma-Leninisma pri TsK KPSS, Gospolitizdat, 1958.

R.S.F.S.R., Commissariat du peuple pour les affaires étrangères. *Correspondance diplomatique se rapportant aux relations entre la République russe et les puissances de l'Entente, 1918*. Moscow: Commissariat du peuple pour les affaires étrangères, 1919.

R.S.F.S.R., Commissariat du peuple pour les affaires étrangères. *Livre rouge: recueil des documents diplomatiques relatifs aux relations entre la Russie et la Pologne, 1918-1920*. Moscow: Edition d'état, 1920.

R.S.F.S.R., Narodnyi komissariat inostrannykh del. *Sbornik sekretnykh dokumentov iz arkhiva byvshago Ministerstva inostrannykh del*. Petrograd: Gosizdat, 1917. (Hoover Library).

R.S.F.S.R., Narodnyi komissariat inostrannykh del. *Vestnik*, 1917–20.

Sed'moi ekstrennyi s'ezd RKP(b), mart 1918 goda; stenograficheskii otchet. Moscow: Institut Marksizma-Leninizma pri TsK KPSS, Gospolitizdat 1962.

Seymour, Charles (ed.). *The Intimate Papers of Colonel House*. Vols. III–IV. New York: Houghton, Mifflin Co., 1926–28.

Shafir, I. M. (ed.). *Secrets of Menshevik Georgia; the Plot Against Soviet Russia Unmasked: Documents*. London: Communist Party of Great Britain, 1922.

218

Shliapnikov, A. G. (ed.). *Kto dolzhnik? sbornik dokumentirovannykh statei po voprosu ob otnosheniiakh mezhdu Rossiei, Frantsiei i drugimi derzhavami Antanty*. Moscow: Avioizdat, 1926.

——. (ed.). *Les alliés contre la Russie avant, pendant et après la guerre mondiale: faits et documents*. Paris: A. Delpeuch, 1926. (essentially the same as *Kto dolzhnik?*).

Shlikhter, A. G. (ed.). *Chernaia kniga: sbornik statei i materialov ob interventsii antanty na Ukraine v 1918-1919 gg*. Kharkov: Gosizdat Ukrainy, 1925.

Subbotovskii, I. (ed.). *Soiuzniki, Russkie reaktsionery i interventsiia; iskliuchitel'no po ofitsial'nym arkhivnym dokumentam Kolchakovskogo pravitel'stva*. Leningrad: Vestnik Len. soveta, 1926.

Sumbatov, Prince. *Memoire soumis par le prince Soumbatoff, délégué du gouvernement georgien, aux représentants des Puissances alliées à Berne au mois de novembre 1918*. Paris, 1918. (Hoover Library).

Tashleva, Sh. (ed.). *Turkmenistan v period inostrannoi voennoi interventsii i grazhdanskoi voiny, 1918-1920 gg.: sbornik dokumentov*. Ashkhabad: Gosizdat T.S.S.R., 1957.

Tolokonnikov, T. (ed.). *Frantsuzskaia burzhuaziia i Iuda Vrangel' (dogover Frantsii s Vrangelem)*. Moscow: Gosizdat, 1920.

United States, Department of State. *Papers Relating to the Foreign Relations of the United States, 1918, Russia*. 3 vols. Washington: Government Printing Office, 1931-32.

United States, Department of State. *Papers Relating to the Foreign Relations of the United States, 1919, Russia*. Washington: Government Printing Office, 1937.

United States, Department of State. *Papers Relating to the Foreign Relations of the United States, 1919*. Vol. II. Washington: Government Printing Office, 1934.

United States, Department of State. *Papers Relating to the Foreign Relations of the United States, 1920*. Vol. III. Washington: Government Printing Office, 1936.

United States, Department of State. *Papers Relating to the Foreign Relations of the United States: The Lansing Papers, 1914-1920*. 2 vols. Washington: Government Printing Office, 1939-40.

United States, Department of State. *Papers Relating to the Foreign Relations of the United States: The Paris Peace Conference, 1919*. 13 vols. Washington: Government Printing Office, 1942-47.

United States, Department of State, *Russian Series*, No. 3 *Documents Relating to the Organisation and Purpose of the Anti-Bolshevik Forces in Russia*. Washington: Government Printing Office, 1919.

U.S.S.R., Komissiia po izdaniiu diplomaticheskikh dokumentov pri MID SSSR. *Dokumenty vneshnei politiki SSSR*. Vols. I-III. (November 1917-March 1921). Moscow: Gospolitizdat, 1957-9.

Varneck, Elena, and Fisher, H. H. (eds.). *The Testimony of Kolchak and Other Siberian Materials*. Stanford: Stanford University Press, 1935.

Velikaia Oktiabr'skaia sotsialistichezkaia revoliutsiia i pobeda Sovetskoi vlasti v Armenii. Erevan: Gosizdat ASSR, 1957.

Volunteer Army (Dobrovol'cheskaia Armiia). *Kratkaia zapiska istorii vzaimootnoshenii Dobrovol'cheskoi armii s Ukrainoi*. Rostov-on-Don: Tip. 'Donskogo akts. o-va. pech. i izd. dela,' 1919. (Hoover Library.)

Volunteer Army, General Staff of the Armed Forces of South Russia. *Ocherk' vzaimootnoshenii vooruzhennykh sil' Iuga Rossii i predstavitelei frantsuzskago komandovaniia*. ('Orange Book'). Columbia University Russian Archive and *Arkhiv Russkoi Revoliutsii*, Vol. XVI, pp. 233–62. Berlin: Izdatel'stvo 'Slovo,' G. V. Gessen, 1925.

Volunteer Army. *Sobranie uzakonenii i rasporiazhenii previtel'stva*. 2 vols. Rostov-on-Don: Osobym Soveshchaniem pri Glavnokomanduiushchem Vooruzhennymi Silami na Iuge Rossii, 1918–19. (Hoover Library).

Volunteer Army. *The Voluntary Army as a National Factor in the Renaissance of Great Russia, One and Indivisible*. Ekaterinodar: Volunteer Army, 1919. (Hoover Library).

Voronovich, N. (ed.). *Zelenaia kniga: sbornik materialov i dokumentov. Istoriia krest'ianskago dvizheniia v Chernomorskoi gubernii*. Prague: Izdanie Chernomorskoi Krest'ianskoi Delegatsii, 1921.

West Ukrainian People's Republic. *The Book of Bloody Cruelties: Returns Concerning the Invasion of the Poles into the Ukrainian Territory of Galicia in 1918–1919*. Vienna: H. Engel and Son, 1919. (Hoover Library).

Woodward, E. L., and Butler, R. (eds.). *Documents on British Foreign Policy, 1919–1939*. Vols. II–III. London: H. M. Stationery Office, 1949.

Selected Bibliography (Printed)

Adams, A. E. *Bolsheviks in the Ukraine, The Second Campaign, 1918–1919*. New Haven: Yale University Press, 1963.

Alekseev, S. A. (ed.). *Denikin, Iudenich, Vrangel*. Moscow: Gosizdat, 1927.

——. (ed.). *Nachalo grazhdanskoi voiny*. Moscow: Gosizdat, 1926.

——. (ed.). *Revoliutsiia na Ukraine po memuaram belykh*. Moscow: Gosizdat, 1930.

Allen, W. E. D. *The Ukraine*. Cambridge: Cambridge University Press, 1940.

Anishev, A. *Ocherki istorii grazhdanskoi voiny, 1917–1920*. Leningrad: Gosizdat, 1925.

Al'f, I. (Seimovich, I.) et al. *Antanta i Vrangel: sbornik statei*. Moscow: Gosizdat, 1923.

Antonov-Ovseenko, V. A. *Zapiski o grazhdanskoi voine*. 4 vols. Moscow: Gosvoenizdat, 1924–33.

Arshinov, P. A. *Istoriia Makhnovskogo dvizheniia, 1918–1921*. Berlin: Gruppa russkikh anarkhistov v Germanii, 1923. (*L'histoire du mouvement makhneviste, 1918–1921*. Paris: Editions Anarchistes, Librairie internationale, 1924).

Atlas, M. L. *Bor'ba za sovety: ocherki po istorii sovetov v Krymu v 1919 g.* Simferopol: Krymgosizdat, 1933.

Azan, Paul Jean Louis. *Franchet d'Esperey*. Paris: Flammarion, 1949.

Balabanoff, Angelica. *My Life as a Rebel*. London: H. Hamilton, 1938.

Bazhanov, B. (ed.). *Pokhischchenie generala A. P. Kutepova bol'shevikami*. Paris: no pub., 1930.

Bechhofer-Roberts, C. E. *In Denikin's Russia and the Caucasus, 1919–1920*. London: W. Collins, Sons and Co., Ltd. 1931.

Beliaevskii, V. A. *Pravda o gen, Denikine: prichiny prekrashcheniia belogo dvizheniia na iuge Rossii v 1920 g.* San Francisco: no pub., 1959.

Benegin, M. F. *Revoliutsiia i grazhdanskaia voina v Krymu*. Simferopol: Krymgosizdat, 1927.

Beneš, Edvard. *My War Memoirs*. Translated by Paul Selver. Boston: Houghton Mifflin, 1928.

Bertie, F. L. *The Diary of Lord Bertie of Thame, 1914–1918*. 2 vols. Edited by Lady Algernon Gordon Lennox. London: Hodder and Stoughton, 1924.

Blair, Dorian, and Dand, C. H. *Russian Hazard: The Adventures of a British Secret Service Agent in Russia*. London: Robert Hale, 1937.

Bochagov, A. K. *Milli Firka; natsionalnaia kontr-revoliutsiia v Krymu*. Simferopol: Krymgosizdat, 1930.

Borshchak, Il'ko. *L'Ukraine à la conférence de la paix, 1919–1923*. Paris: no pub., 1938.

Bradley, J. F. N. *La légion tchécoslovaque en Russie, 1914–1920*. Paris: Centre National de la Recherche Scientifique, 1965.

Bubnov, A. S., Kamenev, S. S., and Eideman, R. P. (eds.). *Grazhdanskaia voina, 1918–1921*. 3 vols. Moscow: Gosizdat, 'Voennyi Vestnik,' 1928–30.

Buchan, John (ed.). *The Baltic and Caucasian States*. Boston: Houghton, Mifflin Col, 1923.

Buchanan, Sir George. *My Mission to Russia and Other Diplomatic Memories*. 2 vols. London: Cassell and Co., Ltd., 1923.

Budennyi, S. M. *Proidennyi put'*. 2 vols. Moscow: Voennoe izdatel'stvo, 1965.

Buiskii, A. *Bor'ba za Krym i razgrom Vrangelia*. Moscow: Gosizdat, 1928.

Bullitt, W. C. *The Bullitt Mission to Russia*. New York: R. W. Heubach, 1919.

Bystrianskii, V. A. *Antanta, Rossiia i revoliutsiia*. Petrograd: Gosizdat, 1920.

——. *Iz istorii grazhdanskoi voiny v Rossii*. Petrograd: Gosizdat, 1921.

Cambon, Paul. *Correspondence, 1870–1924*. Vol. III (1912–24). Paris: Editions Bernard Grasset, 1946.

Carr, E. H. *The Bolshevik Revolution, 1917–1923.* Vol. III. London: Macmillan Co., 1953.

Chamberlin, W. H. *The Russian Revolution.* 2 vols. New York: Macmillan Co., 1935.

——. *The Ukraine: A Submerged Nation.* New York: Macmillan Co., 1944.

Chebaevskii, F. V. *Razgrom vtorogo pokhoda Ananty.* Moscow: Znanie, 1952.

Chernov, V. *The Great Russian Revolution.* Translated and abridged by P. E. Mosely. New Haven: Yale University Press, 1936.

Chicherin, G. V. *Stat'i rechi po voprosam mezhdunarodnoi politiki.* Moscow: Izdatel'stvo sotsial'no-ekonomicheskoi literatury, 1961.

——. *Two Years of Foreign Policy: The Relations of the Russian Socialist Federal Soviet Republic with Foreign Nations from November 7, 1917, to November 7, 1919.* New York: Russian Soviet Government Bureau, 1920.

Chikalenko, Eugene. *Spohadi.* Vols. II and III, Lviv: no pub., 1925–26.

Churchill, W. S. *The World Crisis: The Aftermath.* London: Thornton Butterworth, Ltd., 1929.

Clemenceau, Georges. *Grandeurs et misères d'une victoire.* Paris: Plon, 1930.

Coates, W. P., and Zelda K. *Armed Intervention in Russia, 1918–1922.* London: V. Gollancz, Ltd., 1935.

Coates, W. P., and Zelda K. *A History of Anglo-Soviet Relations.* London: Lawrence and Wishart, The Pilot Press, 1944.

Coen, Antonio. *La verité sûr l'affaire Sadoul.* Paris: Comité pour la défense de Jacques Sadoul, 1919.

Dan, F. *Dva goda skitanii, 1919–1921.* Berlin: no pub., 1922.

Davatts, V. K. *Gody: ocherki piatiletnei bor'by.* Belgrade: no pub., 1926.

Deborin, G. A. *Sovetskaia vneshniaia politika v pervye gody sushchestvovaniia sovetskogo gosudarstva, 1917–1920 gg.* Moscow: Izdatel'stvo Pravda, 1951.

Delert, D. *Don v ogne.* Rostov-on-Don: no pub., 1927.

Denikin, A. I. *Kto spas' sovetskuiu vlast' ot gieli.* Paris, Izdanie Soiuz' Dobrovol'tsev, 1937.

——. *Ocherki russkoi smuty.* 5 vols. Berlin: Russkoe Natsional'noe Knigoizdatel'stvo 'Slovo' and Paris: J. Povolozky et Cie., 1921–26.

——. *The Russian Turmoil.* London: Hutchinson and Co., 1922.

——. *The White Army.* Translated by Catherine Zvegintzov. London: J. Cape and Co., 1930.

——. *World Events and the Russian Problem.* Paris: Imprimerie Rapide, 1939.

Denisov, S. V. (ed.). *Belaia Rossiia.* New York: Izdatel'stvo glavnago pravleniia zarubezhnago soiuza Russkikh voennikh invalidov, 1937.

——. *Zapiski: grazhdanskaia voina na iuge Rossii, 1918–1919 gg.* Constantinople: Izdanie avtora, 1921.

Deutscher, I. *The Prophet Armed: Trotsky: 1879–1921*. New York: Oxford University Press, 1954.

Deygas, F. J. *L'Armée d'Orient dans la guerre mondiale, 1915–1919*. Paris: Payot, 1932.

Dnistrianskii, S. *Ukraine and the Peace Conference*. Berlin: Ukrainian Delegation, 1919.

Dobrynin, V. *Bor'ba s bol'shevizmom na iuge Rossii: uchastie v bor'be donskogo kazachestva*. Prague: Slavianskoe Izdatel'stvo, 1921. (*La lutte contre le bolchevisme*. Prague: Imp. 'Melantrich,' 1920.

Dobrzhinskii, G. V. *Osvobozhdenie Kryma*. Moscow: Vsesoiuznoe obshchestvo politikatorzhan i ssyl'no-poselentsev, 1932.

Dolenga, S. *Skoropadshchyna*. Warsaw: M. Kunytsky (Nakladom Modesta Kunits'kogo), 1934.

Dolgorukov, P. D. (Prince). *Natsional'naia politika i partiia narodnoi svobody*. Rostov-on-Don: Osvag, 1919.

Doroshenko, D. *Istoriia Ukrainy, 1917–1923 gg*. 2 vols. Uzhhorod: Nakladom d-ra Osipa Tsiupki, 1930–32.

——. *Moi spomyny pro nedavne-mynule, 1914–1918*. 4 vols. Lvov: Chervona Kolyna, 1923–1924.

Dotsenko, Oleksandr. *Litopis Ukrains'koi revoliutsii*. Vol. I. Kiev: Nakladom avtora, 1923.

Drozdovskii, M. G. *Dnevnik*. Brelin: Knigoizdatel'stvo Otto Kirkher, 1923.

Dubreuil, Charles. *Deux années en Ukraine, 1917–1919*. Paris: Paulin, 1919.

Efremoff, I. N. *The Cossacks of the Don*. Paris: Imp. L. Fournier, 1919.

Egorov, A. I. *Razgrom Denikina, 1919*. Moscow: Gosvoenizdat, 1931.

Eideman, R., and Kakurin, N. *Hromadians'ka Viina na Ukraine*. Kharkiv: Derzhavne vidavnitstvo Ukraini, 1928.

Erde, D. *Godi buri i natiska*. Kharkov: Gosizdat Ukraini, 1923.

Evain, Emmanuel. *La problème de l'indépendance de l'Ukraine et la France*. Paris: F. Alcan, 1931.

Filippov, N. *Ukrainskaia kontr-revoliutsiia na sluzhbe u Anglii, Frantsii i Pol'shi*. Moscow: Moskovskii Rabochii, 1927.

——. *The Soviets in World Affairs*. 2 vols. Princeton: Princeton University Press, 1951.

Fleming, Peter. *The Fate of Admiral Kolchak*. New York: Harcourt, Brace and World, 1936.

Footman, David. *Civil War in Russia*. London: Faber and Faber, Ltd., 1961.
——. (ed.). *Soviet Affairs*. Number Two. St Antony's Papers, Number Six. New York: Praeger, 1959.

Franchet d'Esperey, L. F. M. F. *Histoire militaire et navale de la nation française: la grande guerre, 1914–1918*. Vol. VIII of *Histoire de la nation française*, edited by G. Hanotaux. Paris: *Plon-Nourrit et Cie.*, 1927.

Francis, D. *Russia From the American Embassy*. New York: Scribner, 1921.

Ganetskii, Iakov S. *Angliiskii imperializm i SSSR*. Moscow, Gosizdat, 1927.

General Kutepov: sbornik statei. Paris: Izdanie komiteta imeni generala Kutepova, Imp. d'art franco-russe, 1934.

Gleichen, E. (ed.). *The Baltic and Caucasian States*. Boston: Houghton-Mifflin Co., 1923.

Gollin, A. M. *Proconsul in Politics: A Study of Lord Milner in Opposition and in Power*. New York: Macmillan, 1964.

Golovin, N. N. *Rossiiskaia kontr-revoliutsiia v 1917-1918 gg.* 5 vols. Paris: Biblioteka 'Illiustrirovannoi Rossii,' 1937.

Golubev, A. (ed.). *Perekop i Chongar*. Moscow: Gosvoenizdat, 1933.

——. *Shturm Perekopa*. Moscow: Izdatel'stvo TsK VLKSM, Molodaia gvardiia, 1938.

——. *Vrangelevskie desanti na Kubani, Avgust-Sentiabr, 1920*. Moscow: Gosizdat, 1929.

Gooch, G. P., and Ward, A. W. (eds.). *The Cambridge History of British Foreign Policy, 1783-1919*. Vol. III. Cambridge: Cambridge University Press, 1923.

Goode, W. T. *Is Intervention in Russia a Myth?* London: Williams and Norgate, Ltd., 1931.

Graubard, S. R. *British Labour and the Russian Revolution, 1917-1924*. Cambridge: Harvard University Press, 1956.

Grenard, F. *La révolution russe*. Paris: A. Colin, 1933.

Gukovskii, A. I. *Antanta i oktiabr'skaia revoliutsiia*. Moscow: Gosudarstvennoe sotsial'no-ekonomicheskoe izdatel'stvo, 1931.

——. *Frantsuzskaia interventsiia na iuge Rossii, 1918-1919*. Moscow: Gosudarstvennoe sotsial'no-ekonomicheskoe izdatel'stvo, 1928.

——. (ed.). *Lenin ob interventsii*. Moscow: Ogiz 'Mosk. rabochii,' Tip. 'Krasnyi proletarii,' 1931.

——. Malakhovskii, V., and Melikov, V., (eds.). *Razgrom Vrangelia, 1920: sbornik statei*. Moscow: Gosvoenizdat, 1930.

Gul, R. *Ledianoi pokhod*. Berlin: no pub., 1921.

Gusev-Orenburgskii, S. I. *Kniga o evreiskikh pogromakh na Ukraine v 1919*. Petrograd: Z. Grzhebin, n.d.

Haumant, Emile. *Le problème de l'unite russe*. Paris: Editions Bossard, 1922.

Heifetz, Elias. *The Slaughter of the Jews in the Ukraine in 1919*. New York: Seltzer, 1921.

Hill, G. A. *Go Spy the Land: Being the Adventures of I. K. 8 of the British Secret Service*. London: Cassell, 1932.

Hodgson, J. *With Denikin's Armies*. London: L. Williams Co., Ltd., 1932.

Hoffmann, M. *War Diaries and Other Papers*. 2 vols. London: Martin Secker, 1929.

Iakushkin, E. E., and Polunin, S. *Angliiskaia interventsiia v 1918–1920 gg.* Moscow: Gosizdat, 1928.

Iakushkin, E. E. *Frantsuzskaia interventsiia na iuge, 1918–1919.* Moscow: Gosizdat, 1929.

Iaroslavskii, E., and Radek, K. *Delo Borisa Savinkova: ispoved', protsess, i sbornik statei* Moscow: Gosizdat, (1924?).

Ignat'ev, V. *Nekotorye fakti i itogi chetirekh let grazhdanskoi voiny, 1917–1921.* Moscow: Gosizdat, 1922.

Ilovaiskii, V. *God puti: zhizn' Dobrovol'cheskoi armii.* Rostov-on-Don: Tip. 'Obnovlenie,' 1919.

Ilovaiskii, V. *God puti: zhizn' Dobrovol'cheskoi armii.* Rostov-on-Don: Tip. 'Obnovlenie,' 1919.

Ioffe, Ia. *Organizatsiia interventsii i blokady Sovetskoi respubliki, 1918–1920.* Moscow: Gosizdat, Otdel voennoi literatury, 1930.

Isproved' Savinkova: protsess Borisa Savinkova, Avgust 1924. Berlin: Izdanie zhurnala 'Russkoe Ekho,' 1924.

Ivanis, Vasil'. *Stezhkami zhittia: spogadi.* Vols. II and III. Neu-Ulm: 'Ukrainski Visti,' 1959.

Ivashin, I. F., and Zuev, F. G. *Mezhdunarodnye otnosheniia v period provedeniia velikoi Okt'iabrskoi sotsialisticheskoi revoliutsii: vneshniaia politika sovetskogo gosudarstva v gody inostrannoi voennoi interventsii i grazhdanskoi voiny.* Moscow: Vyshaia partiinaia shkola pri TsK KPSS, 1955.

Jeanneret, P. *En campagne contre les Bolcheviks.* Lausanne: Bibliothèque universelle et revue suisse, 1919.

Kakhovskaia, I. Kl *Souvenirs d'une revolutionnaire.* Translated by M. Livane and J. Newman. Paris: F. Rieder et Cie., 1926.

Kakurin, N. *Kak srazhalas' revoliutsiia.* 2 vols. Moscow: Gosizdat, 1925.

Kalinin, I. M. *Pod znamenem Vrangelia.* Leningrad: Rabochee izdatel'stvo 'Priboi,' 1925.

———. *Russkaia vandeia.* Moscow: Gosizdat, 1926.

Kalvari, M. A. *Interventsiia v Krymu.* Simferopol: Krymgosizdat, 1930.

Kandidov, B. P. *Religioznaia kontr-revoliutsiia 1918–1920 gg. i interventsiia: ocherki i materialy.* Moscow: Izdatel'stvo obshchestva 'Bezbozhnik,' 1930.

Kantorovich, V. A. *Frantsuzy v Odesse.* Petrograd: Biblioteka Izdatel'stvo 'Byloe,' 1922.

Kapustianskii, M. *Pokhid ukrainskikh armii na Kiiv-Odesu v 1919 rotsi.* 2 vols. Munich: 'Khvil'ovogo,' 1946.

Kashen (Cashin), M. *Frantsiia organizator interventsii.* Moscow: Ogiz 'Mosk. rabochii' tip. Izdatel'stvo 'Der emes,' 1931.

Kazimirski, K. M. *Bor'ba imperialisticheskoi Anglii s Respublikoi Sovetov.* Kharkov: 'Proletarii,' 1927.

K desiatiletiiu interventsii- sbornik statei. Moscow: Gosizdat, Obshchestvo sodeistviia zhertvam interventsii, 1929.

Kennan, G. F. *Russia and the West Under Lenin and Stalin.* Boston: Atlantic-Little, Brown and Co., 1960.

——. *Soviet-American Relations, 1917–1920.* 2 vols. Vol. I: *Russia Leaves the War.* Princeton: Princeton University Press, 1956. Vol. II: *The Decision to Intervene.* Princeton: Princeton University Press, 1958.

Kerenskii, A. F. *The Catastrophe: Kerensky's Own Story of the Russian Revolution.* New York: D. Appleton, 1927.

——. *The Crucifixion of Liberty.* New York: John Day, 1934.

——. *The Prelude to Bolshevism: The Kornilov Rebellion.* London: T. Fisher Unwin, 1919.

Kerzhentsev, P. M. *Les alliés et la Russie.* Moscow: Edition du Groupe Communiste française, 1919.

Khrystiuk, P. (ed.). *Zamitky i materialy do istorii ukrains'koi revoliutsii.* 4 vols. in two. Vienna: Ukrains'kii Sotsiol'ohichnii Instytut, Drukernia J. N. Vernay, 1920–21.

Khovanskaia, A. S. *Vosstanie frantsuzskogo flota na chernom more.* Moscow: Gosizdat, 1929.

Kin, D. *Denikinschchina.* Leningrad: 'Priboi,' 1927.

Kirimal, E. *Der Nationale Kampf der Krimtuerken, mit besonderer Beruecksichtigung der Jahre 1917–1918.* Emstetten: Verlag Lechte, 1952.

Kiritchesco, C. *La Roumanie dans la guerre mondiale, 1916–1919.* Translated by L. Barral, Paris: Payot, 1934.

Kluev, L. *Bor'ba za Tsaritsyn.* Moscow: Gosizdat, 1928.

Knox, Sir Alfred W. F. *With the Russian Army, 1914–1917.* 2 vols. London: Hutchinson and Co. Ltd., 1921.

Komarnicki, Titus. *Rebirth of the Polish Republic.* London: W. Heinemann, 1957.

Konovalets, Eugene. *Prichinki do istorii ukrains'koi revoliutsii.* 2nd ed. N. p.: no pub., 1948.

Korff, S. A. *The Constitution of the Cossacks.* Paris: L. Fournier, 1919.

Korostovetz, V. *Seed and Harvest.* Translated and abridged by Dorothy Lumby. London: Faber and Faber, Ltd., 1931.

Korotkov, I. S. *Razgrom Vrangelia.* Moscow: Voennoe Izdatel'stvo Ministerstva Vooruzhennykh sil, 1948.

Kouchnire (Kushnir), M. *L'Ukraine, l'Europe orientale et la conference de la paix.* Paris: Bureau de presse Ukrainien, 1919.

Kovtiukh, E. *Ot Kubani do Volgi i obratno.* Moscow: Gosvoenizdat, 1926.

Krasnov, P. N. *Kazach'ia 'samostiinost'.'* Berlin: 'Dvuglavyi Orel,' 1921.

Kritskii, M. A. *Kornilovskii udarnyi polk'.* Paris: Imp. 'Val,' 1936.

Kroupensky, A. N. *The Rumanian Occupation in Bessarabia.* Paris: Imp. Lahure, 1920.

Kutiakov, I. *Razgrom Uralskoi beloi Kazachei armii.* Moscow: Gosvoenizdat, 1931.

La Chesnais, P. G. *The Defense of the Cossacks Against Bolshevism.* Paris: L. Fournier, 1919.

Ladokh, G. *Ocherki grazhdanskoi voiny na Kubani.* Krasnodar: Burevestnik, 1923.

von Lampe, A. A. (ed.). *Beloe delo; letopis beloi bor'by.* 7 vols. Berlin: Russkoi natsional'noe knigoizdatel'stvo, 'Mednyi Vsadnik,' 1926–28.

——. (ed.). *Glavnokomanduiushchii russkoi armiai general baron P. N. Vrangel: sbornik statei.* Berlin: Knigoizdatel'stvo 'Mednyi Vsadnik,' 1938.

——. *Prichiny neudachi vooruzhennago vystupleniia belykh.* Berlin: Otdel'nyi ottish iz zhurnala 'Russkii Kolokol'.' 1929.

Laserson, Max. M. *The Curzon Line.* New York: Carnegie Endowment for International Peace, 1944.

Lenin, V. I. *Lenin o vneshnei politike sovetskogo gosudarstva.* Moscow: Institut Marksizma-Leninizma pri TsK KPSS, Gospolitizdat, 1960.

——. *Ob inostrannoi voennoi interventsii i grazhdanskoi voine v SSSR, 1918–1920 gg.* Moscow: Gospolitizdat, 1956.

——. *Polnoe sobranie sochinenii.* 5th edition. 55 vols. Moscow: Institut Marksizma-Leninizma pri TsK KPSS, Gospolitizdat, 1960–.

——. *Vse na bor'bu s Denikinym.* Moscow: Partiinoe Izdat., 1935.

Levidov, M. *K istorii soiuznoi interventsii v Rossii.* Vol. I. Leningrad: Rabochee Izdatel'stvo 'Priboi,' 1925.

Lipatov, N. P. *1920 god na Chernom More; voenno-morskie sily v razgrome Vrangelia.* Moscow: Gosvoenizdat, 1958.

Lishin, N. N. *Na Kaspiiskom more; god beloi bor'by.* Prague: Izdanie Morskogo zhurnala, 1938.

Lisovoi, Ia. M. (ed.). *Belyi arkhiv: sborniki materialov po istorii i literature voiny, revoliutsii, bol'shevizma, belago dvizheniia i t. p.* 3 vols. Paris: no pub., 1926–28.

Liubimov, N. N. *SSSR i Frantsiia.* Leningrad: Rabochee Izdatel'stvo "Priboi,' 1926.

Lloyd George, D. *The Truth About the Peace Treaties.* Vol. I. London: V. Gollancz, Ltd., 1938.

——. *The War Memoirs of David Lloyd George.* Vols. III–VI. Boston: Little, Brown and Co., 1933–34.

——. *Memoirs of the Peace Conference.* Vol. I. New Haven: Yale University Press, 1939.

Lobanov-Rostovskii, A. *The Grinding Mill: Reminiscences of War and Revolution in Russia, 1913–1920.* New York: Macmillan Co., 1935.

Lockhart, R. H. Bruce. *Jan Masaryk, a Personal Memoir.* New York: Philosophical Library, 1951.

——. *Memoirs of a British Agent.* London: Putnam, 1932.

Loginov, P. N. (ed.). *Interventsiia i vnutrenniaia kontr-revoliutsiia, 1917–1918*. Moscow: Fabrik 'Diafoto,' 1932.

Loris-Melikof, J. *La révolution russe et les nouvelles républiques trans-caucasiennes*. Paris: F. Alcan, 1920.

Lotots'kii, A. I. *Simon Petliura*. Warsaw: Nakladom Komitetu dlia vshanu-vannia X richnitsi smerti Simona Petliury, 1936.

——. *Storinki minuloho*. Vols. II–III. Warsaw: Pratsi Ukrains'kogo nauko-vogo institutu, 1933–34.

Lozyns'kii, M. *Halichina v rokakh 1918–1920*. Vienna: no pub., 1922.

von Ludendorff, Erich. *Ludendorff's Own Story: August 1914–November 1918*. 2 vols. New York: Harper and Brothers, 1919.

Lukomskii, A. S. *Memoirs of the Russian Revolution*. Translated and abridged by Olga Vitali. London: T. F. Unwin, Ltd., 1922.

——. *Vospominaniia*. 2 vols. Berlin: Otto Kirchner, 1922.

L'vov, G. E. *A nos frères ainés*! Paris: Edition de l'Union, 1919.

Lykholat, A. V. *Razgrom natsionalisticheskoi kontrrevoliutsii na Ukraine, 1917–1922 gg*. Moscow: Gospolitizdat, 1954.

Machray, Robert. *The Poland of Pilsudski*. London: George Allen and Unwin, Ltd., 1936.

Maillard, M. *Le problème russe; le mensonge de l'Ukraine séparatiste: notes d'un témoin*. Paris: Imp. Berger-Levrault, 1919.

Maiskii, I. M. *Demokraticheskaia kontr-revoliutsiia*. Moscow: Gosizdat, 1923.

——. *Vneshniaia politika RSFSR, 1917–1921*. Moscow: Gosizdat, 1923.

Makarov, P. V. *Ad'iutant General Mai-Maievskogo; iz vospominanii nachal'nika otriada krasnykh partizan v Krymu*. Leningrad: Rabochee Izdatel'stvo 'Priboi,' 1929.

Makhno, Nester I. *Pod udarami kontr-revoliutsii*. Paris: Izdanie komiteta N. Makhno, 1936.

——. *Russkaia revoliutsiia na Ukraine, ot marta 1917 po aprel 1918*. Paris: Izdanie komiteta N. Makhno, 1929.

——. *Ukrainskaia revoliutsiia*. Paris: Izdanie komiteta N. Makhno, 1937.

Makhrov, P. *Kto i pochemu mog' pokhitet' gen. Kutopova i gen. Millera?* Paris: no pub., 1937.

Maklakov, V. A. *Rechi, sudebniia, dumskiia i publichniia lektsii, 1904–1926*. Paris: Izdanie Iubileinago komiteta, 1949.

Makoshin, R. *Chto sdelala Dobrovol'cheskaia armiia*. Rostov-on-Don: Osvag, 1919.

Malchevskii, I. S. (ed.). *Vserossiiskoe uchreditel'noe sobranie*. Moscow: Gosizdat, 1930.

Mannerheim, Carl. *The Memoirs of Marshal Mannerheim*. Translated by Count Eric Lawenhaupt. London: Cassell and Co., Ltd., 1953.

Mantoux, Paul. *Les délibérations du Conseil des Quatre (24 Mars–28 Juin 1919)*. 2 vols. Paris: Editions du Centre National de la Recherche Scientifique, 1955.

BIBLIOGRAPHY

Mantoux, Paul. *Paris Peace Conference, 1919.* Geneva: Droz, 1964.

Marchand, René. *Why I Support Bolshevism.* London: British Socialist Party, n.d.

Margolin, A. D. *From a Political Diary: Russia, the Ukraine and America, 1905-1945.* New York: Columbia University Press, 1946.

———. *Ukraina i politika antanty.* Berlin: Izdatel'stvo S. Efron, 1921.

Margulies, M. S. *God interventsii.* 3 vols. Berlin: Izdatel'stvo Z. I. Grzhebina (Z. J. Grschebin Verlag), 1923.

Margulies, Vladimir. *Ognennye gody: materialy i dokumenty po istorii grazhdanskoi voiny na iuge Rossii.* Berlin: Izdatel'stvo 'Manfred,' 1923.

Markhlevskii, Iulian. *Ocherki istorii Pol'shi.* Moscow: Gosundarstvennoe Sotsial'no-Ekonomicheskoe Izdatel'stvo, 1931.

———. *Voina i mir mezhdu burzhuaznoi Pol'shei i proletarskoi Rossiei.* Moscow: Gosizdat, 1921.

Marty, André P. *The Epic of the Black Sea Revolt.* New York: Workers' Library Publishers, 1941. (*La Révolte de la Mer Noire.* Paris: Bureau d'Editions, 1932.)

Masaryk, Tomas G. *The Making of a State, Memoirs and Observations, 1914-1918.* London: G. Allen and Unwin, Ltd., 1927.

Maynard, C. C. M. *The Murmansk Venture, 1918-1919.* London: Hodder and Stoughton, Ltd., 1928.

Mekler, N. *V denikinskom podpol'e.* Moscow: Ogiz Molodaia gvardiia, 1932.

Mel'gunov, S. P. *N. V. Chaikovskii v gody grazhdanskoi voiny: materialy dlia istorii Russkoi obshchestvennosti, 1917-1925 gg.* Paris: Librairie 'La Source,' 1929.

Mel'kumov, A. *Materialy revoliutsionnogo dvizheniia v Turkmenii.* Tashkent: Ispart TsKKPT, 1924.

Michelson, A. M., Apostol, P. N., and Bernatsky, M. W. *Russian Public Finance During the War.* Cambridge: Yale University Press, 1928.

Migal'skii. V. *Vospominaniia.* Odessa: Gosizdat, 1921.

Miliukov, P. N. *Beloe dvizhenie.* Paris: Izdanie Respublikansko-demokraticheskogo ob'edineniia, Imprimerie d'Art Boltaire, 1929.

———. *The Case for Bessarabia: A Collection of Documents on the Rumanian Occupation.* London: Russian Liberation Committee Publication No. 8, 1919

———. *Istoriia vtoroi russkoi revoliutsii.* 3 vols. Sofia: Rossiisko-Bolgarskoe Knigoizdatel'stvo, 1921-24.

———. *La politique extérieure des Soviets.* Paris: Giard, 1934.

———. *Russia and its Critics.* New York: Collier, 1962.

———. *Respublika ili monarkhiia?* Paris: Izdanie Respublikansko-demokraticheskogo ob'edineniia, 1929.

———. *Russia Today and Tomorrow.* New York: Macmillan Co., 1922.

———. *Russia and England.* London: Russian Liberation Committee Publication No. 13, 1920.

Miller, David Hunter. *My Diary at the Conference of Paris.* 21 vols. New York: privately published, 1924–26.

Mints, I. I. (ed.) *.Sovetskaia Rossiia i kapitalisticheskii mir v 1917–1923 gg.* Moscow: Akademiia nauk SSSR, Institut istorii, Gospolitizdat, 1957.

Mordacq, Jean J. H. *Le ministère Clemenceau, journal d'un témoin.* 4 vols. in two. Paris: Librairie Plon, 1931.

Nabokoff, C. *The Ordeal of a Diplomat.* London: Duckworth and Co., 1921.

Naida, S. F. et al. (eds.). *Istoriia grazhdanskoi voiny v SSSR, 1917–1922.* 3 vols. Moscow: Institut Marksizma-Leninizma pri TsK KPSS, Gospolitizdat, 1959.

——. (ed.). *Iz istorii bor'by sovetskogo naroda protiv inostrannoi voennoi interventsii i vnutrennei kontr-revoliutsii v 1918: sbornik statei.* Moscow: Gosizdat, 1956.

——., and Aleksashenko, A. N. *Kommunisticheskaia partiia v period 'inostrannoi voennoi interventsii i grazhdanskoi voiny.* Moscow: Gospolitizdat, 1959.

——. *O nekotorykh voprosakh istorii grazhdanskoi voiny v SSSR.* Moscow: Gospolitizdat, 1958.

——. (ed.). *Reshaiushchie pobedy sovetskogo naroda nad interventami i belogvardeitsami v 1919 g.* Sbornik statei. Moscow: Gospolitizdat, 1960.

Nansen, Fridtjof. *Russia and Peace.* London: Allen, 1923.

Naumenko, V. G. *Iz nedavniago proshlago Kubani.* Belgrade: no pub., 1930.

Nazaruk, Osip. *Rik na Veliki Ukraini, spomini z Ukrains'koi revoliutsii.* Vienna: Vidannia 'Ukrains'kogo praporu,' 1920.

Nazhivin, I. F. *Zapiski o revoliutsii.* Vienna: Knigoizdatel'stvo 'Rus',' 1921.

Nemirovich-Denchenko, G. *V Krymu pri Vrangele.* Berlin: Tip. P. Ol'denburg, 1922.

Nesterovich-Berg, M. A. *V bor'be s bol'shevikami: vospominaniia.* Paris: Imp. de Navarre, 1931.

Nicolson, H. *Curzon: The Last Phase, 1919–1925.* New York: Harcourt, Brace and Co., 1939.

Niessel, Henri. *Le triomphe des bolcheviks et la paix de Brest–Litovsk: souvenirs, 1917–1918.* Paris: Librairie Plon, 1940.

Nizhegorodtsev, A. *Pochemu Dobrovol'cheskaia armita voiuets' protiv kommunistov Lenina i Trotskago.* Kharkov: no pub., 1919.

Noulens, Joseph. *Mon ambassade en Russie Soviétique, 1917–1919.* 2 vols. Paris: Librairie Plon, 1933.

Oberuchev, C. M. *Vospominaniia.* New York: no pub., 1930.

Obolenski, V. A. *Krym pri Vrangele: mamuary belogvardeitsa.* Moscow: Gosizdat, 1927. (Prague: Edition 'Vataga,' 1925.)

Oktiabr' na Kubani i Chernomore. Krasnodar: Istpart, Burevestnik, 1924.

BIBLIOGRAPHY

Oktiabr'skaia revoliutsiia i grazhdanskaia voina v Voronezhskoi gubernii. Voronezh: Istpart, Voronezhskaia Kommuna, n.d.

Osvobozhdenie Kryma ot anglo-frantsuzskikh interventov, 1918–1919. Simferopol: Krymogsizdat, 1940.

Paléologue, Maurice. *An Ambassador's Memoirs.* 3 vols. London: Hutchinson and Co. Ltd., 1923.

Partiia Men'shevikov i Denikinshchina. Moscow: Krasnaia Nov. 1923.

Pasmanik, D. S. *Revoliutsionnye gody v Krymu.* Paris: Imp. de Navarre, 1926.

Pavlovich, M. P. *Sovetskaia Rossiia i kapitalisticheskaia Frantsiia.* 2 vols. Moscow: Gosizdat, 1922. (See also Vel'tman, M. L.)

———. (Vel'tman, M. L.). *Ukraina kak ob'ekt mezhdunarodnoi kontr-revoliutsii.* Moscow: Gosizdat, 1920.

Paz, Maurice. *Les révoltes de la mer Noire.* Paris: Librairie du travail, 1921.

Petriv, Vsevolod. *Spomini z Chasiv Ukrains'koi revoliutsii, 1917–1921.* 4 vols. Lviv: Nakladom vidavnichoi kooperativi 'Chervona Kalina,' 1927–31.

Petrushevskii, I. P. (ed.). *Istorik i sovremennik: istoriko-literaturnyi sbornik.* Vol. II. Berlin: Olga Diakow Verlag, 1922.

Pipes, Richard. *The Formation of the Soviet Union: Communism and Nationalism, 1917–1923.* Cambridge: Harvard University Press, 1954.

Pokrovskii, G. K. *Denikinshchina: god politiki i ekenomiki na Kubani, 1918–1919 gg.* Brelin: Izdatel'stvo Z. I. Grzhebina, 1923.

Pokrovskii, M. N. *Kontr-revoliutsiia za 4 goda.* Moscow: Gosizdat, 1922.

———. *Oktiabr'skaia revoliutsiia i Antanta.* Moscow: Gosizdat, 1927.

———. *Vneshniaia politika Rossii v XX veke.* Moscow: Gosizdat, 1926.

Polovtsov, L. V. *Rytsary ternovago ventsa; vospominaniia o l-om Kubanskom pokhode gen. M. V. Alekseeva, L. G. Kornilova i A. I. Denikina.* Prague: Tip. Griunkhut, 1921.

Poslednie dni Kryma: vpechatleniia, fakty i dokumenty. Constantinople: Tip. 'Pressa,' 1920.

Potemkin, V. P. (ed.). *Istoriia diplomatii.* Vols. II–III. Moscow: Ogiz, Gospolitizdat, 1945.

Pravosudie v voiskakh generala Vrangelia. Constantinople: no pub., 1921.

Price, M. P. *My Reminiscences of the Russian Revolution.* London: G. Allen and Unwin, Ltd., 1921.

———. *Russia, Red or White.* London: S. Low, Marston, 1948.

———. *The Soviet, the Terror and Intervention.* Brooklyn: Socialist Publication Society, 1918.

———. *The Truth About the Intervention of the Allies in Russia.* Belp: Promachos Publishing House, 1918.

Rabinovich, S. *Istoriia grazhdanskoi voiny.* Moscow: Gos. sots.-eko. izdatel'stvo, 1935.

Radek, Karl. *Vneshniaia politika sovetskoi Rossii.* Moscow: Gosizdat, 1923.

Radkey, Oliver H. *The Election to the Russian Constituent Assembly of 1917.* Cambridge: Harvard University Press, 1950.

——. *The Sickle Under the Hammer.* New York: Columbia University Press, 1963.

Radziwill, S. A. *Les Ukrainiens pendant la guerre.* Paris: no pub., 1937.

Rafes, M. *Dva goda revoliutsii na Ukraine.* Moscow: Gosizdat, 1920.

Rakovskii, C. *Bor'ba za osvobozhdenie derevni.* Kharkov: Political Dept. of the Council of the Ukrainian Labor Army, 1920.

Rakovskii, G. N. *Konets belykh ot Dnepra do Bosfora.* Prague: Izd. 'Volia Rossii,' 1921.

——. *V. stane belykh: grazhdanskaia voina na iuge Rossii.* Constantinople: Izdat. 'Pressa,' 1920.

Razgrom Vrangelia, 1920: sbornik statei. Moscow: Gosvoenizdat, 1930.

Reilly, Sidney. *Britain's Master Spy.* London: Harper and Brothers, 1933.

Reshetar, John S. *The Ukrainian Revolution, 1917–1920.* Princeton: ·Princeton University Press, 1952.

Revoliutsiia v Krymu. Simferopol: Istpart, Krymskoe Gosizdat, 1930.

Rosenberg, William G. *A. I. Denikin and the Anti-Bolshevik Movement in South Russia.* Amherst: Amherst College Press, Amherst College Honors Thesis No. 7, 1961.

Rostov, B. *Pochemu i kak sozdalas' Dobrovol'cheskaia armiia i za chto ona boretsia.* Rostov-on-Don: Osvag, 1919.

Rybakov, M. V. *Protiv Denikina. Stranitsy istorii sovetskoi rodiny.* Moscow: Gospolitizdat, 1962.

Sadoul, Jacques. *Notes sûr la révolution Bolchevique, Octobre 1917–Janvier 1919.* Paris: Editions de la Sirène, 1919.

Samurskii (Efendiev), N. *Dagestan.* Moscow: Gosizdat, 1925.

Savchenko, E. *Les insurgés du Kouban.* Paris: Payot, 1929.

Savinkov, B. V. *Bor'ba s bol'shevikami.* Warsaw: Izdanie Russkago Politicheskago Komiteta, 1920.

——. *Memoirs of a Terrorist.* Translated by Joseph Shaplen. New York: Albert and Charles Boni, 1931.

——. *Za rodinu i svobodu: na puti k 'tret'ei' Rossii: sbornik statei.* Warsaw: Izdanie Russkago Politicheskago Komiteta, 1920.

Sazonov, S. D. *Fateful Years, 1909–1916.* London: J. Cape, 1929.

——. *Vospominaniia.* Paris: Knigoizdatel'stvo E. Siial'skoi, 1927.

Schuman, F. L. *American Policy Toward Russia Since 1917.* New York: International Publishers, 1928.

Sejdamet, D. *La Crimée: passé, présent.* Lausanne: G. Vaney-Burnier, 1921.

Serge, Victor. *Mémoirs d'un révolutionnaire, 1901–1941.* Paris: Editions du seuil, 1951.

Sergeev, A. *Denikinskaia armiia samo o sebe; po dokumentam sobrannym na boevykh liniiakh voennym korrespondentam 'Rosta'.* Moscow: Gosizdat, 1920.

Shaumian, S. G. *Stat'i i rechi, 1908–1918*. Baku: Izdat. 'Bakinskii Rabochii,' 1924.

Shchegolev, P. E. (ed.). *Frantsuzy v Odesse; iz belykh menuarov Gen. A. I. Denikina, M. S. Margulies, M. V. Braikevicha*. Leningrad: Izdat. 'Krasnaia gazeta,' 1928.

Shekhtman, I. B. *Pogromy dobrovol'cheskoi armii na Ukraine, 1919–1920*. Berlin, Ostjudisches historisches archiv, 1932.

Shekun, O. (ed.). *Perekop; sbornik vospominanii*. Moscow: Gos. sotsial'noekonomicheskoe izdatel'stvo, 1941.

Shelukhin, Serhi. *Varshavski dohovir mizh Poliakami i S. Petliuroiu*. Prague: no pub., 1926.

Shteifon, B. A. *Krizis dobrovol'chestva*. Belgrade: Russkaia Tip., 1928.

Shtein, B. E. '*Russkii vopros*' *na Parizhskoi mirnoi konferentsii, 1919–1920 gg*. Moscow: Gospolitizdat, 1949.

——. '*Russkii vopros*' *v 1920–1921 gg*. Moscow: Gospolitizdat, 1958.

Shul'gin, Oleksandr (Alexander). *Bez territorii*. Paris: F. Alcan, 1934.

——. (Choulguine, A.). *L'Ukraine contre Moscow*. Paris: F. Alcan, 1935.

——. (Choulguine, A.). *L'Ukraine, la Russie et les Puissances de L'Entente*. Berne: Imp. Réunies S. A. Lausanne, 1918.

Shul'gin, V. V. *Dni*. Belgrade: Knigoizdatel'stov M. A. Suverin i ko., 'Novoe Vremia,' 1925.

——. *1920 g.: ocherki*. Sofia: Rossiisko- Bolgarskoe Knigoizdatel'stvo, 1921.

Simonov, B. *Razgrom Denikinshchini*. Moscow: Gosizadt, 1928.

Skrzynski, Count A. *Poland and Peace*. London: G. Allen and Unwin, 1923.

Slashchev, Ia. A. *Krym v 1920 g*. Moscow: Gosizdat, 1924.

——. (Slashchev-Krymskii, Ia. A.). *Trebuiu suda obshchestva i glasnosti; oborona i sdacha Kryma: menuary i dokumenty*. Constantinople:' Knigoizdatel'stvo M. Shul'mana, 1921.

Sloves, C. H. *La France et l'Union soviétique*. Paris: Editions Rieder, 1935.

Smirnov, A. P. *Soldaty i matrosy Frantsii otkazalis' streliat'*. Leningrad: Ogiz, 'Priboi,' 1931.

Smith, C. Jay, Jr. *The Russian Struggle for Power, 1914–1917: A Study of Russian Foreign Policy During the First World War*. New York: Philosophical Library, 1956.

Smolenskii, S. *Krymskaia katastrofa*. Sofia: Rossiisko-Belgarskoe Knigoizdatel'stvo, 1920.

Sokolov, K. N. *Pravlenie Generala Denikina*. Sofia: Rossiisko-Bolgarskoe Knigoizdatel'stvo, 1921.

Stalin, I. V. *Sochineniia*. Vol. IV. Moscow: Ogiz, Gospolitizdat, 1947.

Stefaniv, Z. *Ukrainski zbroini syly v 1917–1921 gg*. Kolomyia: Vydavnytstvo Nasha Slava, 1935.

Stewart, G. *The White Armies of Russia.* New York : Macmillan Co., 1933.

Strakhovsky, L. I. *The Origins of American Intervention in North Russia.* Princeton: Princeton University Press, 1937.

Struve, P. B. *Razmyshleniia o russkoi revoliutsii.* Sofia: Rossiisko-Bolgarskoe Knigoizdatel'stvo, 1921.

Sukhanov, N. N. *Zapiski o revoliutsii.* 7 vols. Berlin: Z. I. Grzhebin, 1922–23.

Sukhov, A. A. *Inostrannaia interventsiia na Odeshchine v 1918–1919 gg.* Odessa: Izd. Istpart Otdel Odesskogo Okrkoma KPBU, 1927.

Suliatits'kii, P. P. *Narisi z istorii revoliutsii na Kubani.* Prague: Ukrains'kii institut hromadoznavstva v Prazi, 1925.

The Supreme Ruler Admiral of the Russian Nation A. V. Kolchak. Tokyo: Russian Press Bureau magazine, No. 1, 1919.

Suvorin, A. *Pokhod Kornilova.* Rostov-on-Don: Knigoizdat. 'Novyi Chelovek,' 1919.

Suvorin, Boris. *Za rodinoi; geroicheskaia epokha dobrovol'cheskoi armii, 1917-1918 gg.* Paris: O. D. i ko., 1922.

Temkin, Ia, G. *Bol'sheviki v bor'be za demokraticheskii mir, 1914-1918.* Moscow: Gospolitizdat, 1957.

Temperley, H. W. V. *A Brief Summary of Diplomatic Events From the German Armistice to Locarno.* London: The Historical Association, 1926.

——. *A History of the Peace Conference of Paris.* 6 vols. London: H. Frowde, and Hodder and Stoughton, 1920–24.

Timoshenko, V. P. *Rélations économiques entre l'Ukraine et la France.* Paris: Bureau Ukrainien, Imp. Robinet-Houtain, 1919.

Todorskii, A. *Krasnaia armiia v gorakh.* Moscow: Voennyi Vestnik, 1924.

Toynbee, A. J. (ed.). *Survey of International Affairs, 1920–1923.* London: Oxford University Press, 1927.

Tragediia kazachestva. Prague: Biblioteka 'Vol'nogo kazachestva-Vil'nogo kozatstvo,' 1933.

Trotskii, L. D. (Trotsky, Leon). *Between Red and White: A Study of Some Fundamental Questions of Revolution, with Particular Reference to Georgia.* London: Communist Party of Great Britain, 1922.

Trotskii, L. D. (Trotsky, Leon). *The History of the Russian Revolution.* 3 vols. New York: Simon and Schuster, 1932.

——. *Kak vooruzhalas' revoliutsiia.* 5 vols. Moscow: Vysshii voennyi redaktsionnyi sovet, 1923–1925.

——. *My Life: An Attempt at an Autobiography.* New York: Charles Scribner's, 1930.

Trukhanovskii. V. G. *Istoriia mezhdunarodnykh otnoshenii i vneshnei politiki SSSR, 1917–1939 gg.* Vol. I. Moscow: Izdat. I.M.O., 1961.

Ullman, R. H. *Anglo-Soviet Relations, 1917–1921.* Vol. I: *Intervention and the War.* Princeton: Princeton University Press, 1961.

Val', E. G. (von Wahl, E. G.). *Kak Pilsudski pogubil Denikina*. Tallin: Izdanie avtora, 1938.

——. *K istorii belago dvizheniia: deiatel'nost' General-ad'iutanta Schherbacheva*. Tallin: Izdanie avtora, 1935.

——. *Prichiny raspadeniia Ressiiskoi imperii i neudachi russkago natsional'nago dvizheniia*. 4 vols. in 1. Tallin: Izdanie avtora, 1938.

——. *Rol' Ukrainy po opytu 1918–1920 gg*. Tallin: Izdanie avtora, n.d.

Valentinov, A. *87 dnei v poezde Gen. Vrangelia*. Berlin: no pub., 1922.

Vavrik, V. R. *Karpatorossy v Kornilovskom pokhode i Dobrovol'cheskoi armii*. L'vov: Izd. Tip. Stavropgiiskago instituta, pod upravleniem A. I. Ias'kova, 1923.

——. *Frantsuzskii imperializm*. Moscow: Gosizdat, 1926.

——. *Sovetskaia Rossiia i Kapitalisticheskaia Amerika*. Vol. III: *RSFSR v imperialisticheskom okruzhenii*. Moscow: Gosizdat, 1922.

——. *Sovetskaia Rossiia i kapitalisticheskaia Frantsiia*. 2 vols. Moscow: Gosizdat, 1922.

Vetlugin, A. *Trot'ia Rossiia*. Paris: Izdat. 'Franko-russkaia pechat',' 1922.

Villiam, G. *Raspad 'Dobrovol'tsev' ('pobezhdennye'); iz materialov belogvardeiskoi pechati*. Moscow: Gosizdat, 1923.

Vinaver, M. M. *Nashe pravitel'stvo: Krymskiia vospominaniia, 1918-1919 gg*. Paris: Izdanie posmertnoe, 1928.

Vynnychenko, Volodymyr. *Vidrodzhennia natsii*. 3 vols. Vienna: Dzvin, 1920.

Vishniak, M. V. *Chernyi god*. Paris: Izdat. 'Franko-russkaia pechat',' 1922.

——. *Vserossiiskoe uchreditel'noe sobranie*. Paris: Izdat. 'Sovremenniia zapiski,' 1932.

Volin, V. *Don i dobrovol'cheskaia armiia*. Novocharkassk: no pub., 1919.

Volkonskii, Prince P. N. *The Volunteer Army of Alexiev and Denikin*. London: Russian Liberation Committee Publication No. 7, The Avenue Press, 1919.

Volkov, F. D. *Krakh anglisikoi politiki interventsii i diplomaticheskoi izoliatsii Sovetskogo gosudarstva, 1917–1924*. Moscow: Gospolitizdat, 1954.

Vopicka, Charles. *Secrets of the Balkans*. New York: Rand-McNally, 1921.

Vozrozhdenie russkoi armii. Constantinople: Buro russkoi pechati, 1920.

Vulliamy, C. E. (ed.). *The Red Archives: Russian State Papers and Other Documents Relating to the Years 1915–1918*. Translated by A. L. Hynes. London: Geoffrey Bles, 1929.

Vyshevich, K. *Ukrainski vopros, Rossiia i Antanta*. Helsinki: Central Publishing Co., 1918.

Vyslotsky, Ivan (ed.). *Hetman Skoropadsky v osvitlenni ochevydtsiv*. Toronto: Vydavnytstvo 'Ukrainskoho Robitnyka,' 1940.

Warth, R. D. *The Allies and t e Russian Revolution, From the Fall of the Monarchy to the Peace of Brest-Litovsk*. Durham: Duke Univ. Press, 1954.

Wandycz, Piotr S. *France and Her Eastern Allies, 1919–1925*. Minneapolis: University of Minnesota Press, 1962.

Wasilowski, Leon. *La paix avec l'Ukraine*. Geneva: no pub., 1918.

Wheeler-Bennett, J. W. *The Forgotten Peace: Brest Litovsk, March 1918*. London: Macmillan Co., 1938.

Wrangel (Vrangel), Baron P. N. *Always with Honor*. New York: Robert Speller and Sons, 1957. (Published earlier as: *The Memoirs of General Wrangel*. Translated by Sophie Goulston. New York: Duffield and Co., 1930).

Zaitsov, A. A. *1918 god: ocherki po istorii russkoi grazhdanskoi voiny*. Paris: no pub., 1934.

Zhukov, V. K. *Chernomorskii flot v revoliutsii 1917–1918 gg*. Moscow: Molodaia Gvardia, 1931.

Zolotarev, A. *Iz istorii tsentralnoi Ukrainskoi radi*. Kharkov: Gosizdat Ukraini, 1922.

French Bibliography (Printed Sources)

Anet, C., *La Révolution Russe*, 4 vols., Paris, 1917–19.

Bach, L., *Histoire de la révolution russe*, Paris, 1930.

Camon, General, *La Manoeuvre libératrice du Maréchal Pilsudski contre les bolcheviques*, Paris 1929.

D'Avigdor et Windsor, *La Sibérie orientale et le Japon*, Paris, 1922

Dubarbier, G., *En Sibérie après l'armistice*, Paris, 1939.

Dubreuil, C., *Deux Années en Ukraine, 1917–1919*, Paris, 1919.

Gaillard, G., *L'Allemagne et le Baltikum*, Paris, 1919.

Grenard, *La révolution russe*, Paris, 1933.

Grondijs, L., *La guerre en Russie et en Sibérie*, Paris, 1919.

——, *Le cas Koltchak*, Paris ,1919.

Guillaume, General A., *La guerre germano-sovietique, 1941–1945*, Paris, 1949.

Janin, General, *Ma mission en Sibérie*, Paris, 1933.

Kovalevsky, P. E., *Manuel d'histoire russe*, Paris, 1948.

Lasies, J., *La Tragédie Sibérienne*, Paris, 1920.

Laporte, H., *Le premier échec des rouges*, Paris, 1929.

Legras, J., *Mémoires de Russie*, Paris, 1927.

——, *L'armée russe*, Paris, 1934.

Lescure, J., *Les origines de la révolution russe*, Paris, 1927.

Milioukov, Seignobos and Eisenmann, *L'Histoire de Russie*, 3 vols, Paris, 1933.

Montadon, G., *Deux ans chez Koltchak*, Paris, 1923.

Morizet, A., *Chez Lenine et Trotsky, Moscou, 1921*, Paris, 1922.

——, *Documents diplomatiques secrets russes*, (trad. J. Polonsky), Paris, 1922.

——, *La chute du regime tsariste*, (trad. J. Polonsky), Paris, 1927.

Niessel, General, *Le triomphe des Bolcheviques et la paix de Brest–Litovsk*, Paris, 1940.

Nolde, B., *L'ancien régime et la révolution russe*, Paris, 1920.
Noulens, J., *Mon ambassade en Russie soviétique*, 2 vols., Paris, 1933.
Oldenburg, S., *La révolution bolchevique*, Paris, 1928.
Paléologue, M., *La Russie pendant la grande guerre*, Paris, 1923.
Pilsudski, J., *L'Année 1920*, Paris, 1929.
Renouvin, P., *L'alliance Franco-russe*, Paris, 1929.
——, *La crise européene et la grande guerre*, Paris, 1934.
——, *Histoire de relations internationales*, Paris, 1957.
——, *Les crises du XXe siécle*, Paris, 1957.
Rouquerol, *L'aventure de l'amiral Koltchak*, Paris, 1929.
Sadoul, J., *Notes sur la révolution bolchevique*, Paris, 1919.
——, *Quarante lettres de Jacques Sadoul*, Paris, 1922.
Shulgine, A., *Le coup d'état bolchevique 23 octobre-3 décembre 1917*, Paris, 1929.
——, *L'Ukraine contre Moscou*, Paris, 1937.
Sobolevich, E., *Les états baltes et la Russie soviétique*, Paris, 1931.
Steinberg, J., *Souvenirs d'un commissaire du peuple, 1917-1918*, Paris, 1930.
Vaucher, R., *L'enfer bolchevique*, Paris, 1919.
——, *La guerre entre les alliés et la Russie, 1918-1920*, Paris, 1937.
Verge, A., *Avec les Tchécoslovaques*, Paris, 1926.
Vinogradsky, General, *La guerre sur le front oriental*, Paris, 1926.
——, *Les alliés contre la Russie avant, pendant et après la guerre mondiale*, Paris, 1926.
Welter, G., *La guerre civile en Russie*, Paris, 1936.
Xydias, J., *L'intervention française en Russie, 1918-1919*, Paris, 1927.

Czechoslovak Bibliography (Printed)

Babka, A., *Za polární kruh*, Prague, 1924.
Bartošová, Bieberle, Filip, *Boj komunistů olomouckého kraje za obranu Sovětského svazu letech 1917-1945*, Olomouc, 1957.
Beneš, E., *Světová válka a naše revoluce*, 3 vols., Prague, 1927-28.
Beneš, V., *Masarykovo dílo v Americe*, Prague, 1925.
Chechmajstr, A., *O bratru E. Podmolovi padlém u Zborova*, Brno, 1928.
Čechoslováci ve válce a revoluci. Kiev, 1919.
Čermák, J., *Bachmač*. Prague, 1923.
Červinka, K., *Na cestách naší revoluce*. Prague, 1920.
Chab, V., *Bachmač*. Prague, 1948.
Číla, M., *Rozvědky*. Prague, 1924.
Čižmář, J., *Rusko a naše vojsko v revoluci*. Brno, 1926; *V řadách Čs. družiny a Čsl. brigády*. Brno, 1926.
Culka, E., *Boj s rakouskou hydrou*. Prague, 1921.
Deník plukovníka Švece. Prague, 1921.

Dokumenty o protilidové a protinárodní politice T. G. Masaryka. Prague, 1953.

Dokumenty o protisovětských piklech československé reakce. Prague, 1954.

Durich, J., *V českých službách.* Klášterec nad Jizerou, 1921.

Dyma, J., *Anabase.* Prague, 1922.

Fink, P., *Mezi mohylami.* Brno, 1922; *Bílý admirál.* Brno, 1929.

Gajda, R., *Moje paměti.* Prague, 1921.

Haering, V. *Zdravotnictví v armádě na Sibiři.* Prague, 1924.

Halas, F., *Bez legend.* Prague, 1958.

Hanzal, V. *Vyzvědčíci v Haliči.* Prague, 1928.

Hanuš, O. *Marianovka.* Brno, 1924.

——, *O samosprávě a demokracii v sibiřské armádě.* Prague, 1923; *Vláda Sovětů a Čechoslováci.* Prague, 1919.

Hlaváč, J. *Z duše a pera dobrovolce.* Brno, 1926.

Holotík, L., *Štefánikovská legenda a vznik ČSR.* Bratislava, 1958.

Hudec, R., *Cestou osvobození.* Prague, 1924.

Ivičič, V., *Tatranci (7 pluk).* Prague, 1924.

Kaplický, V., *Gornostaj.* Prague, 1936.

Karjansky-Kakhanov, *Rusko a československé legie.* Prague, 1919.

Ke vzniku ČSR. Prague, 1958.

Klecanda, V., *Operace československého vojska na Rusi, 1917–1920.* Prague, 1921.

Kopecký, V., *ČSR a KSČ.* Prague, 1960.

Král, V., *O Masarykově a Benešově kontrarevoluční protisovětské politice.* Prague, 1959.

Kratochvíl, J., *Cesta revoluce.* Prague, 1928.

Krejčí, J. V., *U sibiřské armády.* Prague, 1922; *Návrat sibiřských legií.* Prague, 1920; *Poselství k sibiřskému vojsku.* Prague, 1924.

Křížek, J., *Dvacátý trasport čs. legií.* Prague, 1955.

Kronika 3. střeleckého pluku J. Žižky z Trocnova. Prague, 1927.

Kudela, J., *Aksakovská tragedie.* Brno, 1933; *O Jiřím Klecandovi.* Brno, 1928; *Rok 1913 v dějinách odboje.* Part. I, Brno, 1928; *O starodružníku A. Grmelovi.* Brno, 1926; *Plukovník Švec.* Brno, 1926; *Rok 1918 v dějinách odboje.* Part II, Brno, 1928; *Rok 1917 v dějinách adboje.* Brno, 1927; *Přehled československého odboje do Ukrajiny.* Brno, 1923; *Památce J. Krause,* Brno, 1927; *Profesor Masaryk a československé vojsko na Rusi.* Prague, 1922; *Československý revoluční sjezd v Rusku.* Brno, 1927; (ed.) *Brno v boji za svobodu.* Brno, 1937.

Kunz, J., *Náš odboj v zrcadle rakouské justice.* Prague, 1930.

Kvasnička, J., *Československé legie v Rusku.* Bratislava, 1963.

Mašín, E., *Česká Družina.* Prague, 1922.

——, *Masaryk a revoluční armáda. Masarykovy projevy k legiím.* Prague, 1922.

BIBLIOGRAPHY

Masaryk, T. G., *Světová revoluce.* Prague, 1925.

Medek, R., (ed.). *Za svobodu.* Prague, 1926–29; *Anabase.* Prague, 1927.

Mikolášek, K., *Ze Sibiře kolem světa domů.* Prague, 1928.

Muna, A., *Ruská revoluce a československé hnutí na Rusi.* Kladno, 1919.

Muška, J., Hořec, J., *K úloze československých legií v Rusku.* Prague, 1953.

Na všech frontách. Brno, 1931.

Najbrt, V., *Berezovka.* Brno, 1924; *Rozlet a zlom sibířského bratrstva.* Brno, 1936.

Naše revoluce. Prague, 1923–38.

——, *Penza.* Prague, 1956.

——, *Jaroslav Hašek v revolučním Rusku.* Prague, 1957.

——, Říha, O., *Bez Velké říjnové socialistické revoluce by nebylo ČSR.* Prague, 1951.

Nečas, J., *Úpřimné slovo o stycích česko-ukrajinských.* Prague–Kiev, 1919.

Netolický-Němec, *Za svobodu národa.* Prague, 1922.

Od Zborova k Bachmači, Sborník vzpomínek. Prague, 1937.

Olbracht, I., *Obrazy ze soudobého Ruska.* Prague, 1920.

Olivová, V., *Československo-sovětské vztahy.* Prague, 1957.

Opočenský, J., *Konec monarchie rakousko-uherské.* Prague, 1928.

Památce Jana Volfa. Brno, 1925.

Památce Miloše Wurma. Brno, 1926.

Paměti našich legionářů, vol. I, Mladá Boleslav, 1936.

Pamětní kniha 1. střeleckého pluku. Prague, 1920.

Papoušek, J., *Proč došlo k bojům se Sověty.* Prague, 1928; *Carské Rusko a naše osvobození.* Prague, 1927; *J. Klecanda.* Prague, 1928; *Masaryk a naše revoluční hnutí v Rusku.* Prague, 1925.

Patejdl, J., *Sibířská anabase.* Prague, 1923.

Paulová, M., *Dějiny Maffie.* Prague, 1937.

Pavel, A., *Sibířské úvahy.* Prague, 1925.

Pecháček, F., *Technické oddělení čs. vojska na Rusi.* Prague, 1924.

Peroutka, F., *Budování státu.* 4 vol., Prague, 1934–36.

Petrš, J., *K historii intendantské služby.* Prague, 1926.

Pichlík, K., *Čeští vojáci proti válce.* Prague, 1961.

Pichlík, K., *Bojovali proti válce.* Prague, 1953.

Pisecký, F., *M. R. Štefánik v mém deníku.* Prague, 1934.

Pitra, J., *Z Penzy do Ufy.* Prague, 1922.

Pleský, M., *Dějiny 4. střeleckého pluku Prokopa Velikého.* Turnov, 1927.

Pod Slavnými prapory starodružníků. Prague, 1927.

Polák, J., *Peněžnictví v ruských legiích.* Prague, 1924.

Pravda o legiích v Sibiři. Prague, 1920.

Pražký, F., *Kronika 10. střeleckého pluku Jana Sladkého Kozina.* Brno, 1927.

Řády a resoluce I. sjezdu československého vojska. Ekaterinburg, 1918.

Raše, R., *Evakuace.* Prague, 1923.

239

Řepka, J., *II. sjezd čs. vojska na Rusi.* Prague, 1928.

Říha, O., *Ohlas říjnové revoluce v ČSR.* Prague, 1957.

Ripka, H., *Boj za československou svobodu.* Prague, 1928.

Robl, R., *Taganrog.* Brno, 1928.

Sajdl, J., *Čs. železničáři v sibířské anabasi.* Prague, 1924.

Šeba, J., *Rusko a Malá dohoda.* Prague, 1936.

Seidlerová, B., *Přes bolševické fronty.* Prague, 1924.

Šíp, F., *Několik kapitol o hospodářství naší sibířské armády.* Prague, 1926.

Skácel, J., *Československá armáda v Rusku a Kolčak.* Prague, 1926; *S generálem Syrovým v Sibiři.* Prague, 1923.

Šmíd, J. M., *1. dělostřelecká brigáda Jana Žižky na Ukrajině.* Prague, 1937.

Splítek, J. A., *Národohospodářská činnost československých vojsk na Sibiři.* Prague, 1919.

Steidler, F., *Československé hnuti na Rusi.* Prague, 1922; *Zborov.* Prague, 1922; *Naše vystoupení v Rusku.* Prague, 1923.

Štvrtecký, S., *Bojová pieseň zněla.* Bratislava, 1958.

Svoboda, V., *Soudnictví v čs. vojsku na Rusi.* Prague, 1924.

Sychrava, L., *Duch Legií.* Prague, 1921.

——, *Tragedie Ruska.* Prague, 1922.

Sychrava, L., Werstadt, J., *Československý odboj.* Prague, 1923.

Sýkora, J., *Česká krev,* 2 vol., Vienna, 1927.

Syllaba, T., *T. G. Masaryk a revoluce v Rusku.* Prague, 1959.

Teringl, K., *Desátá rota pod Kazaňi.* Prague, 1935.

Vaněk, V. *Moje válečná odyssea.* Prague, 1925.

Vávra, V., *Klamná cesta.* Prague, 1958.

Vejnar, J., *Úderný prapor.* Prague, 1930.

Velká říjnová socialistická revoluce a naše národní svoboda. Prague, 1950.

Veselý, J., *Češi a Slováci v revolučním Rusku.* Prague, 1954.

Vlasák, F., *Zpráva plnomocníka.* Prague, 1935.

Vlasta, J., *Legionáři socialisté v Rusku.* Prague, 1922.

Vodička, J., *Jak jsme žili a bojovali.* Prague, 1957.

Vondráček, F., *Husité dvacátého století.* Prague, 1922.

Vzpomínáme 1917–1937. Kroměříž, 1937.

Zemek, O., *Z Asie do Evropy,* Brno, 1926.

Zmrhal, K., *Armáda ducha druhé míle.* Prague, s.d.

Znamenáček, J., *Stavba státú.* Prague, 1920.

Zuman, F., *Osvobozenská legenda.* Prague, 1922, 2 vol.

Russian White Sources (Published in foreign languages)

Benckendorf, O., *Last days at Tsarskoe Selo.* London, 1937.

Bing, E. J., *Letters of Tsar Nicholas and the Empress Marie.* London 1937.

Botkine, P., *Les morts sans tombes.* Paris, 1922.

Denikine, General, *La décomposition de l'armée et du pouvoir,* Paris, 1921.

BIBLIOGRAPHY

Gronsky, A., *The war and the Russian government*. London, 1929.
Izvolsky, A. P., *Souvenires de mon ministère*. Paris, 1923.
Kerensky, A. F., *The murder of the Romanovs*. London, 1935.
Kokovtsev, V. N., *Out of my past*. London, 1923.
Lebedev, V. I., *The Russian democracy and its struggle against the Bolshevik tyranny*. New York, 1919.
Melgunov, S., *Das Tagebuch des letzten Tsaren*. Berlin, 1923.
Mihailovich, A., *Once a Grand Duke*. London, 1931.
Milyukov, P., *Memoirs*, 2 vols. New York, 1935.
Noskov, A. A., *Nicolas II, Inconnu*. Paris, 1920.
Rodzianko, M. V., *The reign of Rasputin*. London, 1922.
Sakharov, General K., *Die Tschechischen Legionen in Siberien*. Berlin, 1930.
Sazonov, S., *The fateful years*. London, 1928.
Sokolov, J., *L'enquette judiciaire*. Paris, 1925.
Tchernov, V., *Mes tribulations dans la Russie des Soviets*. Paris, 1921.
Viktoroff-Toporov, V., *La première année de la revolution russe*. Berne, 1919.
Volsky, S. *Dans le royaume de la famine et de la haine*. Paris, 1922.
White, D. F., *Through War and Revolution in Russia*. Philadelphia, 1939.
Witte, S. V., *Memoirs*. Paris, 1921.
Wrangel, N., *Du servage au bolchevisme*. Paris, 1929.
Zenzinov, V., *The Road to Oblivion*. London, 1932.

Polish Bibliography

Bagiński, H., *Wojsko polskie na Wschodzie*. Warsaw, 1919.
——, *Formacje polskie w armii rosyjskiej*. Warsaw, 1918.
Dowbor-Muónicki, J., *Krótki Szkic do historii I Polskiego Korpusu*. Warsaw, 1919.
Dzierzykraj Stokalski, W. *Dzieje jednej partyzenki (1917-1920)*. Lwów, 1927.
Glinka, W., *Pamiętnik z Wielkiej Wojny*. Warsaw, n.d.
Grosfeld, L. *Polskie reakcyjne formacje wojskowe w Rosji 1917-1921*. Warsaw, 1958.
Heltman, S., *Robotnik polski w Rewolucji Razdz. na Białorsui*. Minsk, 1927.
Jablonski, H., *Polityka Polskiej Partii Socialistycznej w czasie wojny 1914-18*. Warsaw, 1958.
Kazmierski, F., *Wojskowi Polacy w Rosji w czasie rewolucji (1917-1918)*. Warsaw, 1935.
Seyda, M., *Polska na przelomie dziejow*. Poznan, vol. 1., 1927, vol. 2, 1931.
Szczesny, W., *Kwestia wojska polskiego w Rosji w 1917 r*. Warsaw, 1936.
Tegoborski, W., *Polacy Zwiqznku Radzieckiego*. Moscow, 1927.
Wasilewski, Z. *Proces Lednickiego*. Warsaw, 1924.
Zatorski, A., *Dzieje pułku białgorodzkiego*. Warsaw, 1960.

Materiafy archiwalne do historii stosuńkow polsko-radzieckich. Warsaw, 1957, vol. 1.

Newspapers and Periodicals

Western:

American Slavic and East European Review (New York).
Le Monde Slave (Paris).
Slavonic and East European Review (London).
The Slavonic Review (London).

Soviet:

Istoricheskii Zhurnal (Moscow).
Istorik Marksist (Moscow).
Izvestiia (Petrograd and Moscow).
Krasnyl Arkhiv (Moscow).
Novyi Vostok (Moscow).
Pravda (Petrograd and Moscow).
Proletarskaia Revoliutsiia (Moscow).
Vestnik N.K.I.D. (Petrograd and Moscow).
Voprosy Istorii (Moscow).

Anti-Bolshevik:

Arkhiv Russkoi Revoliutsii (Berlin).
Peloe Delo (Berlin).
Donskaia Letopis' (Belgrade).
France et Ukraine (Paris).
Golos Minuvshego (Paris).
Istorik i Sovremennik (Berlin).
Khliborobska Ukraine (Vienna).
The New Russia (London).
Osvobozhdenie (Stuttgart).
Posledniia Novosti (Paris).
Rossiia (Velikaia Rossiia) (Ekaterinodar, Odessa, Sevastopol).
La Russie démocratique (Paris).
Vidrodzhennia (Kiev).
Vozrozhdenie (Paris).

INDEX OF NAMES